THE SPIRIT OF TRUTH

THE SPIRIT OF TRUTH

Reading Scripture and Constructing Theology
with the Holy Spirit

EDITED BY MYK HABETS

PICKWICK *Publications* · Eugene, Oregon

THE SPIRIT OF TRUTH
Reading Scripture and Constructing Theology with the Holy Spirit

Copyright © 2010 Wipf and Stock. All rights reserved. Except for brief quotations in critical publications or reviews, no part of this book may be reproduced in any manner without prior written permission from the publisher. Write: Permissions, Wipf and Stock Publishers, 199 W. 8th Ave., Suite 3, Eugene, OR 97401.

An alternate version of chapter 6 appeared as Myk Habets, "Developing a Retroactive Hermeneutic: Johannine Theology and Doctrinal Development," *American Theological Inquiry* 1.2 (2008) 77–89. Used with permission.

Cover image from Mark Compton (mgcompton@gmail.com), *Spirit Empowered*, acrylic on board. Copyright © 2009 by artist. Reproduced with permission.

Scripture quotations, unless otherwise noted, are from the New Revised Standard Version Bible, copyright © 1989 National Council of the Churches of Christ in the United States of America. Used by permission. All rights reserved.

Pickwick Publications
An Imprint of Wipf and Stock Publishers
199 W. 8th Ave., Suite 3
Eugene, OR 97401

www.wipfandstock.com

ISBN 13: 978-1-60899-321-5

Cataloguing-in-Publication data:

The Spirit of truth : reading scripture and constructing theology with the Holy Spirit / edited by Myk Habets

xx + 218 p. ; 23 cm. Includes bibliographical references.

ISBN 13: 978-1-60899-321-5

1. Holy Spirit. 2. Bible—Hermeneutics. 3. Hermeneutics—Religious Aspects—Christianity. I. Habets, Myk. II. Title.

BT121.3.S75 2010

Manufactured in the U.S.A.

Το πνευμα της ἀληθειας—wild, mysterious,
beyond our knowing, gusting down desert wadis,
and through the lives of God's image-bearers

Contents

Preface / ix
Acknowledgments / xiii
List of Contributors / xv
Abbreviations / xviii

Part One: Reading Scripture with the Spirit

1. The Holy Spirit and the Presence of God / 3
   Gary Badcock

2. Spirit, *Geist*, and the Knowledge of God / 22
   Gary Badcock

3. A Pneumatology for an Everyday Theology: Whither the Anonymous Spirit in Luke 10:1–12? / 41
   Steve Taylor

4. Spirit, Interpretation and Scripture: Exegetical Thoughts on 2 Peter 1:19–21 / 57
   Tim Meadowcroft

5. James and the Spirit: Wisdom and Hermeneutics / 73
   Martin Sutherland

6. Reading Scripture and Doing Theology with the Holy Spirit / 89
   Myk Habets

Part Two: Constructing Theology with the Spirit

7 Eastern Promises: Remedying the Pneumatological Deficits of Western Theology / 107
Hugh Bowron

8 Theosis, Yes; Deification, No / 124
Myk Habets

9 Teleology as the Key to Pneumatological Anthropology / 150
Stuart Print

10 "When Groans and Mumblings Are Not Enough": Investigating Being "Slain in the Spirit" in Acts / 168
Darren Ayling

11 Taking the Spirit to Work / 179
Peter McGhee

12 The Spirit and Particularity / 206
Judith Brown

Preface

While some of the following chapters were commissioned after the event, most of the following chapters were first presented at The Spirit of Truth Conference, Laidlaw College, Auckland, New Zealand, August 18–19, 2008. The conference was run by Myk Habets and was held under the auspices of the Laidlaw-Carey Graduate School (LCGS), a cooperative venture between Carey Baptist College and Laidlaw College, evangelical tertiary institutions in New Zealand. The contributors to this volume largely comprise faculty and students of LCGS and represent some of the best evangelical theology in Aotearoa, New Zealand. One exception to this is the presence of Professor Gary Badcock of Canada, who provided expert scholarship and a complementary perspective from another geographical locale. We are grateful to him for his willingness to travel so far and contribute so much.

The aim of the conference was to develop contemporary constructive theologies in which pneumatological concerns were paramount. The result is various studies spanning biblical-hermeneutical, theological, and practical disciplines. The aim of the present volume is not to present an evangelical pneumatology in systematic fashion, nor to present a comprehensive theology of the Holy Spirit. Rather, this volume represents explorations in pneumatology from a variety of evangelical scholars working in varying contexts but each wrestling equally with what the Spirit of Truth is saying to the church today.

Chapters 1 and 2, by theologian Gary Badcock, are reflections on the presence of God by his Spirit and the knowledge of God through his Spirit. Badcock mines the works of Barth, Hütter, Hegel, Wingren, and many others in his quest to establish the locus of a correct knowledge of God. These two chapters provide a fitting introduction to the volume, as Badcock suggests an "ecclesiological imperative" and maintains that neglect of this imperative is an issue of first importance in a dogmatics of the Christian faith and a major impediment to an adequate theology for our time.

In chapter 3 practical theologian Steve Taylor asks how the Spirit may be relevant to contemporary culture. He pursues a much-contested but popular claim that we must befriend theologically the everyday and pop cultural narratives, and that in these narratives we can find a redemptive participation in Christ's work of making God known and the Spirit's work of blessing the life of gift and gratitude that the Son shares with the Father. Thus, a theology of popular culture is a participation in the work of the Spirit that finds depth and coherence as a narration of a profoundly Trinitarian patterning. This chapter is sure to raise as many questions as it answers, and if it does it has achieved part of its goal.

Chapter 4 sees Old Testament and hermeneutics scholar Tim Meadowcroft examining a central text of Scripture on Scripture—2 Peter 1:19–21—in order to gain an appreciation of the work of the Spirit in relation to the canon. It is easy enough to assert in general terms that the Holy Spirit is active at the point of the "inspiration" of the biblical writers, but apparently much more difficult to conceive of the Holy Spirit as active and reliable at each operation through which the words of the Bible came to be and now are experienced as the word of God. Such an appreciation requires a comprehensive sense of the Spirit of God pervasively active in God's word. Tim's proposal is that this dynamic is what emerges from a close reading of 2 Peter 1:19–21.

In chapter 5 historian and theologian Martin Sutherland suggests an understanding of hermeneutics that draws on the nexus of wisdom and virtue in the Epistle of James. Sutherland identifies the role and theological significance of wisdom together with its close association in James, and argues that these connections provide a path into hermeneutics. He then explores the potential parallels offered by the philosophical categories of virtue epistemology. In the light of both wisdom in James and the ambitions of virtue epistemology he proposes an approach to theological hermeneutics that offers a third path which may avoid some of the pitfalls of correspondence theories of truth on the one hand and coherence theories on the other hand.

Part 1 concludes with chapter 6, in which theologian Myk Habets constructs a pneumatological hermeneutic wherein the Spirit brings to mind the words of Christ, primarily in Scripture, and then leads the church into all truth. Habets characterizes this twofold movement as *retro* and *active* and thus suggests a retroactive hermeneutic. He then further explores how this leads the church into doctrinal development that is organic and enriching rather than evolutionary and polluting.

Part 2 opens in chapter 7 with Hugh Bowron's suggestion that the East has resources to help remedy Western pneumatological deficiencies. He looks East and gently chides the West for its pneumatological anemia. In the later part of his essay Bowron considers the now popular theme of *theosis* and uses it as a lens to evaluate his central claims. In chapter 8 Myk Habets carries on with the theme of *theosis* initiated by Bowron and shows how this doctrine is not neglected in the West, before outlining what a thoroughly Western doctrine of *theosis* looks like in contradistinction both to the East and to several of Bowron's earlier suggestions. Habets concludes with ten theses for further reflection.

Chapters 9 and 10 are innovative studies by two young ministers of the gospel. In the first Stuart Print attempts an ambitious program aimed at complementing Logos-dominated discussions of the *imago Dei* with a pneumatologically structured approach. In the process he unearths some patristic insights well worth another hearing today, one of which is the pneumatological dimensions of *theosis*, or human participation in the divine life. Print shows why a teleological orientation to the Breath of Life results in an experience of the divine *koinonia* of God. The way humanity responds to the Spirit mediating the Father's love in *koinonia* relationship shows the good in creation, as we walk with God; the bad in the fall, as we attempt to live for self; the new life in Christ, as we are united to him; and the perfect future, as we experience communion with the Trinity.

In chapter 10 Darren Ayling attempts to objectively consider arguments for the Pentecostal phenomenon known as being "slain in the Spirit." Utilizing biblical, historical, and theological evidence, Ayling asks pastoral questions of the practice and concludes that the phenomenon has more to do with *nature* than it does with *grace*. His style and argument (but not necessarily his conclusions) model the sort of pneumatological approach suggested in earlier essays in this volume.

Chapter 11, by ethicist and lay theologian Peter McGhee, critically adopts Miroslav Volf's conception of a pneumatological approach to work and provides a pneumatological critique of contemporary understandings of spirituality in the workplace, both secular and Christian. He concludes with a constructive argument for how the Spirit is at work amidst the mundane but no-less-important contexts in which believers find themselves employed throughout most of their working lives.

In the final chapter theologian and audiophile Judith Brown explores the contribution the arts have to theology, specifically investigating the claim that the arts can reveal theological truths in ways that formal theology fails to achieve. Creativity is especially the focus of Brown's reflections as she works her way through—to name a few—Hegel, Bloch, Irenaeus, Basil of Caesarea, Bonhoeffer, Tillich, and Barth with her own creative artistry of theological improvisation.

Brown's chapter provides a fitting conclusion to the present volume as it leaves open the landscape into which theologians (and artists of all stripes) are invited to walk in tandem with the Holy Spirit, the *Spiritus vivificans*, Lord and Giver of Life. As the celebrated Roman Catholic pneumatologist Yves Conger wrote at the start of his *magnum opus*:

> Each one of us has his own gifts, his own means and his own vocation. Mine are as a Christian who prays and as a theologian who reads a great number of books and takes many notes. May I therefore be allowed to sing my own song! The Spirit is breath. The wind sings in the trees. I would like, then, to be an Aeolian harp and let the breath of God make the strings vibrate and sing. Let me stretch and tune the strings—that will be the austere task of research. And then let the Spirit make them sing a clear and tuneful song of prayer and life![1]

May the Spirit take what each contributor to this volume has offered and make it a tuneful song of prayer and life.

Myk Habets
Doctor Serviens Ecclesiae
Auckland, New Zealand

---

1. Yves Conger, *I Believe in the Holy Spirit*, 3 vols, trans. D. Smith (New York: Seabury, 1983), 1: x.

Acknowledgments

Various people deserve thanks for help in the preparation of this manuscript for publication. Peter Benzies helped with the initial formatting of the text, the contributors on the whole were timely in the preparation of their chapters, and Wipf & Stock has seen the work through to publication in an efficient manner. Thanks also go to Laidlaw-Carey Graduate School for continuing to support academic scholarship in New Zealand, especially Martin Sutherland, first Dean of LCGS and Vice-Principal (Academic) at Laidlaw College. A word of appreciation goes to Paul Windsor, former principal of Carey Baptist College, and Charles Hewlett, the current principal, for their commitment to producing pastor-scholars, a number of whom appear in this volume. Finally I want to thank my wife Odele and our children, Sydney and Liam, who constantly remind me of the Holy Spirit's wider work in the world.

Contributors

Darren Ayling [BEd, Dip Tchg (SLT), BAppTheol]
After 15 years as a speech and language therapist working with head and neck cancer patients, Darren returned to New Zealand from the UK in 2005 to study theology at Carey Baptist College, Auckland. Darren's study at Carey led to a change of vocation and he is now minister at Wellington Central Baptist Church, New Zealand. Darren is married and has two children.

Gary Badcock [BA, MA, BD, PhD]
Peache Professor of Divinity, Huron University College, London, Canada. Gary studied philosophy at Memorial University and theology at the University of Edinburgh. He has taught at the Universities of Aberdeen (1991–92) and Edinburgh (1993–99), and at Huron since 1999. His teaching spans the areas of Christian doctrine, philosophical theology, and ethics. In addition to a series of shorter essays in these fields, Gary has written *Light of Truth and Fire of Love: A Theology of the Holy Spirit* (1997) and *The Way of Life: A Theology of Christian Vocation* (1998). He has also recently completed an ecclesiology under the title *The House Where God Lives* (2009). He lives in London with his wife and two daughters.

Hugh Bowron [MA, Dip Theol]
Hugh is Vicar of Holy Trinity Avonside in the Anglican Diocese of Christchurch, New Zealand. Hugh looks back with a sense of whimsy on 28 years as a parish priest in locations as varied as a working-class parish in the Midlands, a country parish in mid Canterbury, and an

inner-city parish in Wellington. Accompanying all this were secondary ministries as a part-time army chaplain, a community development worker, an employee of the Anglican Social Responsibility Commission, and a mental health activist. His current interest is in systematic theology and the history of Christian thought.

Judith Brown [BA (Hons), BD, MTh, PhD]
Judith is occasionally a theologian. She has taught at Laidlaw College, Auckland, and for the Laidlaw-Carey Graduate School. Judith has contributed to such publications as *Music in the Air* and *Reality*, and *Eras* journal, Monash University. She has many things in progress, not least an interesting and varied membership in the Presbyterian church. Judith lives in West Auckland, which in the right light almost reminds her of her rural Southland home.

Myk Habets [BMin, MTh (Merit), Grad Dip Tert Tchg, PhD]
Myk lectures in systematic theology at Carey Baptist College, Auckland, is a faculty member of Laidlaw-Carey Graduate School, and is the director of the R. J. Thompson Centre for Theological Studies at Carey. He has published numerous articles in constructive systematic theology in international journals, and is the author of *Theosis in the Theology of Thomas Torrance* (2009) and *The Annointed Son* (Pickwick, 2009). Myk is married and has two children.

Peter McGhee [NDA, MBS (Hons), MEd (Hons), Grad Dip Professional Ethics, PhD (cand.)]
Peter is a senior lecturer in the Center for Interdisciplinary Studies in the Faculty of Business at the Auckland University of Technology. He has taught at AUT for 10 years in various areas such as business ethics, applied ethics, organizational behavior, and human resource management. His PhD explores the relationship between spirituality in the workplace and ethical decision making. He has had articles published in management and applied ethics journals covering workplace spirituality, virtue ethics, and professional ethics. Peter is married with two children, is a member of his local Baptist church, and is on the board of The Leprosy Mission, New Zealand.

Tim Meadowcroft [MA, BD, PhD]
Tim is a senior lecturer in biblical studies in the School of Theology at Laidlaw College, Auckland, where he has been since 1994, and also

a faculty member of Laidlaw-Carey Graduate School. He has made a particular study of the books of Daniel and Haggai, on which he has published commentaries as well as articles in a range of journals. This reflects his interest in the Second Temple period. He has also published a number of articles on issues in hermeneutics, and is currently working on a volume on *The Message of Scripture* for IVP. He is married and has four adult children and four grandchildren.

Stuart Print [BAppTheol]
Stu is a pastoral leadership graduate of Carey Baptist College and is now pastor of Wellington South Baptist Church, Island Bay, New Zealand. Prior to attending Carey, he was a sharemilker for 13 years in the Manawatu. Stu is married and has two children.

Martin Sutherland [BTheol, BA (Hons), PhD]
Martin is Vice Principal (Academic) at Laidlaw College. He has published widely on Baptist history and thought as well as on theological method and ecclesiology. He is editor of the *Pacific Journal of Baptist Research*.

Steve Taylor [BHort, BTheol, MTheol (Hons), PhD]
Steve is Director of Missiology, Uniting College, Brooklyn Park, Australia, and a former senior pastor of Opawa Baptist Church in Christchurch. He is the author of *The Out of Bounds Church?: Learning to Create a Community of Faith in a Culture of Change* (2005) and theological film reviewer for *Touchstone* magazine, with his writing "Highly Commended" at the 2008 Australasian Religious Press Awards.

Abbreviations

AB	Anchor Bible
ACCS	Ancient Christian Commentary on Scripture
CSR	Christian Scholar's Review
EvQ	Evangelical Quarterly
FC	Fathers of the Church
GOTR	Greek Orthodox Theological Review
HTR	Harvard Theological Review
IJST	International Journal of Systematic Theology
Int	Interpretation
ITQ	Irish Theological Quarterly
JETS	Journal of the Evangelical Theological Society
JPT	Journal of Pentecostal Theology
JSNT	Journal for the Study of the New Testament
JSSR	Journal for the Scientific Study of Religion
JSNTSup	Journal for the Study of the New Testament: Supplement Series
LCC	Library of Christian Classics
NAC	New American Commentary
NICNT	New International Commentary on the New Testament
NIVAC	NIV Application Commentary
NPNF1/2	Philip Schaff, ed., *Nicene and Post-Nicene Fathers*, Series 1/2 (1886–1900)
NTDSup	Das Neue Testament Deutsche Supplement
NTS	New Testament Studies
PG	J.-P. Migne, ed., *Patrologia graeca*, 162 vols. (1857–86)

PL	J.-P. Migne, ed., *Patrologia latina*, 217 vols. (1844–64)
SBT	Studies in Biblical Theology
SJT	*Scottish Journal of Theology*
SP	Sacra pagina
TDNT	*Theological Dictionary of the New Testament*
ThTo	*Theology Today*
TNTC	Tyndale New Testament Commentaries
TynBul	*Tyndale Bulletin*
WBC	Word Biblical Commentary
WTJ	*Westminster Theological Journal*

Part One

Reading Scripture
with the Spirit

1

The Holy Spirit and the Presence of God

by Gary Badcock

Both at the level of ordinary Christian awareness, and in that second-order level of formal theological reflection that we call Christian theology, talk of the Holy Spirit is commonly reckoned to be concerned with God as present and active today.[1] The Holy Spirit is, after all, the one sent after the departure of the Lord Jesus, so that while for a time we cannot see him, the Spirit whom he sent is present forever (John 14:16; 16:5-16). But what, exactly, do we mean by this idea of the "presence" of the Spirit? This seemingly simple question is, in fact, far from simple to answer, for a cluster of issues of the greatest moment begins to emerge at this point on closer inspection. For instance, does the presence of the Spirit constitute something unique over against the presence of Christ, or alternatively, is talk of the presence of the Spirit shorthand for the presence of what we might call "God-in-general"? Again, if the Spirit is said to be present, are we, by this affirmation, committed to the idea that the Spirit is present not only *in the present* (this being the fundamental sense of the word "presence") but also in a particular place; in short, is

---

1. For a fuller argument on what follows see my study in ecclesiology, *The House Where God Lives: The Doctrine of the Church* (Grand Rapids: Eerdmans, 2009).

the Holy Spirit present *in space* as well as *in time*? And if so, then in what space, or where, exactly, is it possible to encounter the "present" Spirit of God? Ought this space itself thereby to have theological significance, along with the time as well with which it is to be taken together? Large questions, then, are summoned forth from ordinary Christian awareness at this point, and it is the task of the present essay to begin to unpick strands of the knot implicit in some of them, at least, as we seek to understand what it is that we believe.

PRESENCE AND OMNIPRESENCE

Several distinct *loci* from the classical theological tradition will serve as our point of departure. To begin with, let me quote some well-worn words from the eighth-century theologian John of Damascus. God, John teaches in a famous argument, "is his own place" (*topos*).[2] Though this claim has recently been read (rather unsurprisingly, by an exponent of panentheism) as meaning that, for John of Damascus, "the world's spatial-temporal existence is opened by and embraced by God's unimaginable 'roominess,'" the point is in fact rather different.[3] For John, it is both possible and necessary to speak of the "place" of God because while God fills and energizes all things without mixing himself with any one thing, the same God is said to dwell especially in those places that have a greater share in his energy and grace than others. Heaven is such a place, the place of God's throne, while earth, for its part, is relativized as God's footstool; equally, John observes, the "sacred flesh" of Christ and the church can be spoken of as special places in which God is present. In general, in fact, he argues that we are able to speak of anywhere that the divine energy becomes manifest to us as the place of God, not because of the special dignity of the space itself, but solely because of the God who dwells there by way of his transcendent power. That God is *his own* place means, in effect, that God dwells where he wills—but also that God does dwell there in the sense that to the place of dwelling is given to share in his energies.

2. John of Damascus *De Fide Orth.* 1.13 (PG 94:852).

3. Niels Henrik Gregersen, "Three Varieties of Panentheism," in *In Whom We Live and Move and Have Our Being*, ed. Philip Clayton and Arthur Peacocke (Grand Rapids: Eerdmans, 2004), 20.

Medieval theology in the Latin tradition took a slightly different approach, but was, in general terms, preoccupied with the same questions. On the one hand, we might say that the classical divine attribute of divine omnipresence, according to which God is present *everywhere*, made the answer to the question of the possibility of divine presence *somewhere* rather obvious: God's presence in one place or person in particular is grounded in his generic presence in all things. On the other hand, this raises a clear problem, for if God really is present everywhere, then in what possible sense could it be said that God also can indwell one person, people, or place any more than the next? Is there, in a word, no difference between God's presence in the sinner and in the saint?

The importance of these issues was widely recognized in medieval discussions of the presence of God. Thomas Aquinas, for example, argues that God, the cause of all things, dwells in everything in a generic sense *per essentiam, potentiam et præsentiam*.[4] Metaphysically, the presence of God can be seen as an implication of the doctrine of creation, and falls under the heading of what in Catholic theology is called the "presence of immensity." God's creative power is such as not only to generate all that came to exist in the beginning, but also to hold all things in existence at every instant of created time.[5] Yet Thomas is also well aware that God is said to be present to and in the human person in another way that surpasses the divine creative presence, by virtue of the Son or the Holy Spirit's being "sent" to dwell with, in, or among the saints in a more intimate way. Thus there comes about, as he puts it, "a special presence consonant with the nature of an intelligent being." In Thomas's theology, this presence is tied, as one might expect, to the life of conscious faith and of moral obedience. In spiritual creatures who apprehend by faith the truth of God, he maintains, God comes to be present "as the object known by the knower and as the one beloved of the lover" (*cognitum in cognoscente et amatum in amante*), so that, by acts of knowing and loving, a person is said to touch God himself, who dwells in the person "as in his temple."[6] In a strikingly beautiful exposition, Thomas speaks

---

4. Thomas Aquinas, *Summa Theologiae*, ed. and trans. T. C. O'Brien, Blackfriars ed. (London: Eyre & Spottiswoode; New York: McGraw-Hill, 1976), vol. 7, Ia.43.3 *res*. The formula is a traditional one.

5. Antonio Royo and Jordan Auymann, *The Theology of Christian Perfection* (Dubuque, IA: Priory, 1962), 566.

6. Thomas Aquinas *Summa Theologiae* Ia.43.3.

of a process of divinization, or of being made like God by virtue of this specific form of divine presence:

> By grace the soul takes on a God-like form. That a divine person be sent to someone through grace, therefore, requires a likening [*assimilatio*] to the person sent through some particular gift of grace. Since the Holy Spirit is Love, the likening of the soul to the Holy Spirit occurs through the gift of charity and so the Holy Spirit's mission is accounted for by reason of charity. The Son in turn is the Word; not, however, just any word, but the Word breathing Love; *The Word as I want the meaning understood is a knowledge accompanied by love* [citing Augustine *De Trinitate* 9.10]. Consequently not just any enhancing of the mind indicates the Son's being sent, but only that sort of enlightening that bursts forth into love; the kind, namely, that *John* describes, *Everyone that hath heard from the Father and hath learned, cometh to me*; and the *Psalm, In my meditation a fire shall come forth.* [This] points to a kind of experiential awareness and this precisely is what wisdom is, a knowing that, as it were, is tasted . . .[7]

It would seem that Thomas forgot at least this little nugget of gold when, towards the end of his life, and for whatever reason, he famously confessed that all that he had written seemed like straw to him.[8]

There is, however, a residual problem, for Thomas, in speaking of the sending of the Son and of the Holy Spirit as the basis of the distinctive presence of God to the saints, is unable to admit that such a sending involves in any sense that God should come to be located somewhere new. What it means to say that the Son or the Spirit is sent is not that God literally moves to be with or in someone or some place (for as the axiomatically omnipresent one, he must already have been there), but rather, that *the creature* has come to God. What the missions of the Son and of the Holy Spirit amount to, in short, is a change in the relation of the creature to the divine source of the "sending," whereby, according to that peculiar use of language that is theology, God is said to be made present. Thus Thomas speaks of the likening of the creature to the Trinitarian person "sent" as constitutive of the divine presence. Two things emerge

---

7. Thomas Aquinas *Summa Theologiae* Ia.43.5 *ad* 2.

8. Simon Tugwell, ed. and trans., *Albert & Thomas* (New York: Paulist, 1988), 266. Cf. Brian Davies, *The Thought of Thomas Aquinas* (Oxford: Clarendon, 1993), 8–9.

from this treatment that are worth noting: first, as has been indicated, the creature rather than God is changed, for there can be nothing new for God; while secondly, and crucially, the presence of God is conceived in Trinitarian terms, for the change in view is a likening of the creature to the Trinitarian person said to be "sent," and it is this likening that effectively defines the presence of God.

Expanding upon these Thomistic ideas in his pneumatology, the twentieth-century Dominican theologian Yves Congar argues that since God must be spoken of as already both everywhere and nowhere (everywhere because he cannot be confined to one space, and nowhere for precisely the same reason), it is necessary to have recourse to this traditional argument in order to avoid taking the concept of presence too crudely.[9] What takes place when God becomes present to a person, Congar maintains, is that the person is placed in a certain relationship with God, who becomes present now not only implicitly, but explicitly and spiritually as the object of love and knowledge. It is not that a change in God's location is effected; rather, there has come about a change in the person concerned, or more precisely, in his or her conscious relation to God. God's presence, precisely because it is by way of and in a certain logical sense identical with his transcendence, is unalterable. "Where can I go from your spirit? Or where can I flee from your presence?" asks the 139th Psalm (v. 7), and the answer given, of course, is that there is nowhere that God is not, and therefore no such place to which we can flee and hide, or no pit in which we cannot be found by him. That there are those for whom the thought of the presence of God is meaningless, and many for whom the presence of God is impossible to discern, would mean on this account that there are people for whom, and times in which, that Thomistic *assimilatio* of the person to God that comes about by grace is for whatever reason either something dormant or hidden or somehow unrealized. It is not this way, however, because God has himself been objectively absent, since that would be to abandon the metaphysical attribute of omnipresence, and make God out to be something less than God.

What is surprising about this argument is the idea that it is not so much that God becomes present, as that God's presence becomes explicitly known to us, and this shapes the theology of the presence of God

---

9. Yves Congar, *I Believe in the Holy Spirit*, trans. David Smith, 3 vols. (London: G. Chapman, 1983), 2:83–84.

in this central strand of the tradition. God, existing outside of all finite, spatial limits, can neither change nor indeed move from one "place" to another. Whatever change or movement occurs when God becomes present in a life, let us say, can only occur for the creature, who is raised up to grasp what amounts to a primordial presence that is assumed always to have existed.

The trouble with the theory, of course, is that it appears to make much of what we believe at the level of ordinary Christian consciousness, and more decisively, much of the biblical account of the presence of God, seem rather misleading. Rather like the God of St. Anselm's *Proslogium*, who is loving only in terms of human perception, but not in himself,[10] talk of the presence of the Son who is sent into the world in the biblical witness as an individual man "born of a [particular] woman" and only "when the time had fully come," and of the Holy Spirit who is poured out upon the church at Pentecost in fulfillment of prophetic expectation concerning the "last days," is not quite accurate. "The things that you're liable / To read in the Bible / It ain't necessarily so," the immortal lines from George Gershwin's *Porgy and Bess*, we tend to think of as one of the siren songs of modernity, but it is disarming to think of them as applying to the likes of an eleventh-century pillar of orthodoxy like Anselm. (Anselm, indeed, stands among the foremost spokesmen for the view that God cannot in the strict sense be said to be present in *any* place or time, but only in every place and in every time as the creative and sustaining principle of all places and all times.)[11] The presence of God the Holy Spirit consists, on this view, in the drawing of the creature into some new relationship to the Creator, since for God there can, in the strictest possible sense, be nothing new. At Pentecost, therefore, it is not so much that the Spirit was poured out upon all flesh, as that all flesh was enabled to soak up the already present supply: Pentecost was, therefore, something new in human experience, but not, as it were, in God's.

By way of response to this theory, and for our final *locus* in what is now firmly part of the theological tradition, Karl Barth's far more revolutionary approach to the doctrine of God, developed in volume II of his *Church Dogmatics*, merits attention. The account of the doctrine of God that Barth provides is breathtaking in scope, and presents us with,

---

10. Anselm *Proslogium* 8.
11. Anselm *Monologium* 20–24.

among other things, a fundamental re-examination of the idea of God's presence and omnipresence.[12] For instance, omnipresence in the history of Christian theology has traditionally been treated as a "relative" attribute of God, as distinct from the "essential" or "absolute" attributes of eternity, aseity, and so forth, by virtue of their belonging to the sphere of God's relation to the world, rather than to that of God in himself. In the classical view, therefore, God, who is in himself spaceless, can be present only in and to those things that came into being in space and time. God is not "present" (here and now) to himself, but only to creation.[13] In the *Church Dogmatics*, however, Karl Barth develops the view that God's presence does not denote merely his relation to the cosmos. Barth argues, rather, that true presence exists first of all in God himself, before its analogue exists in the created world. The outward manifestation and realization of this divine presence in the cosmos would be inconceivable, he maintains, were it not for the fact that God already in himself is the eternally omnipresent one.[14]

Barth's argument is fleshed out in the context of an exposition of the Johannine statement that "God is love" (1 John 4:16), and in the context of a wider treatment of the love of God that occupies several hundred pages of closely argued text in *Church Dogmatics* II/1. Barth's thesis is that the text literally defines the being of God as the one who is *capable of* sending his Son intot the world. God is, as such, "the one who loves in freedom."[15] The Anselmian view that God appears as the loving one of Christian revelation only to us, whereas in himself God must be conceived in dispassionate terms, is therefore dismissed. Rather, the deepest implication of the text, and in many ways the fundamental claim of the Barthian doctrine of God, is that there is a relationship of love in God which is the source of all that is, and against which all that is must finally be measured. This relationship between the Father and the Son in the Holy Spirit exists eternally in God in a way that is logically prior to there being any relationship between God and creatures, and is indeed

---

12. Karl Barth, *Church Dogmatics*, eds. G. W. Bromiley and T. F. Torrance, trans. T. H. L. Parker et al. (Edinburgh: T. &. T. Clark, 1957), II/1:440–90 (§31.1). Hereafter *CD*.

13. For a discussion, cf. Luco J. van den Brom, *Divine Presence in the World* (Kampen: Kok Pharos, 1993), 170–230.

14. Barth, *CD* II/1:462.

15. Ibid., 257, in the section title; cf. 275–97 in particular.

the ground of all those relationships that come to exist outside of it at the level of creation.

The Barthian thesis leads, in the end, to the conclusion that there is presence *in God himself*, or as Barth puts it, otherness and distance as well as unity and nearness,[16] prior to there being a presence of God in the world. The implication is also that there must correlatively be in God a kind of "space"—God's own space, to be sure, as opposed to creaturely space—within which the mutual presence of the Trinitarian persons can be realized. Language is used here that we have encountered before, in John of Damascus, but in Barth's theology it is used to rather different effect. The theme of the love of God, once consistently thought through, becomes a Trinitarian one. Reflection on it leads to a re-examination of the whole problem of the doctrine of God. For our purposes, the main outcome is the claim that the triune God is first of all present to himself, which in turn means that God is always somewhere rather than nowhere, and indeed, that it is precisely because from all eternity God is present somewhere that, in time, God can also be present *here*.[17]

Barth accordingly maintains that God's presence is not at all generic, but individual and particular. Thus a differentiated presence of God in the world becomes theologically possible, according to which God's presence to one is different than it is to another, and this not only from the subjective standpoint of its appropriation by the creature concerned in the moment of *assimilatio*, or spiritual transformation, but objectively *for God*. Again, Barth picks up on two major biblical concepts in his argument, maintaining in the first instance that the language of the "throne" of God in Scripture needs to be taken with the utmost seriousness. Rejecting the accusation of anthropomorphism, Barth maintains that what this language represents is something profoundly real—indeed, what it represents is reality as such: the primordial "space" in which God dwells, and which is "the principle of space itself, real space *par excellence*."[18] Secondly, Barth turns to the double idea of the tabernacle/temple, arguing that the sheer particularity of the place in which God is said in Scripture to dwell, both in the Exodus wanderings and in the temple in Jerusalem, is essential to

---

16. Ibid., 463.
17. Ibid., 471.
18. Ibid., 475.

the distinctively biblical understanding of God.[19] He thus rejects the idea that the special presence of God with one people or one person is a matter of the subjective recognition or appropriation of a generic presence in all things. Indeed, the *particular* presence of God theologically precedes the general, for the purpose of God is always particular. God is not an abstract infinite substance, but the personal, loving God encountered in revelation, the one who "gives" his only begotten Son and who summons the human creature to the faith and obedience of Christ. God's purpose is eternally oriented to this rather than (as we might well say of an Anselm or a Thomas) to everything in general and nothing in particular; indeed, it is only because God takes an interest in the particular that he can be said to be committed to creation at all.

SPIRIT AND "SPIRITUALITY": THE SUBJECTIVE TURN

These are, of course, deep waters—to which we will need to return—but for the present, we move from such questions of theological speculation to what has become, since the revolutions of the twentieth century in particular, more familiar territory: the notion of "spirituality," which by convention has come to be regarded as the point of talk of the Holy Spirit. "Spirit" and "spirituality" have come, in other words, to be closely associated in much recent Christian theological thought. The turn to the "study of spirituality," which has been powerfully reinforced not only by the thousands of popular books on the subject which weigh down the shelves of the religious booksellers, but also by massive scholarly efforts producing fruit in more than a hundred volumes jointly represented in the *Classics of Western Spirituality* series, the parallel *Classics of Eastern Spirituality*, and the lesser-known series *World Spirituality*, make this dimension of the pneumatological question difficult to ignore. Such scholarly work builds upon the general consensus found in much academic work on religion that the purely functional approach to religion that dominates in social scientific approaches fails to take seriously the one thing that actually matters, the unique and irreducible element within religion—what Mircea Eliade, for instance, calls "the sacred."[20] Accounts

---

19. Ibid., 478–83.

20. For a fuller treatment see, Ewart Cousins, "Spirituality in Today's World," in *Religion in Today's World*, ed. Frank Whaling (Edinburgh: T. & T. Clark, 1987), 306–34.

of the presence of God in Christian theological writing that take a similar line abound: the "encounter with the sacred and the ultimate," in short, has become a normative genre of theological discourse, directly touching (in some hands, at least) on the problem of pneumatology.

My contention in what follows, however, will be that this association of the theology of the Holy Spirit with the concept of spirituality is more hindrance than help in any attempt to work out an adequate pneumatology, and that the cluster of assumptions that surround it have far more to do with the dominant assumptions of modernity than they do either with biblical revelation or, indeed, with the deepest traditions of Christian thought. Of particular concern in this context is the fact that such an interest in the concept of spirituality in Christian theology tends to divorce it from the church and from the regulative framework of doctrine—and yet, in creedal terms, the Holy Spirit, the common confession of faith, the church and the communion of saints are to be taken together.

To begin with, it is important to state flatly, though no doubt controversially, that both in the classical tradition and in much of the modern era, Christians cannot unambiguously be said to have something that they and we together would jointly recognize as a "spirituality." Though the Latin word *spiritualitas* appears in the late patristic and early medieval period in abstract references to the Pauline distinction between the "spiritual" and the "carnal," and though it might be argued that this at least *approaches* the sense of the inner dimension of the person at stake in contemporary discussion, there are also lengthy periods of Christian history in which the word denoted something else altogether. At one time, for instance, it meant merely the clerical estate, as a separate rank (*ordo*) or priestly caste within Christian societies. There have also been significant periods during which the word has not been used at all.[21] Owing to the anti-religious polemic of the Enlightenment, for instance, the word *spiritualité*, which had come in seventeenth-century French culture to refer to the affective relationship with God (and which, as such, was already theologically suspect because it did not fall under ecclesiastical control) came to be associated with irrationality. "Spirituality" and "enthusiasm" thus hung together as words denoting the superstition that infects religion. It so passed out of common discourse as an unmentionable, and

---

21. Bernard McGinn, "Introduction," in *Christian Spirituality: Origins to the Twelfth Century*, eds. Bernard McGinn and John Meyendorff (New York: Crossroad, 1985), xv.

in fact, it was only in the early twentieth century that the word began to make a reappearance. This came first in French sources, then in English translations of French sources, and finally in works written in English, where, interestingly, it was associated with a rejection of the idea that religious faith is to be associated with a body of doctrine, and with the contrary contention that religious faith is rooted in people, and that it grows from their own inward experience. Thus experience, in the distinctively modern concept of spirituality, becomes the criterion of religious authenticity.

In light of these observations, it is, as I have already suggested, important to recognize in any attempt to develop a Christian pneumatology that the claim that what we are about is fostering an authentic Christian spirituality is not necessarily normative. Even the classic liberal Protestant theologian Friedrich Schleiermacher, who is widely regarded as the prophet of modern "religious experience," took the view that what is distinctive about the presence of the Holy Spirit lies in what is collective rather than what is merely individual. According to Schleiermacher, talk of the Spirit has to do with the consciousness of being bound together with others in one bond in the fellowship of Christ.[22] The Spirit is thus "the common Spirit animating the life in common of believers."[23] Individual self-realization in the religious sphere thus fails, for Schleiermacher, to do justice to the distinctive teaching of the Christian religion on the subject of the Holy Spirit, which is clearly referred more to what is public and ecclesial than to what is private and inward—to that "spiritual core" which is "the deepest centre of the person," where we experience "ultimate reality," as one prominent commentator on the idea of spirituality puts it.[24] On the contrary, for Schleiermacher, the work of the Spirit is ecclesial, and as we know (since the fact is so plainly inescapable in all ages), there is much in the church as an empirical, public body that has little to do with any spiritual core, very often much that plainly refuses to appeal to the deepest center of the person, and, far more often that we might care to admit, a famine of ultimate reality. If it were not so, we would scarcely

22. Friedrich Schleiermacher, *The Christian Faith*, eds. H. R. Macintosh and J. S. Stewart, trans. D. M. Billie et al. (Edinburgh: T. & T. Clark, 1928), 565–85.

23. Ibid., 59.

24. Ewert Cousins, "Preface to the Series," in *Christian Spirituality: Origins to the Twelfth Century*, eds. Bernard McGinn, John Meyendorff et al. (New York: Crossroad, 1985) xiii.

spend so much time praying for and awaiting renewal. Nevertheless, the full depth of the question, once understood, thus requires a paradoxical and far more deeply challenging reference to ecclesiology, for it is *the church*—which is to say, the church that we can see around us, with all its flaws and failings—that is the sphere of the Spirit's action.

Let me thicken the plot by referring to one of the writers and books that have led me to this particular conclusion, and reflect for a moment on its significance. I refer to the radical American Episcopalian bishop, John Shelby Spong, and to his little book *Why Christianity Must Change or Die*.[25] The argument Spong presents in this study is at one level amusing, being so profoundly out of touch with the demographic reality of even his own ecclesial tradition, but on the other, it can serve as a kind of canon for theological honesty about the nature of "life in the Spirit" in the present context. Spong, who does not believe in God as a "being," who denies that salvation comes about through the incarnation, death, and resurrection of Christ, or really in any of the usual things that Christians broadly believe as matters of creedal confession, nevertheless clearly develops a vision of Christian "spirituality," following the example of Jesus as an inclusive, open, and fully human paradigm for life. Jesus was one who loved unselfishly, who welcomed the outcast, and who gave himself to and for others. By symbolic identification with him, Christians come to an authentic selfhood that can be said to be defined by his story. They find wholeness in such authenticity and openness, and insofar as the God-principle represents this inner moral quality, they can even be said to be reconciled with "God."

Spong's theology represents a popular version of that non-objective theism developed in more serious theological work such as that of the British theologian Don Cupitt—though in Spong's case the position developed is far less intellectually subtle, and filtered through a set of generic American cultural ideals concerning social inclusion. What is important about it for our purposes, however, is the fact that a version of Christian spirituality can indeed be constructed on the foundations laid. I do not hesitate to acknowledge, in fact, that the quality of John Shelby Spong's own "spiritual life" (as it is called) might well surpass mine (as I am, in point of fact, more or less wholly indifferent to the question).

---

25. John Shelby Spong, *Why Christianity Must Change or Die* (San Francisco: Harper, 1998).

Spong has, after all, spent a lifetime nurturing the sense of selfhood of which he writes, through the considerable liturgical disciplines of the church to which he belongs, and it would be churlish as well as dishonest and insulting to suggest that all of this has had no effect, or that his account of it is in the final analysis plainly dishonest. What it is possible to deny, however, is that his particular vision of Christian spirituality is rooted in an adequate pneumatology, or that the doctrine of the Holy Spirit does not open up to anything more than this fundamentally anthropological dynamic. One might well ponder, for instance, whether the authentic spiritual selfhood of which Spong writes could not be arrived at by other means: let us say, via New Age spirituality (since the latter is in very significant ways so similar), or Wicca, or even that little trinity of materialist supreme ends: money, sex, and power. Indeed, I would go so far as to suggest that when we find people telling us that they do not need to go to church, and that the same sense of personal satisfaction that Christians claim to find in it, they simply find in other ways, we really ought to believe them. They are telling the truth, and reveal by it that some of what we think we mean when we speak of the Spirit's work we cannot possibly mean at all—or at the very least, we surely must be capable of saying something more.

THE WORD AND THE SPIRIT: THE TRINITARIAN QUESTION

There are, however, two separate errors that need to be avoided if this "something more" is ever to be adequately put. The first is, of course, the one already encountered: the tendency to reduce the question of the Spirit's presence to an anthropological dynamic rather than to a properly theological event. There may be some kernel of truth here, in the sense that it is possible to maintain that the *Spiritus Creator* is present in and to every finite thing. However, particular dangers attend the attempt to make such an understanding of the presence of the Spirit normative and theologically regulative. The second mistake appears on the surface to be the polar opposite of the first, whereas in fact it is only the theological "negative," as it were, from which the first is developed. It is the thesis, long developed in Christian theology, according to which our starting point is the generic doctrine of divine omnipresence, and that all the particular apprehensions of the presence of God by creatures are just that—apprehensions or conscious and intentional appropriations of what is in fact everywhere and at all times given. In common with Karl Barth, I wish to argue that this fails to do justice to biblical revelation, which requires a more subtle approach to the question, made possible by a redevelopment of the themes of Trinitarian theology on the one side, and made much more specific by reference to the problem of ecclesiology on the other.

Let me begin to make an ending, then, with another text from Congar, who writes in terms so extraordinary that they must cause us to take notice. "The Church," Congar writes,

> . . . is the fruitfulness, outside God, of the Trinitarian processions. We *see* the Church in the manifestations of its ordained ministry, its worship, its assemblies, works and undertakings. We *believe* that the profound life of that great body, which is both scattered and one, is the culmination and the fruit, in the creature, of the very life of God, the Father, the Son and the Holy Spirit. . . . This idea can also be extended to the authentic unity, holiness, catholicity and apostolicity that is sought and that exists in the ecumenical movement—insofar as this is God's, it is also dependent on the Trinity and is the fruit or the term, outside God, of the processions of the Word and the Spirit.[26]

This passage—weaving together a series of themes from Congar's wide-ranging reflections over many years, from conscious generosity towards the Christian East and the many varieties of Protestantism, to his interest in the problem of the Spirit and the Trinitarian question, to his exploration of Scripture and his abiding interest in the theme of ecclesiology as something properly *theological* rather than merely pragmatic or pastoral in character—will serve as our point of departure in what follows. I shall call this turn the "ecclesiological imperative" and maintain that neglect of this imperative as an issue of first importance in a dogmatics of the Christian faith is a major impediment to an adequate theology for our time. We will find, however, that when the Trinitarian approach taken is deepened by reference to the theology of the cross (a theme that is strangely absent in Congar's theology), the vast ecclesiological ideas towards which the argument moves must appear ever more unexpected and more profound than even in Congar's formulation.

26. Congar, *I Believe in the Holy Spirit*, 2:8.

Congar helps us, I think, to escape the self-referentiality implicit in so much of what passes for ecclesiology by beginning with God. He maintains in particular that the Holy Spirit, in its role as "co-instituting" the church, has a series of critical functions to play, all of which are the "fruit" in the creature of the divine Trinitarian relations that are extended into time in the Spirit's mission. These functions include making the church *one* as the principle of ecclesial communion, *holy* as the principle of its holiness, *catholic* as the principle of wholeness, and *apostolic* as the principle of faithful witness. Thus, for example, the work of the Spirit is the foundation of the communion of saints that is, in a sense, the very life of the church. The Spirit's work, like the Spirit's very being, is one of sharing and participation: sharing, in that through the Spirit the love of God "has been poured into our hearts" (Rom 5:5); participation, in that what is given to one member of the community is given for the benefit also of others.[27] Communion is thus not a purely anthropological or sociological phenomenon; it is, rather, rooted in our participation by grace in the life of God. Experience of the Spirit can also, of course, be intensely private, but priority must be given to the ecclesial dimension, for the gifts of the Spirit are meant to be shared, and the Pentecostal mission of the Spirit is inherently ecclesial in character.

Among other things, Congar's account also offers a corrective for something broadly under-represented in a good deal of Protestant ecclesiology, which tends in many of its manifestations to disregard the idea of the unity of the church grounded in the presence in it of the Holy Spirit. If the effect of this is to downplay the communal dimension of the Spirit's work, its cause is a certain tendency to highlight instead the role of individual experience of the Spirit; the Spirit, on this view, comes to the individual, who only then and only secondarily "congregates" with others. Thus the church is no longer a first- but a second-order theological concept, as it is literally disassembled into the individuals it comprises, becoming an aggregation of what is really primary—individual religious subjects. Rather than existing as a single whole, chosen and called into being by God, it becomes a pragmatic and inherently adjustable arrangement by which a bewildering variety of individual religious "needs" are addressed. In the context of modernity, this ecclesiological weakness came to be further accentuated as what the philosopher John Gray has

---

27. Ibid., 2:59.

called the "paleo-liberal"[28] dogma of the social contract as the basis of all social order took hold, and as agreement on the principle of religious liberty came increasingly to be drawn upon as the basis of religious expression. If all that matters is the satisfying of individual religious aspiration, then we genuinely arrive at a situation in which no distinction can be drawn between a John Shelby Spong, the bishop who does not believe in God, and anyone else in the Christian tradition, for Spong's religious aspirations, and his realization of them, are clearly as real as anyone's.

What Congar is unable to explain, however, is why it is that the divine Trinitarian relations have their "term," when expressed or prolonged into time, in these marks of the church: unity, holiness, catholicity, and apostolicity. The reason, I suggest, is that he has already given the game away by endorsing the Thomist position on the presence of God, which in all its manifestations is reduced to a created effect ("created grace") in the creature rather than a differentiated form of the presence of God. Unlike Barth, for instance, for whom God relates to particular peoples, times, and places, Congar's God is related to particulars only because he is related generically to everything. The question that needs to be asked concerning Congar's position, therefore, is whether he is entitled in the end to claim what he does: that the church represents the fruition, in time, of the relations between the Father, Son and Holy Spirit. Congar has emptied the theology of divine presence of at least much of the specificity that might come of attending to the varied relations in which the persons of the Trinity stand, which come to expression in time in the economy of salvation. There would be, in principle, a number of ways in which this claim could be developed in a full-scale treatment of the theme—in, for instance, an account of how we come to faith, or of how the Christian life is structured by the gospel story, or in attempting alternatively to accommodate or to foster the charisms. It is, however, the ecclesiological imperative that especially interests us here, particularly as enriched by reference to Trinitarian theology.

At this point, Karl Barth's Trinitarian approach to the theology of the divine presence is of particular importance. Barth's claim is that there is in the triune God a here and a there, a first and a second, an I and a Thou, consisting in the relation of love from all eternity between the Father and the Son in the Holy Spirit. The unity of God as Trinity is not monadic, but

---

28. John Gray, *Enlightenment's Wake: Politics and Culture at the Close of the Modern Age* (London; New York: Routledge, 1990), *passim*.

is, rather, both differentiated and relational. What is more surprising and important in Barth's theology is the way that the divine unity is something infinitely capable of embracing difference. The specific difference that the Trinitarian relations assume in the divine outreach to the world, however, grounds the spanning of a bottomless moral and metaphysical abyss in the incarnation, in such a way that this abyss comes thereby to be included in the relations between the Trinitarian persons. What we have here is a doctrine of the triune God according to which God's power is not diminished, but rather most gloriously expressed, precisely in his becoming weak and suffering the death of the cross.

Hans Urs von Balthasar, following precisely this line of reasoning (if departing from a strictly Barthian vocabulary in developing it), speaks of the need to reckon with a *kenosis* of God in the cross of Jesus Christ, insisting that here there is a specific "theo-logic" established by God himself that contradicts the rather more comfortable continuities of theological reasoning found in far too much Christian thought.[29] For Balthasar, it was in his self-emptying in the suffering and death of Christ, when silence swallowed the Word of God, and revelation seemingly broke off, that the Word of God was in fact most emphatically spoken:

> In his self-emptying, God does not divest himself of his Godhead, but rather . . . [gives it] precise confirmation. . . . [The] God-Man can surrender himself to God abandonment, without resigning his own reality as God. . . . By becoming man, he enters into what is alien to him and there remains at the same time true to himself.[30]

In Balthasar's theology, indeed, the possibility of such a divine presence in abasement, or of a theology of glory in what seems by definition to be inglorious, is founded on nothing less than the inner-Trinitarian love of God, the Holy Spirit, who in the divine freedom unites these "opposites" in himself, overcoming their contradiction, and revealing himself in this action as truly the Lord and Giver of Life.

What I would like to suggest in conclusion is that it ought to be key to the whole of the theological enterprise in general, and thus to

---

29. The sources are numerous and lengthy, but the substance of the case is developed in Hans Urs von Balthasar, *Mysterium Paschale*, trans. Aidan Nichols (Edinburgh: T. & T. Clark, 1990), 23–36, 79–83.

30. Ibid., 80–81.

the problem of pneumatology with it, that God's loving outreach to the world in Jesus Christ is such as to involve a genuine encounter with the abyss, in which the Son of God himself not only becomes subject to finitude and the non-being of death, but also to the curse of sin. Christian theology has always been faced with this mystery, but has shrunk from its implication: that it is not something alien to God to be at one with himself in such condescension. The way of the triune God in Jesus Christ involves that radical claim that even in the apparent contradiction of sin and death, the unity of God is deep enough to withstand the contradiction. Jesus dies the death of the cross, crying out in anguish, "Why have you forsaken me?" From this deeper perspective, it is in fact this loss or sundering of relationship that is embraced by God in Christ, so that nothing less than this precisely is to be conceived as "the fruitfulness, outside God, of the Trinitarian processions," for this is what is "assumed" in the love that is deep and broad and high enough to absorb it. In the mystery of the triune life, death and hell themselves are taken up through the death of Jesus into the unity of the triune God, and it precisely in this way that in the gospel story the power of death and hell are broken, and God's great cause with humankind is vindicated.

This general approach has a range of implications for how we understand the presence of the Holy Spirit in the church, and how we relate in practical terms to the church. Our tendency—perhaps one could speak more plainly of our "temptation" and of our "failing"—is to think that the Spirit of God can only be present where the church has reached a certain standard of faith, or pattern of *praxis*, style of worship, numerical strength, pastoral expertise, standard of preaching, or system of government. Some traditions go so far as to lay claim to ecclesial indefectibility (the inability to err) on the basis of having one or more of these. At the other extreme, there are those who find themselves unable to identify with any one, fallible Christian community because of the shortcomings encountered in them all, and who roam the earth, seeking greater perfection for God's sake, or for what they suppose the name of God to mean. The truth of the matter, however, is that God is pleased to dwell with the ill-formed and the half-formed church, the church that knows only in part and the faith of which is fragile. God dwells with sinners, reconciling *them* to himself. Accordingly, it is in imperfect churches that God is found, for there are none other than these, and no other God than the one whose wise patience and gentle mercy we know in Jesus Christ.

THE PRESENCE OF GOD

In the next chapter I develop these ideas further, as a contribution to what it might mean to come to "know" God in Christ, in the power of the Holy Spirit, and in the life of the church. To conclude, however, I must first return to the place from which I began, the theology of the presence of God the Holy Spirit.

What we saw at the outset was that the idea of the presence of the Spirit has historically been conflated with the idea of omnipresence as a relative attribute of God, and furthermore, that the classical theological theme of divine immutability makes it impossible to speak of the Holy Spirit as coming to dwell with or in the creature in any real sense; what takes place, rather, is that the creature is effectively awakened to the primordial omnipresence. I have argued that this represents an unsatisfactory approach to the theology of God's presence, and that, instead, a theological theory that draws much more heavily on the gospel than upon select traditions of philosophical theology allow us to conceive of the presence of the Spirit in ways that are far more interesting and pregnant with possibility.

We have also seen that the theme of the Spirit as present primarily to individuals suffers from certain definite limitations, the most important of which is that it tends to support the very modern thesis that religion is private in character rather than public and social, and not least, the thesis that what is primary is *religious experience* itself rather than the encounter *with the triune God*. In developing a theology of the presence of the Holy Spirit, normative theological significance needs to be accorded instead to the basic narrative that structures Christian faith, namely, the story of the incarnation, death, and resurrection of Jesus Christ, from which there flows, according to the biblical witness, the subsequent story of Pentecost, the church of Jew and Gentile, and (still to come) the decisive events of eschatology. In the context of the "ecclesiological imperative," as I have called it, what this means has, at heart, simply to do with the fact that God reaches out to and dwells with sinners, and that the church is the place where this presence is proclaimed and known.

2

Spirit, *Geist*, and the Knowledge of God

by Gary Badcock

THE CHURCH: LOCUS OF THE KNOWLEDGE OF GOD?

In a recent work, the German-American theologian Reinhard Hütter has argued that theology in our time has the responsibility to remind the church of its role as the unique setting in which it is possible to come to know God as the one who draws us into relationship with himself through his Word and Spirit.[1] Though this may seem at first glance an innocuous thesis, Hütter argues that in the context of modernity, much of the church has come to understand itself very differently. Owing to a kind of Babylonian captivity to Western political and social liberalism, which for a long time now has been the single most powerful cultural force on the planet, the church has tended to regard itself as rendering service to the sovereign individual of liberalism rather than to God. It is

---

1. Reinhard Hütter, *Suffering Divine Things: Theology as Church Practice*, trans. D. Stott (Cambridge: Eerdmans, 2000); cf. Reinhard Hutter, "The Church," in *Knowing The Triune God: The Work of the Spirit in the Practices of the Church*, eds. J. J. Buckley and D. S. Yaego (Cambridge: Eerdmans, 2001), 23-47.

in such fashion that the individual in modernity has become, in effect, the end of the church. Over against this, Hütter seeks to restore to the church an awareness of its true ground in the Word and Spirit of God, and so of its participation in the Trinitarian economy by which we are reconciled and redeemed. Complaining alike of "the service-jargon pervasive in contemporary church growth talk," and of "the kind of free metaphorical constructivism characterizing especially North American Protestant theology in its more progressive representatives," Hütter lays a counter-emphasis on the distinct practices of the proclamation of the Word of the gospel of grace and the celebration of the sacraments, by which alone the God of the Christian revelation can be known, obeyed, and enjoyed.[2] In Hütter's judgment, in both of these ecclesiological distortions, and in a good many more that are not so expressly mentioned, the importance of these practices has been belittled in favor of the religious aspirations of the individual, the consequence of which has actually been general spiritual and theological impoverishment.

There are several features of the Hütter thesis that are of interest in the present context. The first and most obvious is his focus on pneumatology, both because the church is the sphere of the Spirit in the creedal and theological sense, and because Hütter explicitly maintains that what is received, or "suffered" as he puts it, in the practices of the church (proclamation and sacrament) is nothing less than the work of the Holy Spirit. It is, of course, said in Christian theology to be the distinct work of the Holy Spirit to draw us into fellowship with God through Jesus Christ, and it is upon this general theological conviction that Hütter builds his case. The point is essentially that the work of the Holy Spirit in the Christian life cannot be equated with the goal of authentic religious selfhood found in contemporary expressions of Western Christianity, nor with the more general and underlying realization of the ideal of human freedom and individual flourishing as understood in the liberal state. It is, rather, something expressly and rather narrowly defined and mediated by what we might call the instruments of grace, to which really *all* attention in the life of the church needs to be directed.

A second feature of interest is the clear Trinitarian reference implicit in the whole argument and explicit in much of it; Hütter thus assumes, for example, the mantle of those before him such as Karl Barth (of whom

---

2. Hütter, *Suffering Divine Things*, 23.

he is otherwise intensely critical) who set the doctrine of the Trinity at the very center of the theological enterprise. Hütter's Trinitarianism, however, is not especially well developed. Like many analyses of the work of the Spirit, furthermore, there is something rather wooden about Hütter's approach, which makes it incapable of handling certain of the subtleties of the pneumatological question. Entirely absent, for example, is any awareness of the Spirit as anointing Christ and so also the church, with the result that the christological dimension of the work of the Spirit, deepened by reference to his life of obedience, his passion, his resurrection, and the mysterious transition made in the New Testament from the strictly historical to the ecclesial body of Christ, is all alike wanting.

A third feature of note is how the work of the Spirit appears to be enclosed within the church in its proclamatory and sacramental practices in Hütter's theology. Inevitably, we are led to ask if the Spirit can also be encountered *outside* of these practices, whether within or beyond churchly practices as such. Can the Spirit not be found in a church meeting, a synod or a Council, for instance? It is certainly the *claim* of the tradition that the Spirit is found in such things, though it might well be the *experience* of many that the claim is questionable, but beyond this issue of the Spirit's presence and guidance in church affairs, other and perhaps even greater questions loom large. Is the Spirit, for instance, not to be discerned in the beauty of an exemplary Christian life? What of the witness we encounter there? There would surely be something missing from a theology that was not able to say that the Spirit is at work in and through this too, so much so that this missing piece might well be taken to threaten the whole account offered.

And fourthly, what about all those who so much of the time seem to find the church something of a *barrier* to discipleship and to fellowship with God? To say nothing of the many bad experiences had in suffering the life of the church in meetings and in witnessing the myriad disappointing examples of the Christian life as empirically lived, what of all those many plainly false sermons endured, or those instances of sacramental malpractice that daily or weekly mar the face of the church and impair its work and witness? Are these also the ways in which the Spirit comes to us, or something else altogether?

In the previous chapter I argued that the story of the gospel warrants development of a theology in which God's presence can be found in what is inglorious, and that recognizes that God is present in ways that must seem unexpected. To insist on this is merely to keep in step with a certain definite strand within the biblical narrative. We read, for example, of God's choice of an elderly, childless couple as the ones through whose "seed" he would bless all the peoples of the earth, or further on, of the place of a woman like Rahab the harlot in the plans of God, or of the illiterate agricultural peasants to whom the birth of the Lord's Messiah is announced, of the crucified Lord of glory, and in the end, of the rag-bag of his followers upon whom "the end of the ages" had come, and who accordingly became bearers of the Spirit and heralds of the ingathering of the Gentiles. It is not all like this, to be sure, but the claim of Scripture in these matters is very often revolutionary, threatening to establishments past and present, and it is also well capable of putting off the righteous, once they see it as it is. For of course the righteous not unnaturally tend very often to a sense of superiority over all the mess and sheer helpless need that God is said to save people from, as if once rescued from shipwreck and ensconced in the lifeboat of faith, they were *beyond it all*. Things are, however, not like that, and it is accordingly fundamental to the task of ecclesiology, part and parcel of the "ecclesiological imperative," as I called it, and so to the doctrine of the Holy Spirit which shapes ecclesiology, to recognize and try to account for these things.[3]

SPIRIT AND *GEIST*

Hütter's focus on the theme of the knowledge of God is not, of course, at all unique. In the theology of the twentieth century, it was Karl Barth more than any other who set the problem of the knowledge of God at the center of the pneumatological question. Although Barth's dogmatics of the Holy Spirit was never fully developed, the Spirit was nevertheless a lifelong interest, with work on the subject punctuating the whole span of his theological career.[4] As a pneumatoligist, Barth is best known, how-

---

3. The same thing can, of course, also be done in other ways, through the Augustinian distinction between the visible and the invisible church, for instance, or through the Lutheran insistence on the principle *simil justus et peccator*, but these standard arguments from the tradition do not go far enough because they are not conceived pneumatologically, and so fail to make their stand on the native soil, as it were, of the doctrine of the church—for church and Spirit belong together in the third article of the Creed and in the structures of Christian theology.

4. The most sympathetic account in English is John Thompson, *The Holy Spirit in the Theology of Karl Barth* (Allison Park, PA: Pickwick, 1991).

ever, for his treatment of the Spirit as the "Revealedness" of revelation in *Church Dogmatics* I/1, where he sets the doctrine of the Trinity at the forefront of the entire theological enterprise, and treats it as arising necessarily from the fundamental dynamic of the encounter with God in Jesus Christ.[5] The doctrine of the Trinity arises in the first instance, for Barth, in an analysis of the act of outreach to the world through which God makes himself known: God is (as he famously puts it) not only the Revealer, but is also, in the one dynamic "event" of grace, the Revelation itself and also its Revealedness. It is *through God alone that God is known*—a favorite maxim of Barth's—and this applies not merely to the hidden being of God the Father from which the source of the knowledge of God flows, but also to the content of this knowledge (God the Son is himself the content, or the Revelation itself) and to the mode of its apprehension by human beings (God the Holy Spirit is the realization of this knowledge, or its Revealedness by virtue of the presence of the Spirit in the human creature). That on the level of conscious, intelligent, moral existence we come to God through Jesus Christ, or that we trust and obey in obedient faith, is for Barth the function of the ministry of the Holy Spirit in the world, without which we would be thrown back on our own devices. One might in fact go so far as to say that Barth's doctrine of the Holy Spirit is what frames both his final answer to the vexed problem of natural theology, and his approach to revelation and faith. It is because the trajectories of the two are so divergent that he exhibits such mistrust of the methods and claims of natural theology—not so much because of any doctrine of the "darkened intellect" inherited from Calvinist orthodoxy, in short, as because of the utterly unexpected turn that the revelation of God gives to human claims to the knowledge of God.

In a study published in the 1950s, the Lutheran theologian Gustaf Wingren complained of Barth's "Enlightened" preoccupation with the problem of knowledge rather than with the biblical conceptions of sin and righteousness, and claimed on these terms that there was still much work to be done in theology after the earthquake precipitated by the Barthian movement.[6] Wingren wrote before the publication of the largely pneumatological material of *Church Dogmatics* IV/3-4, while

---

5. Karl Barth, *Church Dogmatics*, eds. G. W. Bromiley and T. F. Torrance, trans. G. W. Bromiley, 2nd ed. (Edinburgh: T. & T. Clark, 1975), I/1:8–12. Hereafter *CD*.

6. Gustaf Wingren, *Theology in Conflict: Nygren, Barth, Bultmann* (Edinburgh: Oliver and Boyd, 1958), 28ff.

what might have come had Barth attempted a volume V on the doctrine of redemption will always remain unknown. Strangely, Wingren also neglected the extensive engagement with ethics that can be identified through the length and breadth of Barth's theology, which is concerned in some ways with questions of sin and righteousness. In broad terms, however, Wingren does put his finger on a certain quality in Barth's theology that someone standing at a distance from Barth's thought might find difficult to accept, and that a good many of the most "scholastic" Barthians, who by instinct would wish to locate themselves as close as possible to the Barthian position, characteristically tend to ignore. For Barth believes that God can *genuinely* be known, and in fact, insists upon the idea of the *rationality* of God as central to the Christian theological enterprise. Indeed, I would go so far as to state flatly that Barth himself, and several of the varieties of Barthianism that have developed in the decades after his death in 1968, are especially marked by the depth of their commitment to the knowability of God. This is so much the case, I would suggest, that more is actually claimed to be known of God in the Barthian tradition than ever before in Christian thought.

There are two sides to this confidence in the knowledge of God that need to be teased out before we move on. The first and most important perhaps, is that the basis claimed for this knowledge is simply that *God has given himself to be known*. The knowledge of God here is said, in short, to rest upon revelation. To take one prominent example, the reserve with which classical Christian theology approaches the Johannine proposition "God is love" (1 John 4:16), and which is explicable on the basis of the idea that nobody, the Apostle not excepted, could ever *really* say what "God is," tends to be abandoned in the tradition to which Karl Barth gave rise, in which God *is* indeed love, as the one whose eternal being is opened to the world in the sending of his Son in Jesus Christ and in the gift of the Spirit. Working on the basis of a variety of adaptations of the principle that the economic and the immanent Trinities are one, the very being of God is seen in the Barthian tradition to be disclosed in the acts of love in which God approaches us and comes near. Resort to a doctrine of the hidden being of God in face of the clarity of such revelation is said to amount to a fundamentally pagan commitment, formed far more by Hellenism as represented in Platonic or Aristotelian thought than by the content of biblical revelation (the claim appears, for instance, in the theology of Robert W. Jenson).[7] Whereas, therefore, God in Christian antiquity is ultimately beyond conception,[8] in much contemporary theology God is conceived much more exactly in terms drawn from the story of salvation. To return to the Barthian roots of the new paradigm, while the tradition at the level of formal systematic theology spends much of its time telling us why we *cannot* know God except distantly in images or by analogy, Karl Barth is able to devote literally thousands of pages to the development of positive theological content, the dominant assumption of which is that God's very being is not only *revealed*, but actually *defined* in what the name of Jesus Christ represents in his theology.

The second feature of this new confidence in knowing God that needs to be made explicit is that it is generally hostile to philosophical elaboration, and in particular to philosophical corroboration. We might "know" the very being of God, in other words, but this knowledge is neither our achievement nor something that can be brought under the *aegis* of purely human thought (the Barthian critique of natural theology looms large at this point). For instance, in his breathtaking theology of the cross developed in *Mysterium Paschale*, Hans Urs von Balthasar insists that the logic of revelation is not reducible to the structures of human reasoning or to philosophical expression. There is no way to "collapse" the fathomless content of revelation into a dialectical system, in terms of which the mystery of God, and the utterly unexpected message of the cross in particular, can become something merely "understood."[9] Balthasar, who is intensely and paradoxically aware of the European philosophical tradition, quite clearly has the philosopher Hegel in view in this criticism, as someone who (it is generally assumed, and certainly assumed by Balthasar) presumed to have claimed to understand the ways and works of God in just this fashion, collapsing the mystery into the limits of a philosophical system.[10] Barth treated Hegel similarly, though maintain-

---

7. Robert W. Jenson, *Systematic Theology* (New York: Oxford University Press, 1997), 8, 10.

8. Jaroslav Pelikan, *Christianity and Classical Culture: The Metamorphosis of Natural Theology in the Christian Encounter with Hellenism* (New Haven: Yale University Press, 1993), 40–73.

9. Hans Urs von Balthasar, *Mysterium Paschale*, trans. Aidan Nichols (Edinburgh: T. & T. Clark, 1990), 82.

10. Some years ago, I argued that this polemic misrepresents Hegel's position in "Divine Freedom in Hegel," *ITQ* 61.3-4 (1995) 265–71.

ing, interestingly, that the real problem with Hegel is not so much that he *attempted* to grasp the mystery of God as something amenable to human thought, but that his methods of doing so involved relinquishing the freedom of God, or what Barth calls God's ontic and noetic autonomy, which are the very marks of deity (this is what is sometimes spoken of in Barthian terms as the "Godness of God"). The mystery of God, for Barth, is revealed and so given to us, and can genuinely be *known* as such, but it is yet never placed within our grasp in such fashion as to be properly subject to human logic.[11]

It would be worth our while posing the question whether anything is lost or gained by taking this hostile stance against philosophical understanding. In Hegel's philosophy, for instance, it is seemingly possible to grasp the logical relations in which God and the creature stand—and in this context, to grasp the logic of the incarnation itself. The great question would be whether or not Hegel thinks that this rational grasp of the ways of God is complete or something possible only in fragments, and at a distance from the source—"in a mirror, dimly"—since it is necessarily mediated in human thought and by human speech. The common assumption is that Hegel believed a complete grasp of this logic possible, perhaps because of the extraordinary conceptual athleticism that characterizes his writing as much as anything, so that it becomes possible, in effect, to think the categories that exist in the mind of God. (I note here in passing that, in principle, this claim is actually a commonplace of Western philosophy, or at least of philosophy of the Platonist-Realist-Rationalist variety, and that, against this background, such confidence in reason is scarcely a radical or novel thought. In this tradition, that $1+1=2$ is as true for God as it is for me, its truth being contained within the wisdom of God itself, *to which we have at least this measure of access*.) The result is that Hegel is assumed to speak in a totalizing manner of all reality, albeit in a philosophical system informed by a range of Trinitarian and incarnational ideas.[12] This can lead an undiscerning reader to conclude that

---

11. The source here is Barth's essay "Hegel," in Karl Barth, *Protestant Theology in the Nineteenth Century: Its Background & History*, trans. B. Cozens and J. Bowden (London: SCM, 1972), 384–421.

12. It is in this sense that, in Hegel's philosophy, the Christian doctrines of incarnation and Pentecost represent, even if only in the "pictorial" terms of religious *Vorstellung*, the absolute truth, and it is the vocation of the Hegelian philosopher to conceive of this truth in speculative philosophical reasoning as working itself out as

Hegel believed the logical concept as apprehended by the philosopher is more fundamental than the being, will, and action of the living God. This is what also led some of Hegel's less circumspect and certainly more radical disciples to assert that it is the human grasp of these things in the "moment" of thought alone that matters. Theologically, the implication would be that as the "idea" of the incarnation of God is all we need, it is no longer necessary to think of it as ever having actually *taken place* once and for all in Jesus of Nazareth. Thus, e. g., David F. Strauss famously maintains that it is the *myth* of God incarnate that we need, not the fact of it in the sense maintained in the Christian tradition—and indeed, that it is only when its quality as myth is recognized that its true power, its universality we might say, can be unleashed in such a way as to make the story told truly effective. It is as myth alone that the doctrine of the incarnation transcends the scandal of particularity.[13]

Though Hegel claimed no such thing, it is this strand of interpretation that has typically dominated the imagination of theologians and of philosophers with religious interests who write about him. A recent example is William Desmond, who in *Hegel's God: A Counterfeit Double* argues against what he sees as the all-too-Enlightened rational domestication of the living God of Christian revelation in Hegel's thought, even while managing to avoid the worst excesses of the aforementioned Straussian gloss.[14] I should like to state for the record at this point that I believe that Hegel can be defended against much of this, but to make such a case for the defense is well beyond the scope of this chapter;[15] for the present, I wish to develop a rather humbler argument. Let me observe in

---

it weaves itself through the processes of human history. In Hegelianism, it is owing to Christian revelation, in which God is truly revealed, that one can know the truth of everything. The qualification (often forgotten) is that Hegel is basically interested in how these ideas are woven into the fabric of the world and of human thought rather than in God himself, so much so that he seldom speaks of God directly, but more commonly of the rather formal concept of the Absolute. He is not, in short, so much a *theologian* as a *philosopher*. On this latter point, a theologically perceptive work by one of the "British Hegelians" of the late nineteenth and early twentieth centuries is helpful: Andrew Seth, *Hegelianism and Personality* (Edinburgh: W. Blackwood, 1887), 170ff.

13. David F. Strauss, *The Life of Jesus, Critically Examined*, ed. P. C. Hodgson, trans. G. Eliot (Philadelphia: Fortress, 1972), 757ff.

14. William Desmond, *Hegel's God: A Counterfeit Double?* (Aldershot: Ashgate, 2003).

15. A monograph on the subject is projected.

passing, however, that it is not only Hegel or Hegelianism which seeks to realize the universal significance of the incarnation. This, one might state flatly, is really only an adaptation of the most basic of all Christian faith claims. On the question of the knowledge of God, as we have seen, the Barthians too affirm a true knowledge of God, *as he is in himself* no less, while also demonstrating a remarkable capacity to weave the particular logic of the incarnation through the wider fabric of human thought—Thomas F. Torrance on physical science springs instantly to mind, but there are parallels to this that can be identified in theological writing on everything from bioethics to politics—and so are far from confining the basic concept for which they stand to some world of purely private, religious interest. For a Barthian, after all, creation itself takes place on the basis of the covenant, while the covenant is conceived in thoroughly christological fashion. If, in short, the incarnation stands at the center of God's relation to the cosmos, then insofar as it is possible to speak of God's relation to nature at all, it is not only possible, but obligatory, for us to throw light upon it by reference to what stands at its center as its true organizing principle, its *logos*—Jesus Christ the God-man.

It was, as is well known, what seemed to him to be the absurd overreach of the Hegelian philosophical system that led Søren Kierkegaard to conclude that, while conceptual castles are all well and good, one has actually to live in the world as a finite individual, and accordingly, to maintain against Hegel that the great man's life had in fact been rather more mundane than the system he constructed. This might perhaps be taken to be the upshot of the Barthian critique of Hegel also, except that, in the light of the preceding observations, we might well ask whether a similar criticism could not be leveled against Barth and his disciples also. A secularist, for instance, might have no difficulty in making this allegation, or in arguing a case against the intrusion of an explicitly religious conceptuality into the proper domain of rational science. The Kierkegaardian critique, furthermore, can be construed in such a way as to give it a distinctly anti-Barthian edge, despite Barth's early interest in existentialism, since Barth is in general notoriously disinterested in the quality of religious experience, or in the choices made by the individual, and tends to regard an obsession with such things as a variation on that "invention of the anti-Christ," so ancient and so new, that is natural theology. As early in his theological career as 1934, Barth had uttered a clear and resounding "*Nein*" to all of that, in response to the more sympathetic line taken towards it by his contemporary, Emil Brunner.[16]

What is the importance of this? The fact is that the realm of spirit is commonly conflated with the human capacity for rational or spiritual self-awareness, typically in the form of art, religion, and similar cultural exercises. On one level, Hegel is rightly taken to be a major representative of just such a position. Yet, on the other, Hegel's treatment of Spirit refuses to be confined within these narrow limits. In the Hegelian system, after all, it is of fundamental significance that the Christian religion is revealed, that in Christian revelation God becomes human, and that from his "self-othering" in so doing there comes about the reconciliation of infinite and finite; in the God-man, even the absolute limit of finitude in death is met and overcome. Hegel, trained as a pastor in late scholastic Lutheran orthodoxy, does not dwell long on these themes for their own sake, but what we find in his thought is a procession through what is conventionally known as thesis to antithesis, arriving finally at a stage of thought that transcends both, a kind of *coincidenta oppositorum*. This last is the substance of the concept of *Geist* in Hegelian conceptuality. In *Geist*, apparent contraries are reconciled, not only logically or by way of intellectual principle, but in concrete actuality, as they come to be taken up in a higher unity that shows their earlier formulations to be abstraction. In human terms, at any rate, the reconciliation is something embedded in a stance that involves the suspension of the earlier conflict. Ultimately, since for Hegel ideas are always secondary to life, such a *coincidenta oppositorum* takes place primarily in the formation of a culture, a form of human life that realizes this reconciliation in actual existence (though always incompletely, since thought and being are identical only in God). It is also for this reason that Hegel can speak of the "labor" and "pain" of such development, and thus it is too that in a work like the famously difficult *Phenomenology of Spirit*, the transition from one category to the next is often anything but an easy one, spanning centuries of painstaking change.

---

16. Karl Barth, *Nein! Antwort an Emil Brunner*, Theologicische Existenz Heute 14 (Munich: Kaiser, 1934).

THE SPIRIT OF CHRIST AND THE SPIRIT IN THE CHURCH

We began with Reinhard Hütter's thesis concerning the church as the place in which it is uniquely possible to know God, and noted the limitations of that thesis, which lie chiefly in the pneumatological restrictions that it places upon us, and indeed, upon God. Nevertheless, Hütter's theology has the merit of emphasizing that the knowledge of God is both something that involves being drawn into the divine Trinitarian economy, and that this event is inextricably bound up with the worship and life of the church, as the *locus* of divine action in the world. "Knowledge" may be a poor word for what Hütter has in view, but it is the word he uses, and as there is extensive reference to the propositional (biblical and creedal or confessional) content of faith in his approach, there are good grounds for persevering with his usage. On the other side, we have the philosopher Hegel, whose position is frequently taken to represent a gnosticizing threat to the gospel, and in some interpreter's eyes, its wholesale reduction to a system of ideas as opposed to faithful trust in the mighty acts of God in salvation history. Yet, I wish to argue that Hegel, that dangerous and often almost incomprehensible sage of the early nineteenth century, can help us to deepen our grasp of what it is that takes place in coming to know God in the life of the church, and in particular, to see that what is mediated by the Spirit is something that extends beyond our "suffering" of Word and sacrament in the public ministry of the church.

To make this point, let me refer briefly to the Augustinian theory on which both Hütter and Hegel appear to rely: that the Holy Spirit in the divine Trinitarian life can be understood as the "bond of love" between the Father and the Son. St. Augustine developed this pneumatological theory soon after his conversion, but lent it particularly massive support in one of the great works of his old age, which also ranks among the most important works of Latin patristic theology generally—his *De Trinitate*.[17] This theory, which later became Latin doctrine in the form of the *filioque* gloss on the Latin text of the Nicene Creed, lies at the heart of the Western Christian understanding of the relation, not only between the Father and the Son, and between Christ and the Spirit, but also between Christian and Christian. It grounds, for instance, the theory that the Spirit is source of the church's internal communion; in Augustine's hands, this notion

---

17. For an account, see my *Light of Truth and Fire of Love: A Theology of the Holy Spirit* (Grand Rapids: Eerdmans, 1997), 66–81.

appears in the idea of the Spirit as the church's animating principle, or "soul."[18] To have one such soul implies that we are to live as one, for the common soul of the church is the eternal principle of unity itself, the Trinitarian *vinculum caritatis*.

In the first half of the theology of the twentieth century, the Augustinian "bond of love" theory came to have a particularly important place in official Roman Catholic ecclesiology,[19] while a more speculative adaptation of the tradition appeared in the era of the Second Vatican Council in the work of the influential pneumatologist Heribert Mühlen. For Mühlen, the Spirit's work is that of one person, the third person of the Trinity, with, among, and in many persons—first in the divine Trinitarian life, and derivatively in the church.[20] This role of the Spirit as the one in the many is ultimately grounded, of course, in the relation of the Spirit to the other divine persons in the eternal Trinitarian life, for here the Spirit is something common to the Father and the Son, and ultimately the Spirit of both, *qui procedit ex Patre Filioque*. Mühlen describes the work of the Spirit in "personological" terms, maintaining that the Spirit maintains relationship first of all between the Father and the Son as their corporate We, next by extension between the Father and Christ in his human nature, then between the Holy Spirit and the church as the fruit of Christ's incarnate work, and finally among the baptized themselves. The call of God to faith, love, and obedience is, therefore, a call to new relationship above all, relationship that is both fully personal and also corporate and fully ecclesial. To be a Christian is to be given a share in the dynamic, "personological" life of the triune God himself, and to be invited into this is to be invited also to new life together with others.

What we can clearly see from the constructive pneumatology of a thinker like Mühlen is that there is still, to say the least, a strand of vitality in these ancient formulations from which we may still stand to learn and to benefit. There is, however, also something missing from it, a lack which is equally and paradoxically so serious that it renders much of what is

---

18. Augustine, "Sermon 267.4" (PL 38:1231) and "Sermon 268.2" (PL 38:1232).

19. In particular, the idea is taken up and developed in Pius XII's encyclical *Mystici Corporis Christi*.

20. The main works are Heribert Mühlen, *Der Heilige Geist als Person: in der Trinität, bei der Inkarnation und im Gnadenbund: Ich, du, wir*, 5th ed., Münsterische Beiträge zur Theologie 26 (Münster: Aschendorf, 1988); and especially Heribert Muhlen, *Una Mystica Persona*, 2nd ed. (Paderborn, Ger.: Schöningh, 1967).

said profoundly deadening. The problem, indeed, is so far-reaching that it ought to raise doubts in good Christian minds concerning what counts as pneumatological orthodoxy. For what is missing is nothing less than the *pathos* and alienation of the cross, the fact that in the crucified Christ, God is found in his contrary, glory in the highest in what is inglorious by definition—or, to paraphrase the rightly famous lines of St. Paul, "wisdom in what looks foolish and supreme power in utter helplessness." In short, God in Christ is found where he is supposed *not* to be, and yet, in face of this, one must also say that as "God was in Christ," the Spirit who is the bond of love between the Father and the Son also binds together the Father and the crucified one, even at the limit of suffering and in the estrangement of death. That the Holy Spirit is involved in the passion of the Lord is, it is true, a kind of common knowledge—in that we read that "through the eternal Spirit [he] offered himself without blemish to God" (Heb 9:14), and in that this has always been "acknowledged" on the basis of the abstract principle, *opera ad extra trinitatis sunt indivisa*—except that there has been so little said at this point that it is hard to say whether anything has really *ever* been understood of it. For it is not only the case that, in the womb of Mary, or in the baptism in the Jordan, or in his rejoicing in the Spirit, or in his casting out demons by the finger of God, the Holy Spirit is present and active, spanning the abyss of being the divides the Creator and the creature. Again, it is not only the case, as Yves Congar puts it in one place, that the Spirit mediates the incarnation at each stage of Jesus' life, according to which there is a progressive realization in Jesus himself of what he was from the beginning.[21] For it is also the case that, at the point at which the abyss seems most threatening, when the Word of God falls silent in death and the life of the one in whom all things hold together has been broken apart, that *there* we see the height and depth, the wealth and the richness of the love of the Son for the Father, and yes, of the Father for the Son. For in this he is not let go; it is in this event above all others that the Word of God rings out in the God-man with special clarity, and there above all that the unity of this one with the Father is raised up high for all to see. The Spirit of God is rich enough to span the gulf that is opened at this point, to breathe life into death, and yes, to preserve the unity of God the Father and the Son, even in the scream of the crucified, "Why have you forsaken me?"

21. Yves Congar, *The Word and the Spirit*, trans. David Smith (London: G. Chapman, 1986), 87, 92.

How to understand this is the problem, for it seems not to fall under any of our neat theological categories, nor to accord with the usual continuities by which we seek to organize the body of Christian doctrine. Things ought to be one way or the other, we like to think, and not both. And yet, there is one voice that tries, at least, to give all of this a sense and a meaning, and indeed, to make that meaning regulative in human thought in general. The voice, of course, is Hegel's, who for all his gnosticizing tendencies, alleged and real, and for all his Enlightened propensity to set aside the Word of God in wrestling with human wisdom and human reason, nevertheless speaks with special clarity of the way in which the concept of Spirit involves always a union realized in the reconciliation of apparent opposites, in the overcoming of the alienation between what is often called, in one of the grosser over-simplifications in the history of ideas, thesis and antithesis, and who accordingly sought out a pattern of thought in which the reconciliation of the infinite with the finite could become something both knowable and known.[22] While by no means wishing to advocate a full-scale renaissance in Hegelian Christianity, I do wish to argue that in the whole matter of our relationship with the Western philosophical tradition, there may yet be some "spoils of Egypt" that lie still undiscovered in this man's forbidding and labyrinthine work.[23]

Let me be more concrete, beginning with the theology of Reinhard Hütter. Hütter has argued that the church is the unique *locus* in which it is possible to come to know God as the one who calls us into fellowship through his Word, in the power of the Holy Spirit. The church is not, as he rightly argues, a venue for self-help or for the peculiar form of spiritual underachievement that hides under the banner of Christian self-realization. It is, rather, to put words into his mouth, "the house where God lives."[24] What Hütter is unable to see or to say, however, is that the power of the Spirit can also be present in those members of the church for whom self-help or self-realization is indeed all; that these too,

---

22. Note, however, that in Hegel's own idiom, such a rational grasp of things is "speculative," whereas the finite concepts of "understanding" must remain forever locked in antinomies.

23. Hans Küng makes a similar point in *The Incarnation of God*, trans. J. R. Stephenson (Edinburgh: T. & T. Clark, 1987), 413–508.

24. This phrase is the title of my latest book, *The House Where God Lives: The Doctrine of the Church* (Grand Rapids: Eerdmans, 2009).

even in their most half-baked forms, can yet be prophets through whom the Word of God is spoken to us. Hütter's theology, in short, lends itself to easy continuities, in which what is true and what is false are clearly labeled and clinically separated, whereas the gospel ought to teach us that God loves sinners, failures, the foolish, and those in error, and that he takes these and not some ideal humanity to himself as his own.

Similarly, in the theology of a man like Heribert Mühlen, the Holy Spirit as the "We-in-Person" of the Father and the Son grounds the answering We of the church. But what of the sometimes hostile other who refuses to be numbered with this We, let us say, this particular very Roman Catholic We that Mühlen himself clearly had in mind when he wrote these things? What of the one who prefers to remain outside and at a safe distance from its excesses? Is this person—or, to be more exact, are these sorts of Christians, and the separate communities to which they belong—beyond the sphere of the Spirit's power and work? The answer to this (as has been notably and widely recognized even in Roman Catholic ecclesiology since the Second Vatican Council) is clearly "No." It is indeed implicit in the very idea of the church as the body of Christ that this body should be one rather than divided, but what is not true is that, on account of the empirical disunity of this body, the Spirit is not present in it at all, for the Spirit is thankfully rather more capable than are we of comprehending contradiction and of overcoming enmity.

A final concrete example of where such a pneumatology might lead can be seen in a contribution to a volume on evangelical ecclesiology by the Irish-American Methodist William Abraham.[25] Abraham maintains that the American mainline desperately needs the evangelical movement, in order for it to be renewed and reminded of the vitality of faith and the encounter with God that stands at the heart of everything, but he maintains that the evangelicals need the mainline also, in order to rescue them from distortion (and occasionally from rank irresponsibility, e. g., in relation to the teaching of the biological theory of evolution in the schools), and not least, to recall them to attend to questions of justice and social practice. In other words, it can often be in hearing the voice of the other, and very often of *the other for whom we have little or no time or respect*,

---

25. William J. Abraham, "Inclusivism, Idolatry and the Survival of the (Fittest) Faithful," in *The Community of the Word: Toward an Evangelical Ecclesiology*, eds. M. Husbands and D.J. Treier (Downers Grove, IL: InterVarsity, 2005), 131–45.

that the still small voice of the Spirit comes to us. In recent months, I have personally been massively preoccupied with this insight in response to the threatened collapse of the Anglican Communion, which badly needs such a rediscovery of the nature of the church as a balance of tensions and emphases, and of the fact that even those who are plainly wrong still can have something true to say. There are, indeed, times at which it is necessary even for the lie to be pursued to the limit in order for the truth finally to shine forth (the service of the heretics in all ages), and as Hegel would want to teach us, there are times when there is nothing that we can do but remain faithful in the midst of evident distortion, when all around our fellows rush headlong into error. What is left for us is only to bear witness—and wait for them to awaken, or rather, to be awakened, to something higher, richer, and truer. And so it is for each of us also, and while this is no doubt so for each of us in our own measure, there are none of us who escape these limits. One is reminded here of Ephraim Radner's rueful study *The End of the Church*, which perhaps overstates the case to be made, but nevertheless argues that where Christ's body has been broken, and where its brokenness is willfully sustained, there can be no authentic Christian understanding of Scripture, no adequate sense of holiness, nor a truly eucharistic worship.[26] This may go too far, but it is still true that in such a situation the Spirit has been divided, so that a fundamental theological task becomes that of recognizing the brokenness of the church, reminding Christians of the needlessness of their divisions. Amid the theological and spiritual rubble, it is finally in fellowship with the other who stands, for the moment, beyond the ecclesiological pale that we will come to know the triune God.

It is, however, important to remember even here that God's presence in Christ is his presence in a broken world and, at its apex, in his *broken* body. It is in this very brokenness, indeed, that God's power proves to be *God's*. At this point, I cannot resist a reference to my late teacher Alan Lewis's great work *Between Cross and Resurrection*, which argues so forcefully for the presence of God in a church found amid the brokenness and godlessness of the world.[27] This is the very place where God lay

---

26. Ephraim Radner, *The End of the Church: A Pneumatology of Christian Division in the West* (Grand Rapids: Eerdmans, 1998).

27. Alan E. Lewis, *Between Cross and Resurrection: A Theology of Holy Saturday* (Grand Rapids: Eerdmans, 2001), 370.

when Christ was in the grave, and the church as his ecclesial body can scarcely escape the cruciform pattern of existence assumed by its Lord. Our peculiar temptation is to think of the life of the church and of the ways in which the knowledge of God is mediated through it in terms of straightforward continuities: we sign up to, let us say, thirty-nine articles, and not infrequently, we assume that the Spirit's work is best represented only among those who have done likewise, or who might if given the chance. In reality, the Holy Spirit blows wild and free, and is at work beyond our narrow continuities, in ways that confound expectation and that not infrequently contradict our articles of religion, however theologically "pure" they may be.

To be even bolder, I would like to suggest that the gift of the Holy Spirit to the church not only has its effect in the plurality of gifts seen in 1 Corinthians 12, or in the plurality of ministries of Romans 12, but also in the kind of plurality so clearly seen in the canon, and superabundantly in the multitude of theologies and theological stances seen in the Christian tradition. It is characteristic of major forms of Christian theology to refer to "tradition" as if it were one thing, whereas in fact, it is many things—a bewildering variety of seemingly contradictory positions and claims that vie for attention and loyalty. Yet, if 1 Corinthians and Romans or the sheer character of the canon itself are to be taken as guides, what we ought to be able to think and say is that the Spirit of God is such as to be present not only in one of these narrower systems, but also in others that seem, on the surface, to be contradictory and alien to it. A theology of the coincidence of opposites is needed at this point, not merely because what contradicts also often corrects, but also because what seems contradictory to us is not necessarily contradictory to God.

Methodological approaches to Christian theology that take up the challenge of these claims are surprisingly rare, but in an important recent study, Kevin J. Vanhoozer makes a case for such a pluriform or polyphonic understanding over that of the monological theological system.[28] Basing his argument on the fact of the canon, Vanhoozer maintains that the "drama of doctrine" is such as actually to *require* tension, action on a number of fronts, and both claim and counterclaim made in a plurality of contexts. There is thus a communitarian and dialogical dimension that needs to be acknowledged as foundational in theology, within which

---

28. Kevin J. Vanhoozer, *The Drama of Doctrine: A Canonical-Linguistic Approach to Christian Theology* (Louisville: Westminster John Knox, 2005), 268ff.

doctrinal pluralism is not only something that can be affirmed on the fringes, but becomes something essential to the subject. The pluralism may not be limitless—for it is the one story that must be proclaimed, and something in particular rather than everything in general is to be believed—but the reality is that the story of Christian doctrine is such that it can only properly be heard when the tale is told from more than one standpoint.

There is, however, need at this point to take realistic account of the fact that such doctrinal pluralism must embrace those with whom we genuinely disagree. To speak, with Reinhard Hütter, of the church as a place in which it is possible to come to know the triune God by the power of the Spirit, means that in the church, we "suffer" the work of the Spirit who is present in the relation of the crucified Christ to the Father and poured out by the Christ who still bears the marks of his suffering, and whose love is therefore no stranger to division. God is the one who reconciles *sinners* to himself, after all, and whose truth is pleased to dwell with the half-formed and the uninformed. This, of course, is a good thing—for we are surely such. And yet, it must also serve as the source of painful recognition of limits, since in the life of the church we find that God accepts as sons and daughters some whom we can scarcely abide and others with whom we cannot and perhaps ought not to share a single mind.

To speak of the Spirit at work in the life of the church as source of the knowledge of God, therefore, requires a great deal of us by way of Christian "life together,"[29] while the knowledge of God must be far more than something cerebral, since it extends so clearly to and through the moral, social, and affective spheres. To cite Thomas Aquinas once more, and to return to the content of my first contribution to the present volume of essays, the true knowledge of God that is born of the Spirit is such as to burst forth in love, transcending our petty rivalries and our cherished positions. For so rich is the work and power of the Spirit, the source of salvation and the gift of God.

---

29. The reference is to Deitrich Bonhoeffer's *Life Together*, in *Dietrich Bonhoeffer's Works*, eds. W. W. Floyd Jr. et al., trans. D. Bloesch and J. H. Burtness (Philadelphia: Fortress, 1996–), 5:25–118.

3

A Pneumatology for an Everyday Theology: Whither the Anonymous Spirit in Luke 10:1–12?

by Steve Taylor

CAN THERE BE AN "EVERYDAY THEOLOGY"?

Moving in quite a different direction, perhaps, from the first two chapters by Gary Badcock, this chapter seeks a pneumatology by which theology might engage with popular culture. Following a brief survey of the current writing in the area of everyday theology, a number of questions are directed at the biblical narrative, specifically Luke 10:1–12. The presence in this text of the Spirit as anonymous is suggested as a narrated patterning which can then be applied when considering a theology among popular and everyday culture.

In 1982, Douglas Hall argued that theology needed to farewell its traditional dialogue partner, philosophy.[1] Instead it needed to turn to popular culture because, for Hall, popular culture was now the main carrier of Western culture's search for meaning. A similar argument is made by David Brown, when he argued for a reconceiving of the sacramental

---

1. Dougls J. Hall, "'Who Tells the World's Story?' Theology's Quest for a Partner in Dialogue," *Int* 36 (1982) 47–53.

because "the Church and its theologians have made a very serious error in withdrawing from theological engagement with large experiences that were once the Church's concern."[2] He challenged the church to conceive a sacramentality by which it might engage with the everyday domains and discourses of popular culture (including food, music, dance, town planning, landscape art and architecture).

Since then contemporary theological exploration of everyday culture has become almost popular. Let me briefly mention four examples. Tom Beaudoin's *Virtual Faith* proposed a contemporary generation formed by popular culture and outlined an everyday theology based on tattoos, cyberspace, body-piercing, and grunge music.[3] He employed the religious scholarship of Eliade to interpret body piercing, the life of Bernard of Clairvaux and the ancient Christian fish symbol to interpret various music videos and show that "theology can shed light on interpreting popular culture, even as popular culture imagines new ways of illustrating, upending, and carrying forward theological themes."[4]

A second example is Vanhoozer, Anderson and Sleasman's, *Everyday Theology. How to Read Cultural Texts and Interpret Cultural Texts*. A lengthy prolegomena by Vanhoozer introduced the argument that Christian theology needs to engage popular culture (what Vanhoozer calls "everyday theology"), followed by case studies in which theological conversations were conducted with items for sale at a supermarket checkout, the life and music of rap singer Eminem, the movie Gladiator, the cyberspace phenomena of blogging, and cultural practices present in contemporary weddings and funerals.[5]

A third example is *A Matrix of Meanings: Finding God in Pop Culture*, in which Craig Detweiler and Barry Taylor explore the spiritual search in the post-Christian Western world. After listening to the messages offered by advertising, celebrities, extreme sports, film, and fashion, they argue these are an embodied theological search. "God did not create extreme

---

2. David Brown, "Re-conceiving the Sacramental," in *The Gestures of God: Explorations in Sacramentality*, ed. G. Rowell and C. Hall (London: Continuum, 2004), 21.

3. Tom Beaudoin, *Virtual Faith: The Irreverent Spiritual Quest of Generation X* (San Francisco: Jossey-Bass, 1998).

4. Ibid., 179.

5. Kevin J. Vanhoozer, Charles A. Anderson, and Michael J. Sleasman, eds., *Everyday Theology: How to Read Cultural Texts and Interpret Trends* (Grand Rapids: Baker Academic, 2007).

sports to proclaim a message. Kids created extreme sports as a subversive form of worship. It is a radically new theology, not a convenient evangelistic opportunity."[6] For Detweiler and Taylor, we need to create a theology out of pop culture, rather than a theology for pop culture.[7]

From the United Kingdom, Gordon Lynch's book *Understanding Theology and Popular Culture* sought to provide a methodological primer for the discipline. It offered an author-focused approach (rap artist Eminem), a text focused approach (an episode of *The Simpsons*) and an ethnographic approach (experiences of people entering into club cultures) in seeking a "full academic engagement with popular culture [that] requires that we engage in a rigorous analysis of the truthfulness, meaningfulness, goodness, justice, and beauty of popular cultural texts and practices."[8]

Such writings raise a number of questions. The first of these is in relation to authorial intent. Reading the various attempts at pop culture theology, one finds at times an almost breathless adulation of "theology" in all things everyday and popular. However, when a Christian theologian names God's presence in a cultural artifact, what place should be given to the intent of the author of that artifact? Can theological reflection on everyday culture find more in a cultural artifact than the creating author intended? In a postmodern world of reader response theory, the authors of popular cultural artifacts might be left with little intellectual room for complaint. However, the ethical question remains of how to avoid a rerun of colonization, in which a theological reader declares the "real" meaning of a cultural artifact.

This raises a second and related question, of the relationship between articulating a theology in popular culture and the inherited theological traditions of the church. In introducing his theology of everyday and popular culture, Kevin Vanhoozer noted, "I think it is a mistake to identify an authoritative speaking of the Spirit apart from Christ and the Scriptures. The Spirit's activity outside the church includes restraining

---

6. Craig Detweiler and Barry Taylor, *A Matrix of Meanings: Finding God in Pop Culture* (Grand Rapids: Baker Academic, 2003), 268.

7. More recently, see Barry Taylor, *Entertainment Theology: New-Edge Spirituality in a Digital Democracy* (Grand Rapids: Baker Academic, 2008).

8. Gordon Lynch, *Understanding Theology and Popular Culture* (Malden, MA: Blackwell, 2005), ix.

sin and even illumining truth, but not speaking words."⁹ Vanhoozer is arguing for a theological shift toward popular culture, yet is unwilling to offer an authoritative status to a speaking that is outside the church. Does this not undermine the very discipline he is seeking to promote?

A third question, captured by the well-known pop cultural phrase, "How low can you go?"¹⁰ is raised by the theological work of Graham Ward. He urged a christological discourse with "conscious reference to the cultural situation in which and to which it spoke,"¹¹ and argued that we need to characterize the work of Christ "in terms of the ordinary human operations of that world—its politics, economics, social and cultural milieu, his friends, his family, his enemies, his admirers."¹² What remains problematic is that Ward's "ordinary world" is the world of Continental philosophy and his dialogue partners are intellectuals including Luce Irigaray and Jean-Luc Nancy. Such "ordinary human operations" seem a long way removed from a Snoop Dog concert or a zombie movie.¹³ Are there places in pop culture that remain too banal or offensive for the theologian to engage in discourse?

This chapter will explore such questions by suggesting a pneumatology in relation to everyday theology, with particular reference to Luke 10:1–12. My argument is that since the Spirit is narrated to us around table and in oil, water, bread, and wine, we must befriend theologically the everyday and pop cultural narratives of "living in a material world" (to use yet another well-known pop culture phrase).¹⁴ In these narratives we can find a redemptive participation in Christ's work of making God known and the Spirit's work of blessing the life of gift and gratitude that the Son shares with the Father. Thus, a theology of popular culture is a participation in the work of the Spirit that finds depth and coherence as a narration of a profoundly Trinitarian patterning. This movement might address the questions raised above regarding the honoring of authorial intent, without negating a reader response, and concerning the relation-

---

9. Kevin J. Vanhoozer, "What Is Everyday Theology?," in *Everyday Theology*, 42n104.

10. Jim Jacobs and Warren Casey, "Born to Hand Jive," *Grease: the Original Soundtrack from the Motion Picture* (Polydor/Umgd, 1978).

11. Graham Ward, *Christ and Culture* (Malden, MA: Blackwell, 2005), 16.

12. Ibid., 12.

13. Kim Paffenroth, *Gospel of the Living Dead: George Romero's Visions of Hell on Earth* (Waco: Baylor University Press, 2006).

14. Madonna, "Material Girl," *Like a Virgin* (Sire Records, 1984).

ship between theological exploration and inherited ecclesiological understandings, no matter how "low" the everyday, popular cultural context.

THE ANONYMOUS SPIRIT AND THE BODY: LUKE 9:29–35

Luke is arguably the Bible's pneumatological theologian *par excellence*.[15] The phrase being "baptised and filled with Spirit" occurs twelve times in his writings, compared to once in each of the Pauline letters. The Spirit is mentioned seventeen times in the Gospel of Luke, in contrast to six times in the Gospel of Mark and twelve times in the Gospel of Matthew. For Stronstad,

> Luke gives the greatest emphasis to this renewal of charismatic or prophetic activity. He did so, no doubt, because he believed that it made a vital contribution toward illuminating the meaning of the gift of the Spirit. . . . For Luke it is impossible to divorce either the mission of Jesus from the activity of the Spirit, or the mission of the disciples from the activity of the Spirit.[16]

In Luke the Spirit is named in the infancy narratives (six references in 1:15, 17, 35, 41, 67; and 2:25–27) and in the inauguration narratives (five references in 3:16, 22; 4:1 (twice), 14). The Gospel also has four other references to the Spirit (10:21; 11:13; 12:10, 12). Of these four, Stronstad makes the astonishing claim that they "make no significant contribution to Luke's theology."[17]

While the above serves to introduce the primary biblical text I wish to engage, Luke 10:1–12, as having "no significant contribution," I want to frame my argument by starting in the chapter before with the account of the transfiguration (9:28–36). It is noteworthy that in both texts, unlike the Lukan infancy narratives or the Lukan inauguration narratives, the Spirit is not named. Instead the Spirit is anonymous. Yet most readings of the transfiguration—theological, liturgical, and pictorial—narrate the Spirit as present.

---

15. Roger Stronstad argued for the literary and theological continuity in Luke-Acts, and the need to read Luke as having a "significant, unique, and independent contribution to the doctrine of the Holy Spirit." Roger Stronstad, *The Charismatic Theology of St. Luke* (Peabody, MA: Hendrickson, 1984), 11.

16. Ibid., 47.

17. Ibid., 46.

Theologically, for Eugene Rogers, in the transfiguration we see a Trinitarian narration. "The condition for the possibility of creating is the Father. The condition for the possibility of creation is the Son. The condition for the possibility of creation's having time and space to be created—to be material and enduring—is the Spirit."[18] Textually, the phrase "listen to Him" (Luke 9:35, NIV) occurs also in Deuteronomy 18:5 and thus links Jesus with the Spirit endowed ministry of Moses. For Stronstad, "In contemporary Judaism both Moses and Elijah were end-times or messianic figures. And so, both singly and collectively, they formed an appropriate model for the charismatic or Spirit-anointed ministry of Jesus."[19]

Similar themes are present in religious art. For instance, in the *Allegory of the Transfiguration* by Saint Apollinaire (c. 540), the three persons of the Trinity are present: the Father in the hand, the Son in the cross, the Spirit in the thin clouds that surround the Son. In *The Transfiguration* by Andrea Previtali (c. 1480–1528), the Father is present in the cloud and speaking via the scroll, while the Spirit is considered present in the symbol of the dove. The Spirit might be anonymous in the text of 9:28–36, but remains present in the narration of grace upon nature.

Such a pattern is similarly narrated through the annunciation, baptism, transfiguration, resurrection, ascension, and Pentecost. In each of these narratives the Spirit is befriending the material: the womb of Mary, the waters of baptism, the bodies of Jesus and humans in resurrection, the human body of Jesus at ascension, and the human bodies of the disciples at Pentecost. "It is characteristic of the Spirit to take up and render holy concrete, physical, sociological structures. . . . It is so that she renders the life of the Trinity in matter, in history, in community, in all their human contingency."[20] The Spirit is a befriender of matter and bodies.[21] (A more nuanced understanding of the plurality of matter and bodies is still required, and will be developed in the next section.) This is a pneumatology of Gift, a Life given to human beings in their narrated materiality, an act of befriending in the desire to draw creation, and

---

18. Eugene Rogers, *After the Spirit: A Constructive Pneumatology from Resources outside the Modern West* (Grand Rapids: Eerdmans, 2005), 179.

19. Stronstad, *Charismatic Theology of St. Luke*, 44–45.

20. Rogers, *After the Spirit*, 137.

21. "To think about the Spirit it will not do to think 'spiritually': to think about the Spirit you have to think materially." Ibid., 56.

the created, into the intimacy of the triune community.[22] As the Spirit befriends materiality, so we realize that "God is not opposed to things human, but first puts them back together by assuming flesh."[23] Applying this narrative patterning, popular culture can be affirmed as a part of the material world which God so loved, the incarnation so "tabernacled" (John 1:14), and the Spirit befriends.

Hence, by starting in Luke 9 with the transfiguration, we note that the Spirit is anonymous while simultaneously noting that this anonymity cannot be construed either as inactivity or absence. Rather, by narrating a Trinitarian patterning, space is made to name the Spirit's work as "the complex, storied, audacious reticence of someone who desires and gives herself to be known only and precisely in the community where she is at home."[24]

In summary, the Spirit is active in the world. It is "in a word, gratuitous. The whole point of grace, after all, is its gratuity, its non-necessity. . . . The Spirit has the non-necessity of things that take and delight in time, like music and liturgy and sex."[25] It is this creative abundance that can narrate and frame Luke 10:1–12.

THE ANONYMOUS SPIRIT AND THE BODY: LUKE 10:1–12

After the baptism of Jesus (3:21–22) came a Spirit-initiated journey (4:1) into the wilderness. After the transfiguration (9:28–36) the anonymous Spirit accompanies another journey, this time toward the wilderness that

---

22. "[I]f [the Spirit] takes possession of a shepherd, He makes him a Psalmist, subduing evil spirits by his song, and proclaims him KIng; if He possesses a goatherd and a scraper of sycamore fruit, He makes him a Prophet [Amos 7:14]. . . . If He takes possession of Fishermen, He makes them catch the whole world. . . . If of Publicans, He . . . makes them merchants of souls," writes Gregory of Nazianzus in *On Pentecost* (NPNF2, 7:384), cited in Rogers, *After the Spirit*, 53.

23. Eugune F. Rogers Jr. "The Stranger," in *Knowing the Triune God: The Work of the Spirit in the Practices of the Church*, eds. James Buckley and David Yeago (Grand Rapids: Eerdmans, 2001), 282. Further, "Christians believe that Christ has become incarnate in a human being, subjected himself, therefore to the human sciences; after his ascension, Christians say that Christ's body is the church—in which Christ subjects himself to sociological analysis. Any theology that rejects the social sciences is anti-incarnational." Rogers, *After the Spirit*, 55.

24. Rogers, *After the Spirit*, 47.

25. Ibid., 180, 182.

is Jerusalem (9:51).[26] The pattern of mission that frames this journey is that of the disciples being sent ahead of Jesus (9:52). The pattern is repeated in 10:1, and as the journey ends in 19:29.[27] While the disciples encounter resistance in 9:54, and plead for judgement, the journey moves on.

The geography of the text in 9:52 is also of theological significance. While the journey to Jerusalem takes ten chapters, all of which are strikingly sparse in geographic detail, the journey begins with a geographic location, that of a Samaritan village.[28] Shillington notes that the "place 'between Samaria and Galilee' is hard to find on the map. It looks like 'no-one's land', a place for *outcasts* or *expendables*."[29] Thus, geographically and theologically, the mission of Jesus in the move toward Jerusalem begins in this "no-one's land." This has relevance given that, for theology, popular culture and everyday life have long been considered a theological extra at best, an outcast at worst.

The pattern of mission from 9:52 is re-narrated in 10:1–12. "After this the Lord appointed seventy-two others and sent them two by two ahead of him to every town and place where he was about to go" (10:1). What is fascinating to note is that the bodies of the disciples continue to precede the body of Jesus. Thus 10:1–12 can be said to pre-narrate ascension and Pentecost. At both occasions, Jesus is standing back from the mission. In doing so, a space is being opened, into which, in the

---

26. James L. Resseguie argued that "[e]xternal terrain is a map of inner terrain. The Jordan, desert, lake, and mountain are not only places plotted on a physical map; they are also spiritual landmarks—threshold experiences, epiphanies, trials, awakenings, and so forth." *Spiritual Landscape: Images of the Spiritual Life in the Gospel of Luke* (Peabody, MA: Hendrickson, 2004), 9. Similarly, "[t]he transfiguration . . . conversation . . . has as it's subject the 'exodus' that Jesus is to 'accomplish' in Jerusalem. So Jesus' journey to take possession of David's city is also a journey laden with tension and foreboding," Brendan Byrne, *The Hospitality of God: A Reading of Luke's Gospel* (Collegeville: Liturgical, 2000), 93.

27. Reinforcing this mission motif, Stronstad notes in *Charismatic Theology of St. Luke* that Luke and Acts have a similar thematic structure, and thus parallels the travel in the Lukan travelogue with the missionary journeys of Peter and Paul.

28. "Only with great difficulty can the journey be sketched on a geographical map; rather it must be plotted on a spiritual map. . . . On the journey he gathers together a new Israel for a new promised land, the kingdom of God." Resseguie, *Spiritual Landscape*, 36.

29. V. George Shillington, *An Introduction to the Study of Luke-Acts* (Edinburgh: T. & T. Clark, 2007), 41.

mission of God, the bodies of Christ are being sent. In 10:1–12, this is in twos, in the hope of kingdom life embodied in the towns and villages. In Acts 2:1–12, this is so that each might hear in "their own language," what Lamin Sanneh calls the translatability of the gospel.[30] In other words, in the christological absence of "no-one's land," we still find bodies being befriended by the Spirit.

Throughout Luke 10:1–12 the Spirit is anonymous. Yet, as in the transfiguration, the Spirit is nevertheless active. Why else might the disciples be instructed to speak peace and look to dwell as that peace is returned in hospitality (10:6–7)? How else could these acts of befriending and being befriended lead to the sick being healed (Luke 10:9)? In response to these unique signs, these particular and indigenous healings, the disciples are to name the kingdom of God as near (Luke 10:9). It is logical, then, to attribute the offering of hospitality, the participation in acts of healing, and the naming of the kingdom all as signs of the befriending work of the (anonymous) Spirit.

Further, because of this Spirit, the body of Christ has now become a surplus, an excess, manifest not only in the body of Jesus, but now also in the towns and villages to which the disciples are sent. Thus, Pentecost is foreshadowed.[31] In the homes, eating and drinking "whatever they give you" (10:7), kingdom community is embodied. As at the transfiguration, the Spirit is active, as the One who desires to be known in "the community where she is at home."[32]

My argument is that Luke 10 continues the narrative patterning of transfiguration and bridges to that of the ascension and Pentecost. The Spirit befriends human bodies, graciously, excessively, inviting them into intimacy.

This leaves a question with regard to discernment. As suggested at the beginning of this chapter, invoking categories of the Spirit at work in "the world" leaves one open to the accusation of "How low can you go?" and of being on the slippery slope toward liberalism. Brown sums it up the criticism well: "The claim is that the world is fallen, and so

---

30. Lamin Sanneh, *Translating the Message: The Missionary Impact on Culture* (Maryknoll, NY: Orbis, 1989).

31. See also Fred Craddock, who writes that "Luke is anticipating the mission to the nations begun at Pentecost after Easter when persons gathered 'from every nation under heaven' (Acts 2:5)." *Luke* (Louisville: John Knox, 1990), 144–45.

32. Rogers, *After the Spirit*, 47.

cannot be read properly unless it is approached from the perspective of the Christian faith and not the other way round. . . . For too long [the doctrine of original sin] has been used to yield selective negative verdicts only on what happens outside the Church."[33] Yet, in contrast to the monolithic nature of such assertions, Luke 10:1–12 offers a plurality of categories with regard to the materiality of "the world." The text simply refuses to baptize all things cultural as Christian. Instead, the kingdom is to be named both in receptivity ("Stay there eating and drinking," 10:9) and in rejection ("Even the dust of your town that sticks to our feet we wipe off against you," 10:11). Discernment must be thus multi-faceted rather than simply the breathless adulation of "theology" in all things everyday and popular.

At this juncture, the nuances offered by Rogers and his application of the narrative patternings of the Trinity are instructive.

> "Nature" introduces multiple ambiguities into discursive and bodily Christian practices. Nature can be unfallen, fallen, redeemed; essential or constructed; individual or corporate. I propose that nature plays a narrative or dramatic role various Christian practices of sacrament and storytelling. . . . Mobile as water, nature is not static, but dynamic. A creature of the Spirit, it is to grow. . . . Christian nature-narratives require a dynamic and differentiated account.[34]

Thus the anonymous Spirit—active at the tables of 10:1–12 and, by narrated patterning, active in and among popular culture—needs to be appreciated as dynamic. It can occupy multiple categories—fallen, redeemed, essential, constructed. Further, befriended by the Spirit, a surplus becomes possible. In other words, culture can change and grow. This introduces a dynamic plurality into the Spirit's befriending of the material and the everyday. Material culture is befriended, but such befriending does not limit the *Pneuema* of God to the existing materiality.[35]

---

33. Brown, "Re-conceiving the Sacramental," 29. Further, "Indeed, despite the prominent position given to the Fall in the opening chapters of Genesis, it is salutary to remind ourselves of how seldom that story is subsequently alluded to later in Scripture and by contrast how often a positive verdict is recorded on the natural world as a mediator of divine knowledge." Ibid.

34. Rogers, *After the Spirit*, 149.

35. "He fills the world, but in His power the world does not contain him." John of Damascus, *Exposition of the Orthodox Faith*, trans. F. Chase, FC 37 (New York: Fathers

While the Spirit might be anonymous in Luke 10:1–12, her activity is underlined when the mission is debriefed. While rejection is prophesied in 10:13–16, receptivity is reported in 10:17–18:

> "The seventy-two returned with joy and said, "Lord, even the demons submit to us in your name."
>
> He replied, "I saw Satan fall like lightning from heaven." (NIV)

The anonymous Spirit is then specifically named in 10:21:

> At that time Jesus, full of joy through the Holy Spirit, said,
>
> "I praise you, Father, Lord of heaven and earth, because you have hidden these things from the wise and learned, and revealed them to little children. Yes, Father, for this was your good pleasure." (NIV).

Like Elizabeth in Luke 1:41, the Spirit has befriended human bodies, and in response inspired proclamation occurs.

THE ANONYMOUS SPIRIT AND THE BEFRIENDED BODY: FURTHER NARRATIVE PATTERNS

The richness of Luke 10:1–12 with reference to a pneumatology of popular culture can be further probed by considering other Biblical narratives with similar themes of anonymity and befriending.

In 10:1–12 Jesus has already befriended the disciples. Now the towns and villagers befriend the disciples, offering hospitality. Such generously gracious acts occur in response to the anonymous Spirit, who has already befriended the towns and villages. In these acts of befriending, new bodies are being created, as those befriended by the Son and those befriended by the Spirit together participate in acts of healing and form community around the kingdom named. Each table is unique in particularities and configurations. Ward puts it well: "True justice only operates in obedience to the economy of friendship that recognises the question in every encounter, 'Who is the stranger?', and realises that answer is: 'Neither of us—while we have each other.'"[36] These relationships of befriendedness have ecclesiological implications. For Ward:

---

of the Church, Inc., 1958), 1:200, cited in Rogers, *After the Spirit*, 59.

36. Graham Ward, "Hospitality and Justice Toward 'Strangers': A Theological Reflection," paper delivered at the symposium "Migration in Europe: What are the Ethical

> The coming together of the two bodies does not create a third body whose location can be determined. It is exactly the opposite: the coming together of the two bodies effects a reciprocal dislocation of both bodies: I am not in you but you are now in me.... A new relation is born, and through (*dia*) this Christic co-indwelling all relations are transformed.[37]

Acts of befriending change the relationship of subject to object and object to subject. In 10:1–12, as humans respond to befriendedness new relationships of indwelling are embodied around table.

This theme of befriending the stranger runs throughout Luke/Acts. Indeed, the mission of God is constantly opened up as the stranger is befriended: on the Emmaus road (Luke 24), as Philip steps up into an Ethiopian chariot (Acts 8:26–40), as Peter encounters Cornelius (Acts 10:1–48), as Paul responds to the invitation from the man from Macedonia (Acts 16:6–10).

Furthermore, in the Luke/Acts narratives such befriending is always a risk, for it crosses boundaries of purity. Peter is offered a vision of "all kinds of four-footed animals, as well as reptiles of the earth and birds of the air" (Acts 10:12, NIV). These are to be killed and eaten, for Peter is "not [to] call anything impure that God has made clean" (10:15, NIV). This vision sets the stage for the sending of Peter to discover God already at work among the Gentiles. Similar themes are at work in Luke 10, with disciples being sent to discover God already at work. Their sending includes the command, "Do not take a purse or bag or sandals" (10:4, NIV). There are intertextual echoes with the narrative of Moses and the burning bush and the command to "Take off your sandals, for the place where you are standing is holy ground" (Exod 3:5, NIV). Might the intertextual echo around the act of not taking sandals suggest that what is holy is based not on boundaries, but in entering, eating, discerning the presence of God in the towns and villages where "workers deserve their wages" (Luke 10:7, NIV)? Furthermore, Resseguie explores how clothing can provide a map of the spiritual life in relation to the injunction to take no bag in 10:4. "To have only one tunic was to risk impurity through spots of various origins, and the impossibility to wash it without being

---

Guidelines for Political Practice?" Katholische Akademie, Berlin, 2003. Online: http://www.katholische-akademie-berlin.de/Veranstaltungen/2003112729/ward_pdf.pdf.

37. Ward, *Christ and Culture*, 106, 107.

put to shame."[38] This narrative patterning of the Spirit relies on boundary crossing and the inevitable risk, loss of purity.

Two further patterns are worth naming; while neither is essential to my argument, both are nevertheless worth pondering. First, Luke 10:1–12 is a continuation of Jesus calling the Twelve in 9:1–6. Both texts instruct the disciples to go in vulnerability and to take no staff, bag, or purse (9:3; 10:4). Both are to rely on the hospitality of the surrounding culture, entering houses to "stay there" (9:4; 10:7). What is worth pondering is the contrast between the Twelve in 9:1–6, who are specifically named, and the seventy-two in 10:1–12, who remain unnamed. In the anonymity of the mission of the seventy-two, there is a narrative echo of the mission of the anonymous Spirit.[39]

Second, of interest is the activity of the Spirit in Numbers 11, when Moses requests seventy (equally unnamed) elders to join him at the Tent of Meeting.[40] "I will take of the Spirit that is on you and put the Spirit on them" (11:17,). The Spirit falls, and seventy are specifically named in 11:24–25. Yet two men "were listed among the elders, but did not go out to the Tent. Yet the Spirit also rested on them, and they prophesied in the camp" (11:16). Brown calls them "additional helpers"[41] while Budd comments, "It is not clear whether this means that Eldad and Medad were two of the seventy. The balance of probability is against that supposition. There is no indication earlier in the story that the seventy are 'registered,' and vv 24–25 seem to assert that all seventy went out and received the spirit."[42] Hence in Numbers 11 the Spirit is considered to have fallen on both seventy and seventy-two. Moses' response to this is to wish "that all the Lord's people were prophets and the Lord would put his Spirit on them!" (11:29). The unexpected and multiple befriending by the Spirit

---

38. Gildas H. Hamel, *Poverty and Charity in Roman Palestine, First Three Centuries C.E.* (Berkeley: University of California Press, 1990), 68, cited in Resseguie, *Spiritual Landscape*, 96.

39. For discussion of the history of textual variants concerning the number of disciples, see Joseph Fitzmyer, *The Gospel According to Luke: Introduction, Translation, and Notes* (Garden City, NY: Doubleday, 1985), 2:845–46. See also Robert Tannehill, *Luke* (Nashville: Abingdon, 1996), 174.

40. Thanks to Paul McMahon for the insight, which contributed to this paragraph.

41. Raymond Brown, *The Message of Numbers: Journey to the Promised Land* (Leicester: InterVarsity, 2002), 100.

42. Philip J. Budd, *Numbers*, WBC 5 (Waco, TX: Word, 1984), 128–29.

is accepted by Moses. In the unexpected surplus of the Spirit's work, the text in Numbers can be read as another part of the Trinitarian narrative patterning coherent with the Spirit's befriending the mission of the anonymous seventy/-two in Luke 10:1–12 and at Pentecost.

A PNEUMATOLOGICAL PATTERNING FOR POPULAR CULTURE THEOLOGY?

Let me start to pull the threads of this chapter together. It has been argued that in Luke 10:1–12 we find an anonymous Spirit befriending those apart from Christ and the Scriptures. This befriending is narrated as a complex and multi-faceted, yet ultimately gracious, interaction in which, in embracing the particularity of the Spirit's befriending work, existing bodies and categories of church and world are dislocated and reformed. Further, it has been argued that such a narrative patterning is consistent with a pneumatology of the Spirit, first in the transfiguration, then in ascension and Pentecost, and finally in echoes of other biblical texts. This narrative pattern is that of the Spirit who befriends those "living in a material world." This suggests a theology of popular culture as a participation in the work of the Spirit. Further, in narrating a Trinitarian patterning, specifically a redemptive participation in Christ's work of making God known and the Spirit's work of blessing the life of gift and gratitude that the Son shares with the Father, it offers a coherence by which one might frame a theology of popular culture. A pneumatological relationship with popular culture is thus conceived in which the Spirit can be anonymous without losing any potential to be named and narrated in ways consistent with patterns of previous anonymous befriending.

This allows us to return to the questions raised at the beginning of this chapter. In light of Luke 10:1–12, as the disciples simply name with honesty the actions in which they see the Spirit's befriendedness, they are honoring authorial intent. As the disciples link the actions of befriendedness with the patterns of the Spirit, a form of reader response is welcomed. The Spirit's befriending as essential to these moments of boundary crossing suggests there are no limits to how "low" a theologian can go with respect to pop culture.

What remains are the ecclesiological questions surrounding who, and how, to discern this anonymous work. Or, in the words of Rogers, "If the knowledge of God belongs with the practices of the community

... what does that mean about apparent knowledge of God outside the community? Does God address the community from without?"[43] When one draws on the pneumatological patterning in which the befriending Spirit is a narration of the Trinity, we can begin to define how we should approach our task. First, in grace. In the Trinity, we see that the other is blessed in relationship. "The Trinity is the paradigm or perfect case of otherness as an exchange of gift and gratitude, that from which all other cases of gift take their derivative meaning."[44] Looking for the Spirit in popular culture is simply seeking the movements of God's grace irrespective of who—inside or outside the church—the actor is.

Second, in redemption. In the death and resurrection of Jesus, we see sin at its worst. Yet in this darkest night of the soul, "the Spirit did not forsake the Son," thus there is "now no part of the world godforsaken."[45] Or, in the words of David Brown, "if God is truly generous, would we not expect to find him at work everywhere and in such a way that all human beings could not only respond to him, however implicitly, but also develop insights from which even Christians could learn."[46] By inference, the lower one goes, the better, for in so doing the fullest extent of the Spirit's grace might be discerned.

Third, knowing the narratives, the patternings of God, can help in recognizing future patterns. By implication, discernment is thus both the Spirit's gift to the church and the practice of ecclesial bodies. So, with regard to the question of who can discern, in opposition to Vanhoozer, this capacity is not limited to the church or to Christians. Nevertheless, the church does have a tradition and a set of practices that aid this discernment, thus affirming the importance and veracity of the church.

Fourth, theologies of popular culture are always contingent, given that material culture is dynamic. The plurality of the gospel/culture relationships in Luke 10:1–12 and the new bodies that emerge remind us that "[n]ature is created with an end in view; it is to grow."[47] As the Spirit befriends popular culture, and as we are willing to receive everyday culture's hospitality, so new sets of relationships becomes possible.

43. Rogers, "The Stranger," 266.
44. Ibid., 268.
45. Ibid., 274.
46. Brown, "Gestures of God," 26–27.
47. Rogers, *After the Spirit*, 151.

Fifth, the narrative patterning of Luke 10:1–12 works against the colonizing tendencies of modernity. Shillington notes how terms like "mission" and "kingdom of God" run "the risk of being interpreted as the divine right of the kingdom-bringers to dominate people groups who do not share the same values as theirs."[48] Yet 10:1–12 subverts such a reading, especially in the vulnerability of those sent on mission and in the practice of shaking the dust, and thus the refusal to impose the kingdom on the other. "From this description of mission 'strategy' we could not possibly draw the notion of domination in any way. . . . It is a mystery how this sense of the text could have escaped colonialist-minded missionaries. The idea of imposing a Christian culture on a receiving culture is foreign to this text."[49] Authors and readers are invited into relationships of vulnerability and hospitality.

Such might be the contours by which a pneumatology of popular culture might proceed, based on reading the narrative patternings of an anonymous Spirit, with particular reference to Luke 10:1–12. Let me end with a prayer, written for all those seeking to be theologians among popular culture

> O God,
>
> Give us humility to befriend your Spirited-work amid the popular and everyday world, of cartoons and popular music, graphic novels and fiction, television, video games, and Zombie movies. Grant us discernment, that we might truly bless the anonymous Spirit at rest on YouTube and Google.
>
> In the name of the One who dwelt so "low," living amid our material world,
>
> Amen.

---

48. Shillington, *Introduction to the Study of Luke-Acts*, 89.
49. Ibid., 89, 90.

4

Spirit, Interpretation and Scripture: Exegetical Thoughts on 2 Peter 1:19–21

by Tim Meadowcroft

In my work with beginning theological students, I find that one of the most difficult questions that many of them face concerns the nature of Scripture as the word of God. It is difficult because it is characteristic of theological education that students come face to face with the humanity of Scripture in the course of their studies. Most, at least where I ply my trade, arrive with some real experience of God speaking to them through the Bible, and as a result have some clearly held if unexamined perceptions as to the divine nature of the Bible. They have not thought very much about such issues as: the role of the church in the formation of the canon; the limitations imposed on Scripture by the humanity and the time- and space-boundedness of its authors; the inescapable fact that any reading and/or translation of the Bible, even one's own, is also an interpretation with its own limitations. Like most of us, they long for certainty and objectivity in the matter of communing with the Divine and hope for the Bible to be an externally generated and objectively verifiable message from the Creator. It is difficult to discover that the ancient and ever new set of documents we call the Bible has a long history of compilation and collection, a variegated track record of authorship, a tendency occasionally to contradict itself, and a distressing ability to call forth competing interpretations from the ranks of its readers. And so students struggle.

Yet they need not, for the struggle usually arises from one of two inadequacies in understanding the way the Christian relates to the Bible. The first is an ironic desire to eliminate the need for faith in living the life of faith. If the Bible is conceived as entirely and reliably a divine word miraculously free from the fingerprint of humanity, each part of which has one meaning, and one meaning only, discernable through the exercise of good method, then the need for faith is eliminated. Thielicke characterizes this anxiety as a "need to establish Scripture which does not dare any longer to seek God's Word in it with the help of the testimony of the Holy Spirit but in the passive attitude of a consumer [wanting] to find God's Word in book form."[1] The second closely related deficiency pertains more directly to the point of this chapter, and it is what I would term an inadequate appreciation of the role of the Holy Spirit in Scripture. It is easy enough to assert in general terms that the Holy Spirit is active at the point of the "inspiration" of the biblical writers,[2] but apparently much more difficult to conceive of the Holy Spirit as active and reliable at each operation through which the words of the Bible came to be and now are experienced as the word of God. Such an appreciation requires a comprehensive sense of the Spirit of God pervasively active in God's word: when the writers wrote, when the editors edited, when the translators translate, when the early church fathers and mothers discerned canonicity, when the scholars study and assemble data, when the commentators write, when readers read, when preachers and teachers preach and teach, and when the church listens. At each point the Spirit is at work bringing the word of God to life. My proposal is that this dynamic is what emerges from a close reading of 2 Peter 1:19–21.

---

1. Helmut Thielicke, *The Evangelical Faith*. vol. 3, *Theology of the Spirit; The Third Article of the Creed; The Manifestation of the Holy Spirit in the Word, the Church, the Religions and the Last Things*, ed. and trans. G. W. Bromiley (Grand Rapids: Eerdmans, 1982), 192.

2. A study of "inspiration" is beyond the scope of this paper, but I cannot escape the need to use the undefined term occasionally.

BACKGROUND

These verses contain interpretive puzzles at almost every turn, and are set within a context that is itself the subject of several ongoing debates. As these are not the focus of this chapter, but do impinge on the points that are about to be made, I simply assert my background assumptions and state some key aspects of the wider message of this short epistle. First, because I do not see that a *prima facie* case has been established for this epistle to be pseudepigraphical, I am persuaded to give the benefit of the doubt in the direction of authorship of 2 Peter by the apostle Peter.[3] Secondly, then, this means, in light of the strong tradition of Peter's death at the hands of the Romans in the mid 60s AD, that the second epistle that bears his name would have been written shortly before that time (see 2 Pet 1:14).[4]

Thirdly, I endorse the challenge to Ernst Käsemann's famous declaration that the epistle reflects an "early Catholic viewpoint."[5] By this he and other writers who adopt this label tend to mean that the epistle reflects a later generation looking back to the apostles as those whose teaching is now the property of the church. With Richard Bauckham I see typically Jewish and Jewish-Christian apocalyptic argument wrestling with the tension between imminence and delay, alongside Hellenist themes.[6] This

---

3. This is contra, for example, John N. D. Kelly, *A Commentary on the Epistles of Peter and of Jude*, Black's New Testament Commentaries (London: A & C Black, 1969), 235–237. The claim of pseudepigraphy is hardly new; the Venerable Bede, writing in the eighth century, commented, "Those who doubt that Peter wrote this letter need to pay careful attention to this verse and to the one which follows, because the eyewitness testimony makes it clear that no one else could have written it." Cited in Gerald L. Bray and Thomas C. Oden, eds., *James, 1–2 Peter, 1–3 John, Jude*, ACCS NT 11 (Downers Grove, IL: InterVarsity, 2000), 140. In support, see the detailed discussion on pseudepigraphy and 2 Peter in J. Daryl Charles, *Virtue amidst Vice: The Catalog of Virtues in 2 Peter 1*, JSNTSup 150 (Sheffield: Sheffield Academic, 1997), 63–75.

4. This position is weak in that reference to "[when] our fathers died" (2 Pet 3:4) can be only to the earliest martyrdoms, such as those of Stephen and James. More difficult, but not impossible, is the assumption that Paul's letters acquired an early authority (2 Pet 3:15). But see the argument of Michael Green, *The Second Epistle of Peter, and the General Epistle of Jude: An Introduction and Commentary* (London: Tyndale, 1968), 129.

5. Ernst Käsemann, *Essays on New Testament Themes*, SBT 41 (London: SCM, 1964), 169.

6. Richard J. Bauckham, *Jude, 2 Peter*, WBC 50 (Waco, TX: Word, 1983), 151. Note, however, that unlike Charles, cited above, Bauckham holds to a late date and a pseude-

reflects to some extent an early Christianity encountering the Gentile world, something that must have been the experience of Peter's church in Rome by the mid 60s.[7]

Fourthly, I assume that the central issues of dispute seem to have been around the necessity of an expectation of *Parousia* and an accompanying impatience with the ethical rigor that arises from that expectation in early Christianity.[8] While these concerns may be one feature among others of a Gnostic viewpoint, Bauckham argues convincingly that they are more likely to reflect pagan thinking arising from the church's interaction with Hellenism.[9] A close reading of the epistle does not suggest a Gnostic background to the concerns of these pagan thinkers.[10]

And so to the verses under examination.

THE WORD OF THE PROPHETS

The nature of the "word of the prophets" (*ton prophētikon logon*, v. 19, NIV) is the concern of these few verses. Contrary to the NIV, it is best to read this phrase with an adjective, hence "the prophetic word" or "the prophetic message" (TNIV, NRSV). The adjective *prophētikos* is rare in the New Testament, its only other occurrence being in Rom 16:26, where it modifies the plural noun *graphai*, hence "prophetic writings."[11] In the

---

pigraphical authorship for 2 Peter (ibid., 131–35). From another perspective, Charles notes the often ignored focus on ethical instruction in 2 Peter, a feature held in common with the other general epistles. See Charles, *Virtue Amidst Vice*, 30–43.

7. This forms an interesting contrast with Jude, which, despite its evident links to 2 Peter, seems to reflect a more Palestinian context.

8. Käsemann considered that the opponents of the writer of the epistle were Gnostics. He argues that their rejection of Christian eschatological expectations of a parousia derives from their Gnostic sense of release from transitory human nature. Käsemann, *Essays on New Testament Themes*, 171.

9. Bauckham, *Jude, 2 Peter*, 154–57. "Only insofar as eschatological disillusionment may have contributed to the rise of the Gnostic movement can the opponents in 2 Peter be seen even as forerunners of Gnosticism" (157).

10. Admittedly, although the developed Gnosticism assumed by Käsemann as the background to 2 Peter did not flower until the second century, many of its elements were in play much earlier. These are drawn out by Green, *Second Epistle of Peter*, 38–39.

11. There is an issue around the authenticity of this section of Romans. James D. G. Dunn, *Romans 9–16*, WBC 38 (Dallas: Word, 1988), 913, considers that the "greater probability lies in favor of post-Pauline addition," contra Douglas J. Moo, *The Epistle to*

singular the same noun, *graphē*, may also be translated as "Scripture," as it in fact is in v. 20 in most English translations. Which writings Paul exactly had in mind in Romans 16:26 may be debated, but it is generally accepted that he was referring to the authoritative witness of the written Hebrew Scriptures,[12] however delineated at the time of his writing. The phrase employed by Peter in v. 20, *prophēteia graphē* ("prophecy of scripture"), reflects the Pauline usage of Romans 16:26 in that it is likely also to apply to the prophetic message enshrined in authoritative writing.[13] The phrase *ton prophētikon logon* (v. 19, "prophetic word") is a little more ambivalent. It may or may not have a written witness in mind; in that respect the grammatically unsatisfactory translation of NIV, "the word of the prophets," in fact succeeds ironically in conveying the possibility that the phrase may be understood as either a written word or a spoken or symbolic message. The third reference to this type of material is simply to "prophecy" (v. 21, *prophēteia*), a term that can encompass both the written and the spoken or symbolic. This prophecy is the product of a prophet's speaking rather than writing. What all of this adds up to is an apparent understanding of prophecy that has its origins in utterances and actions spoken and enacted by particular individuals which then take up residence in authoritative writings. By including these two threads in his thinking, Peter affirms the activity of the Holy Spirit both in the writings that are described as "prophetic" and in the speaking that leads to these writings. Both their production and their preservation or enscripturation are imbued with the Spirit.[14] So begins a delicate dance

---

the Romans, NICNT (Grand Rapids: Eerdmans, 1996), 937, who is "slightly inclined" to include it as original. In the second and subsequent editions of his commentary on Romans, Karl Barth simply declines to comment on the final verses of the epistle, contenting himself with a long footnote outlining the reasons for his view that they are inauthentic. See Karl Barth, *The Epistle to the Romans*, trans. E. C. Hoskyns (London: Oxford University Press, 1933), 522–23.

12. See for example Moo, *Epistle to the Romans*, 940.

13. Although note that Papyrus 72 appears to separate spoken and written prophecy by the inclusion of a *kai*, hence "prophecy and writing." If nothing else, this textual tradition reflects the ambivalence present in these verses.

14. This means that caution is called for when faced with statements such as that by J. Barton Payne, "The Unity of Isaiah: Evidence from Chapters 36–39," *Bulletin of the Evangelcial Theological Society* 6 (1963) 51, on the matter of the sources of Scripture: "The evangelical assumes nothing about the general character and value or specific inspiration of these sources, insisting only on the validity of their final biblical usage. . ."

between the prophet, the preserved authoritative word of the prophet, and a third element, "interpretation" (v. 20).

The parallel I have just drawn with the terminology in Romans 16:26 begs the question of what Peter may have intended in the passage in question by his use of the term "scripture."[15] Most commentators argue that the "prophetic word" is a reference to the Old Testament, however conceived at the time. It is highly unlikely that a Jew of Peter's time would have seen the general prophetic impulse of the early church as constitutive of sacred writings.[16] At the same time, the apostle Peter refers later in this epistle to the letters of "our beloved brother Paul" (2 Pet 3:15). These letters are in the same category as "the other scriptures" (*tas loipas graphas*), again presumably the Old Testament writings. It is possible then that Peter has in mind some of the earliest Christian writings, such as those by Paul, which are beginning to be ascribed some authority by the believers. Just as for the scriptures of the Old Testament, they too are subject to interpretation. In short, we sense the beginnings of the formation of a wider collection of authoritative writings, which in due course the church came also to recognize as imbued by the Spirit, and themselves the outcome of people carried along by the wind of the Spirit in the writing of them.

This emphasis on the prophetic was probably the most natural way that Peter knew to consider the role of the Spirit with respect to the word of God. In the Old Testament corpus, and indeed other Second Temple Jewish writing, the Spirit is mostly virtually synonymous with the "spirit of prophecy" in the minds of the writers.[17] It would probably have been

---

15. At the time of his writing, the New Testament as we know it was still several centuries short of being a settled collection, with the formation of some parts of it still nearly a generation in the future. Moreover there probably remained questions around some parts of what we now know as the Old Testament canon. Roger T. Beckwith, *The Old Testament Canon of the New Testament Church: And Its Background in Early Judaism* (London: SPCK, 1985), 110–65, argues for an Old Testament canon structured into its three parts and closed "not less than 250 years earlier than the currently accepted date of AD 90 (165)," contra John Barton, *Reading the Old Testament: Method in Biblical Study* (London: Darton, Longman and Todd, 1984), 91–97, who probably represents a majority of scholars with his view that an early concept of canon is essentially anachronistic.

16. See for example Daniel J. Harrington, "2 Peter," in Daniel J. Harrington and Donald Senior, *1 Peter, Jude and 2 Peter* SP 15 (Collegeville, MN:Liturgical, 2003), 257–60.

17. See the survey of this issue by Archie W. D. Hui, "The Spirit of Prophecy and Pauline Pneumatology," *TynBul* 50 (1999) 93–115.

self-evident to Peter that the writing, the *graphē*, has come into being through prophetic activity. And it would also have been self-evident that that prophetic activity was fueled by the Holy Spirit. For that is how it had always been.[18] There could therefore have been no fine distinction made between the written words of Scripture and the prophetic activity at work prior to the fixing of that material into a text.

Inherent in such an environment is the possibility that the spirit of prophecy that brought the Scriptures into being and that informed the words of the prophets continues to be the Spirit behind the words and actions of Jesus and those who bear witness to him.[19] As that witness gradually takes on and is preserved in written form, the enscripturated expression of that Spirit-fueled witness takes on new shape. The beginnings of that process lurk in the background to this pericope, and are reinforced by the eschatological hope of a "light shining in a dark place" (v. 19, NIV).[20] Although what Peter is saying about the "prophetic word" technically does not apply to what we now name the New Testament, the implicit possibility emerges that the "prophetic word" may embrace all of Christian Scripture.[21]

MADE MORE CERTAIN

The prophetic word with which Peter is concerned is said to be "made more certain" (v. 19, NIV), in Greek the comparative adjective *bebaioteron*.

18. David E. Aune, *Prophecy in Early Christianity and the Ancient Mediterranean World* (Grand Rapids: Eerdmans, 1983), 86, comments, "In ancient Israel it was widely believed that the Spirit of God caused the revelatory trance. For this reason a prophet could be popularly designated a 'man of the spirit' (Hos 9:7)."

19. Gene L. Green, "'As For Prophecies, They Will Come to an End': 2 Peter, Paul and Plutarch on 'The Obsolescence of Oracles,'" *JSNT* 82 (2001) 107: "Charismatic activity became a dominant feature of the church's landscape (1 Cor 12–14; 1 Thess 5.19–22) and this activity placed Christianity firmly in the line of the prophetic tradition within Israel, which, by some accounts, had not completely ceased since the last of the writing prophets."

20. This dynamic is more fully explored by Joel B. Green, "Narrating the Gospel in 1 and 2 Peter," *Int* 60 (2003) 262–77. He comments that Peter "orients his audience toward the future consummation of God's plan at the same time that he grounds their identity in a divine strategy that predates creation itself. He is already working to collapse the self-evident historical distinctiveness between Israel of old and these communities of Jesus-followers..." (274).

21. A possibility asserted by Thomas R. Schreiner, *1, 2 Peter, Jude*, NAC 37 (Nashville: Broadman & Holman, 2003), 324.

Both the reference and the direction of the comparative are much discussed, as is its force. With respect to its force, the question is whether it is a true comparative or simply an emphatic form. The TNIV takes the latter route with its translation, "something completely reliable," as does NRSV with "more fully confirmed." On balance, however, the evidence suggests that the comparative is intended to join two items. This is highlighted by the word order in the Greek. Reading literally from the start of the verse, "And we have more certain/sure the prophetic word . . . ," the result is a strongly implied connection with the preceding reference to the Mount of Transfiguration and the revelatory experience that occurred there.

The next, and more crucial, interpretive question is, how is the word of prophecy being compared to the revelatory experience of the transfiguration? There are several possibilities: the witness of Scripture is more certain and enduring than the eyewitness experience of Jesus; the eyewitness account is what makes the written witness sure or reliable and the latter is diminished without the former; or the two items of comparison together combine to make for a more certain witness. A case can be made for either of the first two possibilities.[22]

As we have seen above, Peter's deployment of the terms "scripture," "word," and "prophecy" suggest that he sees an interaction between the eyewitness and the text and the interpreter. In that vein, it seems best then to acknowledge that the comparison could work in either direction.

---

22. For Green, *Second Epistle of Peter*, 86, "the Scriptures confirm the apostolic witness," while for Kelly, *Epistles of Peter and Jude*, 320–21, the word of prophecy is made more sure by God's revelation in Christ. Indeed, the exegetical debate reflects an interpretive discussion that continues to this day between different Christian understandings of Scripture and the word of God. Some place a primary emphasis on those things to which the words of Scripture bear witness, and in particular on the one, Christ, to whom they bear witness. Hear for example Karl Barth, "The Doctrine of the Word of God," in *Church Dogmatics*, trans. G. W. Bromiley and H. Knight (Edinburgh: T. & T. Clark, 1936), I/2:514, for whom "the Bible is the Word of God here and now in virtue of the eternal, hidden, heavenly, presence of Christ." Others place more importance on the actual canonized text as the authoritative agent. See "Inerrancy in Current Debate," in James I. Packer, *Beyond the Battle for the Bible* (Westchester: Cornerston, 1980), 37–61. In the twentieth century the Pentecostal tradition has also brought a provocative challenge to the evangelical tendency to fix the word of God in the text. For example James K. A. Smith, "The Closing of the Book: Pentecostals, Evangelicals, and the Sacred Writings," *JPT* 5 (1997) 69, writes, "the same Spirit that guided the first Christian community continues to inhabit the contemporary church and illumines it as a community."

It could be either expressing the superiority of the scriptural witness to the time-bound eyewitness revelation of Jesus, or it could be indicating the dependence of the scriptural witness on the spoken prophetic word and the revelations concerning the earthly Jesus to his disciples and typified by Peter's eyewitness account of the transfiguration. Holding those two apparently contradictory possibilities together then leads to the third option mentioned above, which is that Peter's use of *bebaioteron* is intended to be polyvalent and to work in two directions. Together the stories of Jesus witnessed to by the apostles and the scriptures that foreshadow that witness and subsequently also encapsulate it bring a "more certain" prophetic word.[23]

ABOVE ALL

There is something of primary importance about this prophetic word known in Scripture and through the witness of the apostles. The Greek expresses this with the adverb *prōton*, translated by the NIV in v. 20 as "above all." Not surprisingly, given our experience of this epistle so far, its usage could signify more than one thing. The adverb is most likely to modify the verb "to know," so that what is known is in some way primary. The term could refer to the first thing we know, as in the sense of a primer, or it could refer to the primary, or the most important thing that we know. Both senses could be taken to apply to this context. In that case, Peter is about to say something very important about the prophetic word of Scripture whose importance may be thought of in two different ways that reflect the variability of *prōton*: first, that what is to follow is foundational to our appreciation of Scripture; and, secondly, that what is to follow is the first thing that needs to be said about this Scripture. Thus the reader is introduced to the programmatic comments on the nature of the Scripture with respect to the Holy Spirit.

ONE'S OWN INTERPRETATION

This leads into a consideration of the phrase translated in NIV as "the prophet's own interpretation." In fact the word "prophet" in that phrase

---

23. This is what Bauckham, *Jude, 2 Peter*, 223, means by the "superlative (elative) meaning."

is not in the Greek, as a result of which the statement is more elliptical than the NIV English translation leads one to believe. It may be rendered thus: "no prophecy of Scripture comes into being through/by means of its own interpretation." The NRSV comes close to this with "... is a matter of one's own interpretation." However exactly it is translated, the phrase remains annoyingly out of focus in that it is hard to articulate just what type of distinction between the "prophecy" itself and the "interpretation" is being made. Is prophecy the outcome of interpretation? Or are prophecy and interpretation considered to be two distinct operations, so that prophecy is what the prophet does while interpretation is what the interpreter does? If the former possibility is allowed for, then there is a contrast between interpretation in v. 20 and the work of the Spirit in v. 21. In the case of the latter possibility, then there is a contrast between one's "own" (in Greek *idias*) interpretation and that of the Spirit; prophetic utterance is not idiosyncratic, not the product of a particular human, but owes its coming into being to the work of the Spirit.

Both possibilities can be illustrated from Scripture itself. On the one hand there is plenty of material that seems to arise directly as from an omniscient narrator, somebody who knows the truth of what he or she is writing. In that case, there is no evidence of a process of interpretation giving rise to the writing. Much of the Pentateuch is of that order. In narrative terms, the words of the omniscient narrator come unmediated to the reader; interpretation lies in their reading, not their production. On the other hand, much apocalyptic material is explicitly about interpretation in that the task of the seer is to interpret events and symbolic messages with the help of heavenly "messengers" (*mal'achim*). This phenomenon of "messengers" pushes back into the later prophetic material also. For example, there is a widely held view that the figure Malachi is as likely to be the term "my messenger," *mal'achi*, as a proper name. And another prophet of the restoration, Haggai, is also at one point referred to as a "messenger" (Hag 1:13, *mal'ach*). The phenomenon of Old Testament prophecy itself, particularly in the pre-exilic and exilic era, displays both characteristics. The prophet often speaks the unmediated word of the Lord. At the same time, however, as the prophet Amos indicates, the role of the prophet is to sit in the counsel of God and then convey that counsel (Amos 3:7). The language is not explicitly that of interpretation but the process is strongly implied.

Jerome Neyrey illustrates how in the Hellenist setting of this epistle there was an understanding of pagan oracular prophecy that it was partly the result of interpreting.[24] His examples highlight the dynamics of 2 Peter 1, in which Peter as the eyewitness of Jesus' encounter at the Mount of Transfiguration is now also the prophetic figure called to interpret that event. In technical Hellenist terms of the day, "The *mantis* and the interpreter both act as clients of the revealing Deity."[25] Peter in this instance is both prophet and interpreter, as, potentially, are those whose writings have come to constitute the "prophecy of Scripture."

Once again, perhaps the answer is to adopt a both/and approach. It is quite possible to read the phrase "one's own interpretation" as inclusive of the prophetic process. In that case, Peter is asserting that the prophet's message is not the result of a prophet's idiosyncratic ideas. In the context of his use of prophetic language noted above, then, the message is that the Scriptures do not arise merely from the unreliable imaginations of their human authors. The Spirit is active in the authors of Scripture, and the Spirit is active in overseeing the process by which their words come to be established as the authoritative word of God.

At the same time, the Greek is ambiguous enough that an argument could be made that "one's own interpretation" is an activity distinct from the prophecy that brought the Scriptures into being. In that case, this functions as a warning that there is no place for the interpretation of Scripture that is merely idiosyncratic. The classic response to this reading is to distinguish between private and public interpretation with the emphasis that interpretation must be tested by the wider church. While that is certainly the case, it is not necessarily the contrast that is being drawn here. Rather, the distinction is primarily between those who interpret idiosyncratically and those who interpret under the direction of the Spirit.[26] Of course, the difference between the two types of interpretation needs to be discerned by the wider church and over time. To that extent a corollary is indeed that public interpretation moderates private readings. But the

---

24. Jerome H. Neyrey, *2 Peter, Jude: A New Translation with Introduction and Commentary*, AB 37 (New York: Doubleday, 1993), 181–82.

25. Ibid., 182.

26. William Barclay, *The Letters of James and Peter*, The Daily Study Bible (Edinburgh: St. Andrew, 1960), 369, makes the distinction between private and public interpretation. In contrast, Bauckham, *Jude, 2 Peter*, 230, reads the distinction as between one's own interpretation and that of the Spirit.

key distinction is between that which is spoken as from those bearing the Spirit and that which is merely human speculation and reasoning. This emphasizes the role of the Spirit in the work of interpreters of Scripture as distinct from producers of Scripture.

However, caution should be exercised here. That is not the same thing as equating the work of those who interpret Scripture with Scripture itself. Correspondingly, it does not allow for the possibility that interpretive insights under the guidance of the Spirit may subsequently contradict the potential meaning of any portion of Scripture.[27] It does, however, acknowledge that the literature in which Scripture finds itself is in many respects foreign and strange. There is technical work to be done in correctly discerning its possible meaning in its own day: language learning, historical discernment, philological study and so forth. This type of work often comes under the rubric "grammatico-historical." At the same time, the words of Scripture are sometimes tolerant of more than one meaning or emphasis. In that respect, there is a responsibility on the reader to understand how such passages speak meaning into to the lives of those around them. Both processes—the discernment of original meaning and the contemporary selection from more than one possible meaning—may be described as "interpretation." And in both cases the word of God is truly conveyed as its interpreters are "carried along by the Holy Spirit" (2 Pet 1:21, NIV). Theologically, Michael Welker has expressed it thus:

> Talk of the inspiration of Scripture thus applies first of all to the action of God in and through which the various testimonies of the biblical traditions, either individually or communally in more or less complex interconnections, point to God's presence and God's glory. Second, talk of the inspiration of Scripture applies to the action of God through which the testimonies of Scripture evoke in individual human beings or communities' experiences, answers, and reactions to that presence of God to which they attest.[28]

---

27. It is on this point that, notwithstanding his challenging corrective noted above, Smith, "Closing of the Book," 68, moves onto problematic ground with his declaration that "It is not Scripture that is the ultimate norm, but Christ. As such, prophecy is not subject to the standard of written Scripture but rather the *kanon* of the Spirit as it operates in the discernment of the community."

28. Michael Welker, *God the Spirit*, trans. J. F. Hoffmeyer (Minneapolis: Fortress, 1994), 277.

In terms of current debates around biblical interpretation, this means that the technical notion of reader response must be taken seriously in the discernment of reading. Readers do have a responsibility to draw meaning from texts. These meanings must be tested over time and by the church, and must be constrained by the authority of the text, but that does not remove the responsibility for discerning reading.[29] In such an environment, an interpretation is not merely something that comes from an external source; it is also discerned and experienced in the context of a Spirit-fueled relationship with the God who speaks. Such work, if it is to bear the prophetic word of God into its own day, must be undertaken by people "carried along by the Holy Spirit" reading the words of Scripture that in their turn are the outcomes of prophets also "carried along by the Holy Spirit."

CARRIED ALONG BY THE HOLY SPIRIT

But just what does it mean to be "carried along by the Holy Spirit"? It is important to translate this phrase well, and the NIV has not quite done so with "men spoke . . . as they were carried along by the Holy Spirit." The effect of this translation is to play down the will of the speaker, and thus to imply the Hellenist notion of prophecy as an ecstatic activity in which the will of the speaker is taken over by a divine force of some sort. As a counter to that, Bede's comment from the eighth century still bears repeating: "Some interpret Peter's words to mean that the Spirit inspired the prophets in much the same way as the flutist blows into his flute, so that the latter were no more than mechanical instruments in God's hands, saying what the Spirit told them to say without necessarily understanding it themselves. This is ridiculous."[30] A better translation would be: "men being borne by the Holy Spirit spoke from God" (my translation). The NRSV works in the same direction with "moved by the Holy Spirit." It is a commonplace that the word I have translated as "being borne" is a maritime metaphor of a ship being carried along by the wind.[31] It gives a

---

29. For further see Robert M. Fowler, "Who Is 'The Reader' in Reader Response Criticism?" *Semeia* 31 (1985) 5–23.

30. Cited in Bray and Oden, *James, 1–2 Peter, 1–3 John, Jude*, 142.

31. Of many commentators who deploy this metaphor, see for example Green, *Second Epistle of Peter*, 91.

picture of people who hoist their sails to catch the wind of the Spirit that the voice of God may be heard. The will and character and ability of the prophetic agent are fully engaged by the Spirit.

In that understanding there are three dimensions to the Spirit's involvement in the development of the prophetic word. First, the Holy Spirit engages in the lives of those who speak and write the words of Scripture, as people whose wills are set in obedience to God's Spirit. Verse 21 is quite clear that prophecy, this certain and primary prophetic word, comes about through the speaking of people being borne by the Spirit. It cannot in any sense become apart from the human agents who speak it. All that they are as fallen and redeemed human beings is part of the prophetic word that they speak. That is why the interpreter must be aware of the life and limitations of each writer as well as the situation in which each one writes and speaks.

Secondly, though, and perhaps paradoxically, the "word of the prophets" (more literally, "the prophetic word") does exist also as a discrete entity. Once the prophets have spoken and the signs and symbols have been performed, something comes into being that then takes on a life and authority of its own. In a true sense it becomes the word of God. And it does so by means of the activity of the Spirit. It may then be spoken of as "God-breathed" (2 Tim 3:16, NIV). Inseparably related to this is the sense of Scripture coming into being, of its origin. This is found in two different Greek verbs, *ginomai* and *pherō*. The former is represented in the NIV by "came about" (v. 20), and the latter by "had its origin" (v. 21). Both in their own ways carry a sense of being created or formed or produced.[32] As the Spirit imbues the human authors of the words of Scripture, so also the Spirit imbues the very creative process by which these words come into being.

Thirdly, as we have seen, the Spirit is active in the process of interpretation of those prophetic words once they have been spoken and brought into being. Once the artifact of Scripture emerges, God does not cease to be active. God through the Spirit works in those who interpret it.

In the providence of God, this picture is not a tidy one. It does not yield a neat schema for the mechanics of inspiration such as tends to emerge in systematic treatments. Indeed, as Green has pointed out, it is

---

32. Of the latter verb, one of its related nouns is *genesis*. For further on *ginomai* see *TDNT* 1:681–83, and on *pherō* see *TDNT* 9:56–59.

a telling fact that in this passage "no interest should be displayed in the psychology of inspiration. The author is not concerned with what they felt like, or how much they understood, but simply with the fact that they were the bearers of God's message."[33] The message of the ambivalence of this section of Scripture is that readers must be patient with this ambivalence in their reading. We may be clear that the Holy Spirit was at work in the lives of those who wrote the words that we now know as Scripture, and we may be clear that there is a Holy Spirit quality to those words as they were subsequently preserved as the prophetic word. We may also be clear that the Spirit remains active in all that the church subsequently does to hear these words as the word of God: collection, preservation, translation, exposition. All of this may be gathered into the concept of interpretation. Our confidence rests in the all-encompassing activity of the Spirit as we read the words of Scripture whose very being is the product of the Spirit's activity.

THE WIDER ENVIRONMENT OF THE WORK OF THE SPIRIT-BORNE PROPHETIC WORD

The role of the Spirit in the development and hearing of Scripture impacts the past, present, and future of the believer's life and the life of the church. All three are found in 2 Peter 1 as part of the context in which the role of the Spirit in Scripture is affirmed. The present context is seen in the often overlooked ethical concerns earlier in vv. 4–9.[34] The apostle is at least partly interested in the daily life of the follower of Jesus. The Spirit engages with the ethical life of the Christian through the prophetic word of Scripture. The witness of Scripture also points into the past to the life and witness of Jesus himself as conveyed through eyewitnesses, such as Peter, and those who anticipate and reflect on him in Scripture.[35] The Spirit thus also engages with the historical memory on which the Christian faith is founded. Finally, within vv, 19–21, the Spirit witnesses to the future hope of the believer. Scripture comes as a light into a murky

33. Green, *Second Epistle of Peter*, 91.

34. See the discussion in Charles, *Virtue amidst Vice*, of this much overlooked section of the epistle.

35. It is beyond the scope of this essay to explore the nature of the engagement of the words of Scripture with the word of God manifest in Jesus implied in the juxtaposition by Peter of the transfiguration and the prophecies of Scripture.

place anticipating a day when dawn breaks the darkness and the morning star rises in our hearts. The words of Scripture and their formation and reception are soaked in the life of the Spirit. They become a word from yesterday about today and pointing towards the future.

5

James and the Spirit: Wisdom and Hermeneutics

by Martin Sutherland

In this chapter I will suggest an understanding of hermeneutics that draws on the nexus of wisdom and virtue in the Epistle of James. The argument falls naturally into two parts. First, a consideration of recent scholarship on James which identifies the role and theological significance of wisdom together with its close association in the letter with Christian living. James' use of wisdom has functional parallels with more developed understandings of the Holy Spirit. Arguing that these connections provide a path into hermeneutics, I will then explore the potential parallels offered by the philosophical categories of virtue epistemology. Second, in the light of both wisdom in James and the ambitions of virtue epistemology I will propose an approach to theological hermeneutics that offers a third path that may avoid some of the pitfalls of correspondence theories of truth on the one hand and coherence theories on the other.

JAMES AS HERMENEUTICAL GUIDE

Hermeneutics is by origin a Christian discipline. Most commentators link its emergence to the Protestant imperative to develop rules for interpretation robust enough to sustain the authoritative role ascribed to Scripture. As so often in the history of Christian thought, Schleiermacher is a pivotal figure, defining hermeneutics as the art of understanding the meaning of discourse—"at first just as well as and then better than the author."[1] However, because we have no direct access to the author's mind we must engage grammatical and psychological aspects as we can observe them, moving inevitably in a hermeneutical circle between the parts or particulars of each aspect and the whole, using each to interpret and reinterpret the other. Under Heidegger, the spotlight shifts from the author to the recipients, the primary hermeneutical task being to interpret the one who is interpreting the text.

The focus of this essay will ostensibly be on the first, author-focused approach (and, indeed a specialized, theological version of it). At base, Christian hermeneutics is the quest to discover the mind of God. In and of itself this quest pushes beyond us the self-imposed boundaries of Schleiermacher's theory. Schleiermacher put us at one remove from the mind of the human author and, with regard to the Scriptures, a yet further remove from the Spirit who inspired them.[2] However, the mere imagining of a role for the Holy Spirit in the hermeneutical process shifts our understanding fundamentally. The Spirit's presence leads Christians to dare to believe that in fact we *can* gain access to the mind of the divine author, that indeed this mind comes to *us* rather than requiring us to search it out. The hermeneutical task is transformed. We are not merely seeking to understand divine revelation but to know the divine revealer through being known. Heidegger's wider sense of hermeneutics thus also comes into view. To know and be known is transformative. Thus, in Heidegger's terms, hermeneutics is a matter of the potential of being. In James's language, the Christian is "perfected" in this divinely generated process.

The link between Christianity and the discipline of hermeneutics is clear. Ironically, the link between Christianity and the New Testament letter of James has not been so consistently acknowledged. Martin Luther famously concluded that the letter's silence on justification by faith was

---

1. Friedrich Schleiermacher, "Introduction," in *Hermeneutics and Criticism and Other Writings*, ed. and trans. A. Bowie (Cambridge: Cambridge University Press, 1998), 23. Much of this work is concerned with how to interpret Scripture.

2. Ibid., 15–20.

such for it to be dismissed as a "right strawy epistle." John, I John, Romans, Galatians, Ephesians—"these show thee Christ." By comparison, James "has no gospel character to it."[3] Dibelius saw it reflecting the "Christian ethos" whilst lacking the force and scope of Jesus' gospel and being "essentially alien" to the spirit of Paul and John.[4] Sophie Laws proffered the view that, "by contrast with thinkers such as Paul, John or the author of Hebrews, the Christianity of James will inevitably be judged as superficial and undeveloped."[5] James Dunn assessed it to be "the most Jewish, the most undistinctively Christian document in the New Testament."[6] Brevard Childs is more positive, acknowledging that the letter witnesses "to a form of life which is formulated almost entirely in Old Testament terminology . . ." but which is "no less Christian in substance."[7] Patrick Hartin, by contrast, affirms that "of all the New Testament writings the letter of James appears to lie closest to Jesus' spirit and message."[8]

Both Dunn and Hartin can be right of course. When Dunn calls James "undistinctively Christian" he means it does not reflect Pauline and post-Pauline Christianity. He does, nonetheless, acknowledge other models of Christianity, a variety of *kerygmata*, which were potentially valid but failed to flourish beyond a generation or two. Jewish Christianities that failed to develop a strong Christology or that clung to the law were, Dunn suggests, ultimately rejected.[9] James—acceptable, even preferred by some in the first century—represents one of those models that faded. Hartin's comparative optimism about James reflects his interest in faithfulness to the teaching of Jesus. Dunn would not contest this view but would argue that the future of Christianity clearly lay with Paul's and John's interpretations of Jesus.

---

3. Martin Luther, "'Preface' to the 'September Testament' (1622)," in *Luther's Works*, ed. E. T. Bachman (Philadelphia: Muhlenberg, 1960), 35:362.

4. Martin Dibelius, *James: A Commentary on the Epistle of James* (1964. Philadelphia: Fortress, 1976), 50.

5. Sophie Laws, *A Commentary on the Epistle of James* (London: A & C Black, 1980), 3.

6. James D. G. Dunn, *Unity and Diversity in the New Testament*, 3rd ed. (London: SCM, 2006), 271.

7. Brevard S. Childs, *The New Testament as Canon: An Introduction* (Philadelphia: Fortress, 1984), 444.

8. Patrick J. Hartin, *James*, SP 14 (Collegeville: Liturgical, 2003), 1.

9. Dunn, *Unity and Diversity*, 286–87.

The reasons for the thread of suspicion about James's version of Christianity are not hard to identify. There is no cross and no resurrection mentioned or implied in his letter. Two further apparent problems bear on the themes of this essay and warrant closer examination. First is the apparent lack of a pneumatology. James does not directly speak of the Holy Spirit. *Pneuma* appears twice (2:26 and 4:5) but in neither case can the instance confidently be taken to be a reference to the Holy Spirit.[10] What, then, could such a book have to say to the theme of this volume, "reading Scripture and constructing theology with the Holy Spirit"?

In this chapter I will maintain a strong connection between James's use of wisdom and what becomes the orthodox Christian view of the Spirit. In a seminal article in 1969 James Kirk sought to test "whether there is sufficient equality of meaning and terminology to make probable an identical use of Wisdom in James with Spirit in Paul."[11] He cautiously concluded that there was such evidence. Peter Davids is more definite, holding that James ascribes to wisdom the functions of the Spirit, indeed that the letter exhibits a "Spirit Pneumatology."[12] It is of course too simplistic to align James with Paul merely because the "wisdom from above" in James results in a series of virtues (Jas 3:17) analogous to those ascribed to the Spirit in Paul (e.g., Gal 5:22–23). These features may simply imply that James continues the forms and themes of received wisdom literature. There are similar virtue lists in Jewish literature, and indeed the point of Old Testament wisdom is to gain the capacity to live the best life.

---

10. Of the two instances of *pneuma*, Jas 4:5 is the more problematic. Either *pneuma* or God (implied from v. 4 and *katōkisen*) might be held to be the subject of *epipothei* (the one who yearns or desires). If *pneuma* is the subject, then difficulties of the negative connotations of *phthonos* might prevail against it being the Holy Spirit. See Laws, *Commentary on the Epistle of James*, 177–80, and Hartin, *James*, 199–200, following Laws. If God is taken to be the subject, then the notion that the object of that desire in this context is the Holy Spirit as third person of the Trinity, rather than the human spirit created by God, is unsustainable (see discussions in Dibelius, *James*, 223–24; Peter H. Davids, *Epistle of James: A Commentary on the Greek Text* (Grand Rapids: Eerdmans, 1982), 162–65; Douglas J. Moo, *The Letter of James* (Grand Rapids: Eerdmans, 2000), 188–91). Martin, on the other hand, holds *pneuma* to the subject and takes it to refer to the Holy Spirit, suggesting (with some merit) that this would preserve best the flow of the argument from v. 4. Ralph P. Martin, *James*, WBC 48 (Waco, TX: Word, 1988), 149–51.

11. James A. Kirk, "The Meaning of Wisdom in James: Examination of a Hypothesis," NTS 16 (1969–70) 28.

12. Davids, *Epistle of James*, 55–56.

Moreover, a link between wisdom and God's Spirit (e.g., Gen 41:38–39; Isa 11:2) is commonplace in the sapiential tradition. Yet Douglas Moo surely misses much when he concludes that James offers no innovation to the Jewish wisdom tradition.[13] Richard Bauckham and Hartin perceive a distinctly Christian wisdom presented here. Bauckham sees this primarily in James's authentic representation of Christ's teaching.[14] Hartin goes further, identifying a crucial note of dynamic transformation in James's use of wisdom. Wisdom is generously given to all, from above, amounting to a new birth (new creation), an "implanted word" that has the power to save your souls, generating "first fruits" (1:17–21).[15] I will propose a reading of James that supports the cautious claims of Kirk but sees no need to contrive a direct alignment with Paul.

The second obvious problem presented by James is the insistence on the role of works in salvation. "So faith by itself, if it has no works, is dead" (2:17). Luther felt this apparently synergistic soteriology to be counter to the gospel. It has become the basis for a traditional relegation of James in relation to Paul. However, more recent scholarship has, promisingly, sought first to understand this element of James in its own right with fruitful results, although the discussion inevitably returns to the issue of harmony or otherwise with Paul.[16]

Without denying the critical importance of canonical issues and the theological categories of later orthodoxy, the greatest priority is surely to attempt to get within James's skin. It is necessary to read him in his own terms, not just on particular points like justification but in the way his themes interweave and overlap. Given James's call for an integrated Christian life that corresponds with the unalloyed singularity of God we should not be surprised to discover that many of his themes reprise and retell each other. Matters of doctrinal correctness are later concerns; interpretations driven by such questions risk violence to James's message.

Crucial to the argument in this chapter are the following theses: that wisdom plays a pivotal role in the letter, that wisdom is developed in a distinctly Christian manner and that significant functional parallels

13. Moo, *Letter of James*, 34.

14. See Richard J. Bauckham, *James: Wisdom of James, Disciple of Jesus the Sage* (London: Routledge, 1999), 107–8.

15. Hartin, *James*, 79–80.

16. See e.g., Bauckham, *James*, 120–27, 127–40; Moo, *Letter of James*, 37–43; Hartin, *James*, 156–63, 163–72.

can be established between Jacobean wisdom and emerging Christian understandings of the Holy Spirit. Moreover, James's use of his categories is not discrete. Wisdom, word, faith and works feed on and inform one another in ways which support his integrated vision of the complete Christian life.

As these are clearly contested notions, an examination of the keys texts is required.

James 1:2–8: Wisdom as Principal Gift

Sophos is named only twice in James. The first mention (1:5) identifies it as a gift from God; the second (3:13–18) sets up a list of virtues for those who "make peace." If this was the full extent of its treatment then Martin would be right that James is content to stay within the framework set by Jewish teachers,[17] and we would have to acknowledge Moo's conclusion that, "while wisdom certainly has its place in James's theology, it cannot be given the central and integrating role that some scholars have wanted to give it."[18] Yet such interpretations are unnecessarily reductionist. A more dynamic approach yields a far richer understanding of wisdom's function. This begins to emerge when we consider the first direct reference to wisdom (1:5) in its fuller context at the opening of the letter (1:2–8).

The NRSV and a number of commentators separate v. 5 from vv. 2–4.[19] This is unhelpful and fails to take sufficiently into account the linguistic links between vv. 4 and 5. The readers are exhorted to be "mature and complete, lacking [*leipomenoi*] in nothing." The first "lack" (*leipetai*), indeed the only lack to be addressed, is wisdom, leading Davids to suggest that "it is this gift which enables one to be perfect or, in James's conception, to stand the test."[20] Wisdom is thus from the outset a crucial theme. If the contextual problem is persecution (and consequently the pastoral concern of the letter is that the community stands firm) then the spiritual solution is wisdom. Two important features of this divine answer emerge. Firstly the gift is *haplōs*—unalloyed, given with integrity, without reservation. The manner of God's giving is thus directly contrasted

---

17. Martin, *James*, xciii.

18. Moo, *Letter of James*, 34.

19. Dibelius, *James*, 77, for instance, regarded the connection to be "superficial" as he regarded wisdom a minor theme on the way to the principle concern of prayer.

20. Davids, *Epistle of James*, 71.

to the double-mindedness of the doubter, who will not receive anything (vv. 6–8). Secondly, as Davids points out, the eschatological tone of vv. 2–4 signals that wisdom enables endurance not merely because it grants a healthier perspective in this world but specifically because it enables the believer "to see history from the divine perspective."[21] Crucially, this gift of God enables a glimpse of the mind of God.

James calls his readers to seek the gift of wisdom. This wisdom will enable them to stand firm because in it they have the mind of God which is pure, wholly integrated, lacking any dissonance. As a result they themselves will be "mature and complete." With this interpretation the otherwise problematic change of focus in 1:9–11 is potentially clarified. The poor brother can "boast" because he can see that the present reality will pass away. But does the same insight work for the rich? Undoubtedly this unit reflects the eschatological expectation of reversal that surfaces again in 4:6—5:6. Since Dibelius, most commentators would therefore see the call to the rich to boast in humiliation as ironic, "obviously not intended to be taken seriously."[22] Yet it is possible, as Johnson acknowledges (although he concludes differently), "to read the sentence more sapientially."[23] Moo and Hartin favor this view, interpreting the passage to be a call for both poor and rich to be wise, i.e., to see themselves in God's economy. The one is exalted in Christ; the other enters Christ's humility. Both outcomes are true cause for celebration.[24]

James 1:12-21: Wisdom and Word

Returning to the pastoral concern for endurance, this time through temptation, James again asserts the integrity of God (1:12–13). God, in whom there is no dissonance, cannot be the tempter.

There is a complex interconnection signaled here between the divinely gifted wisdom and the "word of truth" which gives (new) birth (v. 18), the "implanted word that has the power to save your souls" (v. 21).

---

21. Ibid., 72.

22. Todd C. Penner, *The Epistle of James and Eschatology: Re-reading an Ancient Christian Letter* (Sheffield: Sheffield Academic, 1996), 209. See Dibelius, *James*, 83–88; Davids, *Epistle of James*, 77; Laws, *Epistle of James*, 62–64; Martin, *James*, 24–28.

23. Luke T. Johnson, *The Letter of James: A New Translation with Introduction and Commentary* (New York: Doubleday, 1995), 191.

24. Moo, *Letter of James*, 63–69; Hartin, *James*, 68–69.

The "word" in these verses may be an allusion to the creative word or to the gospel.[25] It is, however, being more attentive to the discursive structure of the text to recognize the echoes of the principal gift of wisdom. Indeed, 1:12–21 provides crucial links between the two specific mentions of wisdom in 1:2–5 and 3:13–18. Robert Wall identifies a "reflexive conversation" between the opening passage of the chapter and this reprise.[26] Verse 3:17 echoes a number of motifs from the opening passage: perfection (*telion*, cf. v. 4), giving that comes from above, and God's unalloyed integrity "in whom there is no variation [*parallagē*]." Yet the passage also looks forward to chapter 3. Temptation, like double-mindedness, is a failing of those who lack wisdom or seek it elsewhere than "from above." That which is not from above is unspiritual and devilish (1:14–15, cf. 3:14–16). In contrast, that which is from above is true, generates fruit (1:17–18, cf. 3:17), and is linked to meekness (1:21, cf. 3:13).

Wall goes so far as to "take 'word of truth' to be an idiom of wisdom," an association usage with Old Testament precedent (Prov 8:7; 30:5; Eccl 12:10).[27] This identification of the two is ambitious but we may certainly conclude that their features and functions overlap and intertwine. The practical outcome is clear: True wisdom comes only from God and has the divine characteristics of integrity and clarity. The life of the believer and the community alike must reflect this same quality. Just as in God there is no *parallagē*, so the Christian life also will be free of dissonance. However, the Christian's integrity is not merely self-referential; it is reflective of God's unalloyed character. The wise life is lived "in consonance with his nature."[28]

James 2:14–26: Word and Works

A similar interlocking of related concepts emerges in the imperative to apply that which is gifted. The wise will be those who act on the word and whose faith is completed in works. The movement is signaled first in the example of the mirror in 1:22–25. A person's knowledge of their "natural

---

25. So Laws, *Epistle of James*, 75–78, 82; Johnson, *Letter of James*, 202; Martin, *James*, 48–49.

26. Robert W. Wall, *Community of the Wise: The Letter of James* (Harrisburg, PA: Trinity, 1997), 65.

27. Ibid., 67. See also Hartin, *James*, 75–81.

28. Martin, *James*, 38.

face" lasts only as long as they continue to contemplate the reflection. Take your eyes off the image and the reality too disappears. If that is true of the merely natural, so much more is it so of the perfect law. In the case of the mirror, looking is the sum of one's engagement. To employ a mirror validly it is enough to be a looker that looks. With the law however, "looking" is emblematic of much deeper interaction. To engage the law is to be a doer that acts. The outcome is not a fleeting impression but a profound transformation. Persevere in the perfect law and you will be blessed in the doing. There is reciprocity here, a dialectic that leads to completion. The divine gift creates the capacity to be doers of the word, which in turn secures perseverance in the word "that has the power to save our souls" (1:21).

This perfecting dynamic continues in the passage for which James is most prominent in the popular mind: "So faith by itself, if it has no works, is dead" (2:17). Crucially, the doctrine on which James turns his arguments is "that God is one" (v. 19), echoing again his emphasis on divine integrity. The case is clinched with examples from the tradition.

The use of *synergēi* in v. 22a and *teleioun* in v. 22b (cf. 1:4) is profoundly important. Works actively cooperate with faith in order to bring faith to its completion. This synergy between works and faith is not justification by works. Rather, as Hartin suggests, Abraham's case

> is surely a graphic illustration of the point with which James opened his letter (1:3–4): the testing of faith leads to endurance, which ultimately culminates in perfection: maturity, integrity and completeness in a relationship with God. . . . A circular movement occurs in the interaction between faith and works: faith inspires the works and is active together with the works, and in this interaction faith is brought to completion and maturity (2:22).[29]

James's diatribe on works is therefore not a departure from the gospel, as Luther feared. Rather it is a continuation of his concern for integrated authenticity, for completion. It is a theme he has repeated in a number of guises. Wisdom is the gift that enables this perfection (1:5), a divine endowment that finds its perfect parallel in the implanted word which saves (2:21). That word in turn proves salvific for those who do not merely hear but who act (1:25). That same saving dynamic is described

---

29. Hartin, *James*, 159.

in the synergy between faith and works. Wisdom, word, faith, works—all relate to one another intrinsically and without contradiction, without, it should be noted, any attempt to draw fine distinctions between them. To separate them, in fact, would be to undermine the intent. These are all emerging Christian ways to describe the one reality of the life lived authentically as God's "firstfruits." This multi-threaded argument is drawn together around the concept with which it started: a return to wisdom. The dynamic of reciprocity and completion continues, only now instead of works completing faith it is wisdom that completes works.

James 3:13–18: Wisdom and Works

James manifestly maintains the traditional connection with between wisdom and behavior. This is most directly addressed in 3:13–18.

What the NRSV renders as "gentleness" in v. 13 is better taken as "meekness." This meekness is not merely a quality of the works but also (and more importantly) of the wisdom. Wisdom and behavior are inextricably linked but the nature of the wisdom that generates the act is crucial. The concluding phrase *prautēti sophias* ("in the meekness of wisdom," cf. RSV) is, as Hartin and others have noted, "awkward," yet it identifies an essential dynamic.

> [The phrase] is probably a Semitism, with the genitive 'of wisdom' use in place of an adjective, "in meek wisdom." By preserving the two nouns James gives a stress to both concepts, of wisdom and meekness. . . . For James, wisdom is the most important gift that comes down from above (1:5; 3:17). By this gift one shares in God's wisdom and is shown how to act. Wisdom is above all characterized by James as "meekness." The type of life that a follower of Jesus is to embrace is one that emulates Jesus' lifestyle and is characteristically identified as being meek . . .[30]

Christian wisdom is thus imitative both of God (unalloyed and pure) and of Christ (meek). It is, moreover, shown by the "good life." Wisdom in James is a rich and complex Christian conception which takes us considerably beyond the sapiential tradition. It is intimately and inseparably bound with the saving word of truth, with faith and with works. It thus has an energy and force that transcends the mere accumulation of knowledge. Indeed, it begins to look like the Spirit.

---

30. Ibid., 191–92.

There are significant advantages in interpreting James this way. Among modern commentators, Douglas Moo is perhaps the most concerned to reconcile James's portrayal of justification with that of Paul. The answer, he avers, "lies in reading James's teaching about 'works' in light of Paul's teaching that Christian works are themselves the product of God's work of grace through the indwelling Holy Spirit.... While not explicitly taught by James, a monergistic interpretation fits well into the emphasis in chap. 2 on true faith."[31] Although he acknowledges that "James gives evidence of a monergistic view of salvation in his emphasis on the creative power of the new birth in 1:18," Moo has to import Paul's Holy Spirit into his solution. The analysis above of James's densely woven treatment of wisdom, word, faith, and works suggest this is unnecessary.

Davids might be thought to claim too much when he asserts that "if some works have a wisdom Christology, James has a wisdom Pneumatology."[32] We would be unwise for instance to see an implication of the third person of the Trinity in James under the guise of *sophia*. It is enough to recognize in this early Christian discourse a fluid use of available categories, expressing a new truth of the dynamic of divine interaction with humanity. Yet Davids is careful to limit his claim—the analogy is functional—"wisdom in James functions as the Spirit does in Paul: wisdom helps one stand, delivers one from the flesh ... and produces the fruit of the Christian life."[33] Wisdom, indissolubly linked to behavior as in the received tradition, is also revelatory, even salvific. It is thus, I contend, quite appropriate to recruit the wisdom teaching of James in a consideration of the Spirit and hermeneutics, in the Christian quest for the mind of God.

A HERMENEUTICS OF CONSONANCE

It is this completing/perfecting aspect of works in the dynamic of wisdom which suggests the potential of an engagement with the philosophical debate that has emerged since the 1980s under the group of theories classed as "virtue epistemology." Prompted by the work of the American philosopher Ernest Sosa, this approach to the validity of beliefs shifts

---

31. Moo, *Letter of James*, 42.
32. Davids, *Epistle of James*, 55–56.
33. Ibid., 56.

attention from the beliefs themselves to the qualities embodied in the person or community holding the beliefs.

"Normative epistemology" holds that beliefs, even true beliefs, can only properly be called "knowledge" if the reasons for such beliefs are sufficiently cogent. The two dominant means of justifying belief are foundationalism and coherentism. In his 1980 paper "The Raft and the Pyramid: Coherence versus Foundations in the Theory of Knowledge,"[34] Sosa called into question both approaches. A key problem with foundationalist theories, he suggested, was that of infinite regression. How can one ever know that the foundations on which one's epistemic pyramid is built are not merely individual instances of yet deeper principles, and that these, if discovered, are not themselves compromised in the same manner? Coherentism on the other hand he likened to a raft. Knowledge is a structure that floats free of any secure anchor or tie. No part of knowledge is more fundamental than the rest to the overall structure, all of the parts being held together by the ties of logical relations. Very neat as long as the raft stays afloat and you stay on it! But what about beliefs from outside the system, particularly those perceived by the senses? It is certainly possible to build new systems of coherence, but these can proliferate and even become contradictory whilst remaining internally coherent. This result can be counterintuitive, however, since person's sensory experience can challenge coherent systems. Whatever the coherence of the worldview that might insist that headaches are illusory, it is difficult to hold the belief to be justified when one is suffering the very pain one's system denies.

Sosa shifts the focus from the beliefs to the believer and in particular to the "intellectual virtues" of the believer. "An intellectual virtue may be viewed as a subject-grounded ability to tell truth from error infallibly or at least reliably in a correlated field. To be epistemically justified in believing is to believe out of intellectual virtue."[35] Lorraine Code and James Montmarquet seek to develop and reposition Sosa's insight. Both want to shift emphasis more thoroughly from the belief to the believer, from reli-

---

34. Ernest Sosa, "The Raft and the Pyramid: Coherence versus Foundations in the Theory of Knowledge," *Midwest Studies in Philosophy* 5 (1980) 3–25, reprinted in Sosa, *Knowledge in Perspective: Selected Essays in Epistemology* (Cambridge: Cambridge University Press, 1991), 165–91.

35. Ernest Sosa, "Knowledge and Intellectual Virtue," reprinted in Sosa, *Knowledge in Perspective*, 242.

abilism to responsibilism. Code stresses the social context of the knower, requiring thick narratives of social and historical place. Montmarquet conceives of intellectual virtues as personality traits rather than intellectual abilities or capacities. Belief is thus justified if, in the process of coming to believe, the one believing has exhibited appropriate virtues, the key one of which is "epistemic conscientiousness"—essentially a proper motivation or desire to know the truth. However, even this must be shaped by other virtues, grouped by Montmarquet under three heading: virtues of impartiality, intellectual sobriety, and intellectual courage.[36]

Is there, then, any ground for learning from this debate in reflecting on the implications of a picture of wisdom in James in which Christian virtues feed the process of the perfection of faith, the process of wisdom creation which we might (as post-Paulinists) associate with the work of the Holy Spirit? There are immediate questions that call such an association into doubt. Mere cognitive virtues hardly amount to the wisdom virtues of purity, peacefulness, gentleness, etc. Code's social awareness is more promising as particularly are Montmarquet's regulative virtues—the one opening possible links with the grand narrative of divine mission, the other suggesting qualities fitting with Christian morality. But neither truly takes us beyond the knower. John Greco, an advocate for external epistemic justification, nonetheless argues for a virtue epistemology that is secured by "an internalist version of virtue epistemology" which depends on the believer's conformation to those epistemic norms the believer countenances.[37] This acceptance of an external norm has promise, but the result remains an epistemology of the single subject, however socially understood, morally regulated or accepting of norms.

The wisdom of James would seem profoundly different. The virtues are indeed active elements in the dynamic of saving faith, but in the Jacobean understanding the virtues are held to be generated not by the one seeking knowledge, but by the one being known. There are two

36. See Lorraine Code, *Epistemic Responsibility* (Hanover: University Press of New England, 1987), and James Montmarquet, *Epistemic Virtue and Doxastic Responsibility* (Lanham: Rowman and Littlefield, 1993).
37. John Greco, "Virtues and Vices of Virtue Epistemology," *Canadian Journal of Philosophy* 23 (1993) 413–32, reprinted in Ernest Sosa et al., eds., *Epistemology: An Anthology*, 2nd ed. (Oxford: Blackwell, 2008), 454–61. See also John Greco, "Justification Is Not Internal," in Matthias Setup and Ernest Sosa, eds., *Contemporary Debates in Epistemology* (Oxford: Blackwell, 2005), 256–70.

subjects. The defining, enabling action of the divine giver ensures a vision of knowing fundamentally different from the unifocal approach of normative models, whether it be foundationalist, coherentist, or virtue epistemology.

Virtue epistemology, at least as conceived in philosophical debate, is thus only superficially promising as an aid to enrich our understanding of wisdom in James. It does, however, serve to call us beyond both foundationalism and coherence, away from a focus on beliefs themselves. However, merely to shift the focus to the believer is insufficient.

Thomas Aquinas spoke of wisdom as "a knowing that is, as it were tasted" and speaks of the encounter with the Spirit that

> Knowledge is not enough for there to have been a mission. Rather it is necessary that there be knowledge deriving from a gift appropriate to a person, and by which we are united to God after the mode of this person, that is, when the Holy Spirit is sent, through love. And such a knowledge is of the experiential order.[38]

Spirit/wisdom calls Christian knowledge into being. The virtues do indeed promote, even perfect, the knowledge. Crucially, they do so not because they are attributes of the believer, but because they are the qualities of the divine giver. Refining Aquinas, we would want to add a further "gift appropriate to the person" of the Spirit: that of drawing us to Christ. As with virtue epistemology, we are called to shift our focus in knowledge, in hermeneutics, even in our understanding of truth, away from beliefs, interpretations, or facts to a person—but in the Christian case the person is Christ, who is the way, truth, and life.

Bauckham sums up James's connection with the wisdom of Jesus in these terms: "his wisdom is the Jewish wisdom of a faithful disciple of Jesus the Jewish sage. He is the disciple of whom Jesus said 'A disciple is not above the teacher, but everyone who is fully qualified will be like the teacher' (Luke 6:40)."[39] I don't believe this gives full recognition to the power of James's use of wisdom. Hartin is surely closer:

> This gift of wisdom is indeed the perfect gift, for it renders the believer whole and complete, lacking in nothing (1:5). Moreover,

---

38. Both quotations cited in Gilles Emory, *The Trinitarian Theology of Thomas Aquinas*, trans. F. A. Murphy (Oxford: Oxford Univesity Press, 2007), 393.

39. Bauckham, *James: Wisdom of James*, 107–8.

this perfection shines through in the call to friendship with God (4:4). All who experience God's gift of wisdom lead a life that encompasses an exclusive relationship with God.[40]

The virtues of Jacobean wisdom bring us closer to the mind of God because they are in fact instances of the Spirit's work of creating in us the mind of Christ. Here James stands not idiosyncratically or primitively apart from the rest of the New Testament but clearly in the same story. In 1 John 4:7–8 the same intimate dynamic is evident: "Dear friends, let us love one another, for love comes from God. Everyone who loves has been born of God and knows God. Whoever does not love does not know God, because God is love" (NIV). The parallels in Paul are particularly interesting, given the history of perceived dissonance between the traditions. Paul develops similar themes in a number of places. We might call to mind 1 Cor 1:18—2:16; Eph 1; 3:14–21; or Col 1:24—2:5, but it is enough to illustrate the point from Philippians. In Phil 2:5 Paul prays "Let the same mind be in you that was in Christ Jesus," which hope introduces the great Christic hymn describing the humility of the son of God in terms more than reminiscent of James's description of the Christian life. The call is then to "work out your own salvation . . . for it is God who is at work in you, enabling you both to will and to work for his good pleasure" (Phil 2:12–13).

We need to venture a genuinely Christian paradigm for knowledge, interpretation, and truth. This need not replace a focus on grammar or context in hermeneutics, nor should it drive out foundationalism, eschew coherence, or deny correspondence in epistemology. What I propose is an *enrichment* of our quest for the mind of God that settles neither for correspondence nor coherence but seeks *consonance* with the life and mind of Christ.

There are important implications for how we understand the nature of biblical interpretation and theology and in particular their claims to be "true." First, we must assert that absolute truth is not some *thing* that you know, share or experience, but a *person* you meet. Christ is truth. Interpretation and the theology that results can be true, but in the sense that a builder's set square or spirit level, the sights on a rifle, or a compass can be true—that is, they indicate a proper alignment, direction, or bearing. None of these instruments is ever *perfectly* true, but good

---

40. Hartin, *James*, 80.

ones indicate measurements or bearings within acceptable tolerances. Interpretation, similarly, can be better or worse, depending on whether it aligns the individual and the church more or less well to the normative Christ story. The truth of theology therefore is not that of correspondence, which claims an unmediated grasp of reality. Neither is it one of self-referential coherence. Rather theology's truth is that of "consonance," establishing and enabling the harmony of the individual and the church's story with that of Christ.

Bauckham is right to claim the significance of Luke 6:40—"A disciple is not above the teacher, but everyone who is fully qualified will be like the teacher." But this cannot be limited to traditional Jewish understandings. Something new is added. Consonance with Christ is not mere imitation. Theology is more than determining "what would Jesus do" or simply cataloguing scriptural concepts. At stake is a transformation, wrought by the Spirit; a transformation that calls us beyond a mere individual faith to life together. It is not for nothing that James employs his fluid categories to make a case for harmonious living among the people of God. As Hartin notes, the perfecting process "also occurs in the community dimension, where [James's readers] are reborn as God's twelve-tribe kingdom. . . . They are the beginning of the reconstitution of God's people, called to live in friendship with God."[41]

This, for James, is true "wisdom."

---

41. Ibid.

6

Reading Scripture and Doing Theology with the Holy Spirit

by Myk Habets

A RETROACTIVE HERMENEUTIC[1]

The role of the Holy Spirit has largely been neglected in contemporary hermeneutics. Major textbooks on biblical interpretation generally fail to address the role of the Holy Spirit; they simply allude to pneumatology, or at best, offer one- or two-page summaries. Most biblical interpreters, however, intuitively grasp the significance of the Holy Spirit in the process of interpretation, but struggle to articulate it. The present work contributes a partial articulation of the role of the Holy Spirit in interpretation and, in turn, doctrinal development, by adopting something I have termed a *retroactive hermeneutic*.[2] A retroactive hermeneutic recognizes

---

1. An alternate version of this chapter appeared as "Developing a Retroactive Hermeneutic: Johannine Theology and Doctrinal Development," *American Theological Inquiry* 1 (2008) 77–89. Used with permission.

2. A similar hermeneutic can be found in the late Ray S. Anderson, who labels his a "christological hermeneutic." See his *Ministry on the Fireline: A Practical Theology*

that the experienced presence of Christ in the Spirit, post-Easter, brought to mind the life of Jesus; thereby reawakening remembrances of his life, words, and deeds. In this sense, the present and the past correspond such that the present does not contradict the past, nor vice versa. This same retroactive process is available for the exegete today.

Limiting ourselves to the Johannine corpus, we can see this retroactive hermeneutic clearly illustrated. John brings the dialectic between the historical words of Christ and the present experience of the Spirit into sharp focus.[3] In John 14:26 and 16:12ff, the other *Paraclete* fulfills two functions. The first is to continue the ministry of revelation already given—"the Advocate . . . will teach you everything"—and the second is to "remind you of all that I [Jesus] have said to you" (14:26). Hence, the new illumination has the continual ministry of the original revelation: "he will guide you into all the truth" is balanced by "he will not speak on his own" (16:13). And again, "he will declare [*anangelei*] to you the things that are to come" (16:13, cf. 16:15) is balanced by "He will glorify me, because he will take what is mine and declare it to you" (16:14). The key word or concept here is *anangelei*, for it can have the force of *re*-announce or *re*-proclaim. The force of the action is understood in 16:13 to include some further information or meaning.[4] Further meaning is in

---

for an Empowered Church (Downers Grove, IL: InterVarsity, 1993), 111; *An Emergent Theology for Emerging Churches* (Downers Grove, IL: InterVarsity, 2006), 134–35; and *Dancing with Wolves While Feeding the Sheep: Musings of a Maverick Theologian* (Eugene, OR: Wipf and Stock, 2002), ch. 3. Another close example is the "christotelic" hermeneutic being developed by Peter Enns, *Inspiration and Incarnation: Evangelicals and the Problem of the Old Testament* (Grand Rapids: Baker Academic, 2005). This merely highlights the reciprocity between Christ and Spirit.

3. James D. G. Dunn, *Jesus and the Spirit: A Study of the Religious and Charismatic Experience of Jesus and the First Christians as Reflected in the New Testament* (Philadelphia: Westminster, 1975), 351. Cf. the similar theme in Paul (see 2 Cor 1:22 and Rom 8:23), and also in the Petrine epistles (see 1 Pet 1:12). See John Calvin's comments in *Institutes of the Christian Religion*, ed. J. T. McNeill, trans. F. L. Battles (Philadelphia: Westminster, 1960), 1.7.4. We also see evidence of this in Hebrews, where the Holy Spirit takes on an unmediated oratorical function (see Heb 3:7–11; 9:6–10; 10:15–17). See Martin Emmrich, "Pneuma in Hebrews: Prophet and Interpreter," *WTJ* 63 (2002) 55–71. Emmrich points out parallels in other texts, which include Eph 1:17; 1 Cor 2:15; and 1 John 2:27.

4. Commenting on John 16:13, Leslie Newbigin, *The Gospel in a Pluralist Society* (Grand Rapids: Eerdmans, 1989), 78, writes, "To the Church, however, the work of the Spirit will be 'to declare the things that are to come,' to interpret coming events, to be the hermeneutic of the world's continuing history."

effect drawn out of the old by way of reinterpretation.⁵ Consequently, this word presents both inspiration in the present and interpretation of the past as bound up in the framework of illumination.⁶ What this interpretive work of the Spirit meant for John is that he would undoubtedly regard his own Gospel as the product of this inspiring Spirit. His own work was in direct fulfillment of these very promises; in fact those promises may constitute an implicit *apologia* for his Gospel.⁷ Dunn writes, "the way in which John handles the words and deeds of the historical Jesus is typically the way in which the Spirit interprets Jesus to a new generation, guides them into the truth of Jesus."⁸

In 1 John 2:27 the same thought is expressed in the following: "the anointing . . . [that is, the Spirit] abides in you, and so you do not need anyone to teach you . . . his anointing teaches you about all things," and thus the prophecy of Jer 31:34 is fulfilled. But the parallel in 1 John 2:27 implies that the Spirit's teaching is actually a continual reinterpretation of the original message of faith.⁹ Again, in 1 John 4:2–6, present inspiration is expected and known, but a right understanding of Jesus is normative. Finally, in 1 John 5:6–12, we see this same dialectic between the remembrance of the life of Christ and the present communicative role of the Holy Spirit. The Spirit testifies to the truth of the humanity of Christ (vv. 6–7), and the Spirit continues to bear testimony to the anti-docetic *kerygma* (vv. 9–10). The last book of the canon, Revelation, also points to this forward orientation or development as the Spirit catches John of the Apocalypse up and is commanded to write down what he sees and hears and what is to come (Rev 1:10, 19). This is, of course, a natural extension; for in the Gospel of John, the Spirit cannot come until Christ is ascended

---

5. On the retroactive perspective of John see Marianne M. Thompson, *The Humanity of Jesus in the Fourth Gospel* (Philadelphia: Fortress, 1988), 123–28. Thompson uses the term "retrospective" but means the same as my "retroactive."

6. See the same conclusions in Stephen E. Fowl, *Engaging Scripture: A Model for Theological Interpretation* (Malden, MA: Blackwell, 1998), 99–100.

7. What is true of John is also shared by the other evangelists. For example, Matt 13:52 echoes this thought when it relates the teaching of Jesus about the bringing forth of old and new together; the one informing the other, the one anticipating and the other unfolding and unpacking as well as revealing new thoughts and concepts.

8. Dunn, *Jesus and the Spirit*, 352ff.

9. On the Spirit's role as biblical interpreter see Dan McCartney, *Let the Reader Understand: A Guide to Interpreting and Applying the Bible* (Wheaton, IL: Victor, 1994), 75–80.

(John 14:12). Again, in Rev 2:7 we read, "Let anyone who has an ear listen to what the Spirit is saying [*legei*, present tense] to the churches." The canonical authors are consciously writing to and for Spirit-inspired readers.[10]

This last point has been recognized by Markus Bockmuehl and forms the fifth thesis of his proposals for New Testament scholarship.[11] He writes, "The implied reader is drawn into an act of reading that involves playing an active role on stage rather than the discreet spectator on the upper balcony."[12] It is the Spirit of Light who illuminates the significance of the Christ event (*retro*); it is the presence of the Spirit of Life that moves the church on (*active*); and it is the Spirit of Truth who brings the Word of God into new situations (*retroactive*).[13] The Holy Spirit, therefore, is the one who moves the church through history. We see this vividly in Acts, as we see the Spirit enabling the church to make radical countercultural innovations in its missionary activity, encapsulated in Acts 15:28: "For it has seemed good to the Holy Spirit and to us."[14]

---

10. In this sense the neo-orthodox and existentialist schools are correct in realizing that the moment of understanding is at once the moment of response. The words of Scripture in this sense do become the word of God. In the words of Barth, "revelation is reconciliation." According to Barth "Revelation takes place in and with reconciliation; indeed, the latter is also revelation. As God acts in it he also speaks.... Yet the relationship is indissoluble from the other side as well. Revelation takes place as the revelation of reconciliation." *CD* IV/3:8, cited in George Hunsinger, "Karl Barth's Christology: Its Basic Chalcedonian Character," in *The Cambridge Companion to Karl Barth*, ed. J. Webster (Cambridge: Cambridge University Press, 2000), 137.

11. Markus Bockmuehl, "'To Be or Not to Be': The Possible Futures of New Testament Scholarship," *SJT* 51 (1998) 271–306.

12. Ibid., 300. In addition to the already mentioned verses in the Johannine corpus, Bockmuehl includes 1 Thess 2:13 and Matt. 28:20.

13. This terminology has been used by Philip J. Rosato, "Spirit Christology: Ambiguity and Promise," *TS* 38.3 (1977) 444. Anderson, *Ministry on the Fireline*, 35ff., speaks of theology as being both historical [backward or *retro*] and contemporary [future or *active*] due to the work of both Christ and the Spirit.

14. Raymond Brown, *The Gospel According to John* (London: G. Chapman, 1971), 2:716, describes this as "interpreting in relation to each coming generation the contemporary significance of what Jesus has said and done." See Ray S. Anderson, *The Soul of Ministry: Forming Leader's for God's People* (Louisville: Westminster John Knox, 1997), 29–30, who speaks of theological innovation not unrelated to theological antecedent or precedent. Fowl, *Engaging Scripture*, 99–100, provides two examples from the Gospel of John (2:22, and 12:16) where this "remembering" in a theological way (retroactive reading) is evidenced, before going on to illustrate with the aid of Acts 10–15.

This retroactive motif parallels to some degree what Anthony Thiselton has been writing about for some time—the so-called *two horizons*.[15] The first horizon is the text and its world, and equates to our *retro*. The second horizon is that of the reader and her world, and equates to our *active*. In the words of Stephen Fowl,

> The Spirit's role is to guide and direct this process of continual change in order to enable communities of Christians to "abide in the true vine" in the various contexts in which they find themselves.... Because the Spirit speaks this "more" in unison with the Father and the Son, believers can act in ways that are both "new" and in continuity with the will of God.[16]

Traditional scholarship has been good at working in the first horizon—that of the text; however, looking backwards can be hazardous to ones health when seeking to move forward! While retrospection is crucial, it cannot be the totality of biblical hermeneutics. We need to spend more time, Clark Pinnock and others argue, in the world of the second horizon—with how the text is to be interpreted and applied today—and this refers to the *active* element of interpretation which relies on the Holy Spirit.[17] And it is here that much recent Pentecostal scholarship has been contributing. As Pinnock writes in relation to contemporary evangelical thought on the issue,

> The Spirit's goal in the illumination of the Word for the Church is to shed light on her pilgrim way.... Here [Acts 15:28] the Spirit led the community to an important corporate decision, not insight into the faith so much as insight into the mission. The Spirit was guiding the Church to move beyond the confines of Judaism and learn to adapt to a mission among Gentiles. All through Acts the ministry of the Spirit is to direct believers in what to think and where to go.[18]

Pinnock adds that

---

15. Anthony Thiselton, *The Two Horizons: New Testament Hermeneutics and Philosophical Description with Special Reference to Heidegger, Bultmann, Gadamer, and Wittgenstein* (Grand Rapids: Eerdmans, 1980).

16. Fowl, *Engaging Scripture*, 101.

17. See Clark H. Pinnock, "The Role of the Spirit in Interpretation," *JETS* 36 (1993) 491–97.

18. Ibid., 495.

> Evangelical theology has to be a "pilgrim theology." We never pass beyond the necessity of reconsidering our traditional interpretations until the return of Christ. We continually ask where the deep structures of Biblical revelation are pointing. A theology that is not restlessly probing and exploring is not serving the Church well. A theology that takes the path of discovery requires the Spirit's illumination most urgently.[19]

It appears that Pentecostals and evangelicals together are working towards just such a "pilgrim theology." The current chapter is a further attempt in this direction.

THE EXEGETE AND THE SPIRIT

Having established a retroactive hermeneutic that accounts for the mission of the Holy Spirit, we are left with the task of briefly pointing out some of the implications of a pneumatological hermeneutic for the biblical exegete.

There are generally two approaches to the role of the Holy Spirit in interpretation; one focuses on what the Spirit does with the *text*, the other on what the Spirit does with the *exegete*.[20] The first approach, while becoming a popular option in contemporary hermeneutics, is rejected by a retroactive reading of Scripture.[21] Proponents of the first approach aver that the Spirit enables the text to be read in a way that would not have been obvious to the first recipients (a "spiritual" reading) and so in this way attempts to render Scripture of continuing relevance to the church. On this view the Spirit is the creative power behind the fusion of the text's and the reader's horizons, with the second horizon exerting a clear dominance over the first. The second approach, the one adopted here, appeals to the Spirit as the minister of the Word, the one who leads the community into a correct interpretation of the text. The *locus* of the

---

19. Ibid., 496.

20. A third approach is now becoming more popular—the role of the Spirit in the communicative event of reading Scripture and then seeking to apply it. See Timothy Meadowcroft, "Relevance as a Mediating Category in the Reading of Biblical Texts: Venturing Beyond the Hermeneutical Circle," *JETS* 45 (2002) 611–27; and "Between Authorial Intent and Indeterminacy: The Incarnation as an Invitation to Human-Divine Discourse," *SJT* 58 (2005) 199–218.

21. See Kevin J. Vanhoozer, *Is There a Meaning in This Text?* (Leicester: Apollos, 1998), 415ff.

Spirit's re-creative work is not the letter of the text; this is fixed and hence forms our *retro*. Rather the Spirit's re-creative work centers on the life of the interpreter, who, as sinner, is inclined to distort the text insofar as its message is perceived as threatening the *status quo* (hence part of the reason for rejecting the first approach).[22] Given this distortion, the Spirit guides and leads the interpreter to the truth of the text and its correct application into new situations and hence forms our *active*.[23]

Having articulated the difference between these two approaches, it remains to further explicate the actual mission of the Holy Spirit as it relates to the interpreter of Holy Scripture. Roy Zuck provides fourteen propositions related to the Spirit and interpretation which culminate in five elements necessary for properly interpreting the Bible: "salvation, spiritual maturity, diligent study, common sense and logic, and humble dependence on the Spirit of God for discernment."[24] A nice illustration of this in practice is that of William Lane who, in the preface to his commentary on the Gospel of Mark, writes:

> Only gradually did I come to understand that my primary task as a commentator was to listen to the text and to the discussion it has prompted over the course of centuries as a child who needed to be made wise. The responsibility to discern truth from error has been onerous at times. When a critical or theological decision has been demanded by the text before I was prepared to commit myself, I have adopted the practice of the Puritan commentators in laying the material before the Lord and asking for His guidance. This has made the preparation of the commentary a spiritual as well as an intellectual pilgrimage through the text of the Gospel. In learning to be sensitive to all that the evangelist was pleased to share with me I have been immeasurably enriched by the discipline of responsive listening.[25]

Lane, like Pinnock, appeals to the concept of *pilgrimage* as the best way to describe the way in which the exegete receives this ministry of

---

22. Ibid., 415.

23. For Vanhoozer, ibid., 423, the formula is not retro + active but "biblical relevance = revelatory meaning + relative significance."

24. Roy B. Zuck, "The Role of the Holy Spirit in Hermeneutics," *Bibliotheca Sacra* 141 (1974) 130.

25. William L. Lane, *The Gospel According to Mark: The English Text with Introduction, Exposition, and Notes*, NICNT (Grand Rapids: Eerdmans, 1974), xii.

the Word by the Holy Spirit. This pilgrimage, however, is not simply that of the individual exegete but involves the entire faith community. The work of the Spirit is thus a work *in* community and *for* community and so an examination of the communal nature of the of the Spirit's role in interpretation is required.

THE COMMUNITY AND THE SPIRIT

Of special importance is the communal aspect of the reading and interpreting of Scripture.[26] On the basis of Acts 2, James McClendon argues that Scripture is addressed directly to readers *today*: Peter declares "this" (the event of Pentecost) is "that" (the meaning of the prophecy of Joel).[27] Such an interpretation is not merely Peter's human projection but a product of the Spirit's guidance. Only his sharing in the life of the believing community allowed Peter to see "this" as "that."

In a similar way to McClendon, Kevin Vanhoozer notes that when Ezra the scribe opened up the Scripture, the people literally stood under the text (Neh 8:5).[28] Their response to the reading showed that they understood and, as a result, worshipped. Contrast their response with that of earlier kings and priests who had failed to understand or to follow the law (Neh 9:34). A habit of disobedience had made it difficult to understand or to follow the biblical text. Under Ezra, by contrast, there was a week-long feast of reading, followed on the eighth day by a solemn assembly. The Scriptures were read and the people responded in confession and worship (Neh 9:2–3). Here was no dead letter, no tired book, but a text that spoke directly to the people's hearts and minds.[29] Their

---

26. See Gordon D. Fee, *Listening to the Spirit in the Text* (Grand Rapids: Eerdmans, 2000), 15f.

27. James McClendon, *Systematic Theology*, vol. 1, *Ethics* (Nashville: Abingdon, 1986), 31–33. Following McClendon's position would be Richard Hays, *Echoes of Scripture in the Letters of Paul* (New Haven: Yale University Press, 1989), and Stanley Hauerwas, *Unleashing the Scripture: Freeing the Bible from Captivity to America* (Nashville: Abingdon, 1993).

28. Vanhoozer, *Is There a Meaning in This Text?*, 408ff. He also uses Acts 2 as a case study.

29. This relates to Fee's words in *Listening to the Spirit in the Text*, 14: "During the process of exegesis we momentarily reverse these roles, so that we act as subject with the text as object. I would argue that the exegetical process is not completed until we return to the proper posture of objects being addressed by the subject."

reception of the text was the occasion for reformation and renewal, both communal in nature.

While a communal reception of the text under the guidance of the Holy Spirit is acknowledged, when this approach is taken to an extreme it reveals a problem, notably: How can the church know what God is saying through Scripture if what God is saying fails to coincide with the verbal meaning of the text? Hauerwas appeals to the leading of the Spirit.[30] But is this sufficient? The solution has problems. First, the Spirit's leading is often difficult to discern or to distinguish from merely human consensus. Second, it relocates the Word of God and divine authority from the text to the tradition of its interpretation.[31] When individualized, there is the constituent problem of subjectivity. However, when this is done in the context of ecclesial community it is perhaps similar to the early church and their use of the "rule of faith." For Tertullian and Irenaeus, Scripture is rightly understood only in the context of the living tradition handed down through apostolic succession. Ultimately the human criterion for right interpretation is the consensus of the catholic church, best represented by the earliest creeds. On this view, the arbiter of right interpretation is the church, which enjoys not canonical but "*charismatic* authority, grounded in the assistance of the Spirit: *for it seemed good to the Holy Spirit and to us.*"[32] The function of the rule of faith is thus not overturned but placed within its proper context: the community that "stands under" the text of Scripture and the Spirit of Truth.

These issues are only a problem when a pneumatological hermeneutic is not at the same time a retroactive one. A retroactive hermeneutic seeks to hold together the plain sense of Scripture ("what it meant") with its use by the Spirit in the community ("its significance today"). We may now go back to Nehemiah 8 and look again at what was going on. Amidst a community that had departed from the Spirit, the Word held no great attraction for them. However, amidst the missionary work of the Spirit inhabiting the Word of the Law, the people were convicted, revived, and reformed.[33] Here, as Vanhoozer states, "The Spirit's role in

---

30. See for instance Stanley Hauerwas, "The Moral Authority of Scripture: The Politics and Ethics of Remembering," in Hauerwas, *A Community of Character* (Notre Dame: Univesity of Notre Dame Press, 1981), 53–71.

31. These criticisms appear in Vanhoozer, *Is There a Meaning in This Text?*, 411.

32. Cited in ibid.

33. This is why Fowl, *Engaging Scripture*, 113ff., speaks about reading the Spirit and

bringing about understanding is to witness to what is other than himself (meaning accomplished) and to bring its significance to bear on the reader (meaning applied)."[34]

Utilizing speech-act theory,[35] Vanhoozer outlines three aspects of the Spirit's work in bringing readers to understanding. First, the Spirit *convicts* believers that the Bible is divine as well as human locution (and thus to be read as a unified text). This relates to the *testimonium Spiritus sancti internum* by which the reader comes to receive the Bible as the Word of God. Second, the Spirit *illuminates* the letter by impressing its illocutionary force upon the reader. Under the influence of the Holy Spirit believers see and hear the text of Scripture as warnings, commands, promises, and assertions. In so doing the Spirit does not alter but ministers the meaning. "The distinction between the 'letter' and the 'spirit' is precisely that between reading the words and grasping what one reads. Likewise, the difference between a 'natural' and an 'illuminated' understanding is that between holding an opinion and having a deep sense of its profundity."[36] Finally, what does the Spirit illumine—head or heart? Both! The Spirit's illumination of the mind is dependent on his prior transformation of the heart. Vanhoozer concludes:

> Negatively, the Spirit progressively disabuses us of any ideological or idolatrous prejudices that prevent us from receiving the message of the text. The Spirit purges us, first, of hermeneutic sin, of that interpretive violence that distorts the otherness of the text. Positively, the Spirit conforms our interests to those of

---

how that is crucial for the interpretive task. In fact, Fowl writes, "[the] experience of the Spirit's work provides the lenses through which Scripture is read rather than vice-versa. This is perhaps the most significant point the New Testament has to make about the hermeneutical significance of the Spirit; this point runs against the grain of modern interpretive presumptions" (114).

34. Vanhoozer, *Is There a Meaning in This Text?*, 413.

35. Speech-act theory involves three constituent elements: the *locutionary* act is the bare fact of the utterance of the text; the *illocutionary* act is the intent of the utterance or text; and the *perlocutionary* act is the effect on the reader or hearer.

36. Vanhoozer, *Is There a Meaning in This Text?*, 413. I. Howard Marshall, "The Holy Spirit and the Interpretation of Scripture," in *Rightly Divided: Readings in Biblical Hermeneutics*, ed. Roy B. Zuck (Grand Rapids: Kregel, 1996), 69, points to passages such as 1 Thess 1:5 and 2:13 to indicate that Paul's preaching was effective because the Spirit was active in and through the preaching of the Word to produce faith. By this he indicates that understanding Scripture is not only an intellectual task, it is also a spiritual one.

the text. To read in the Spirit does not mean to import some new sense into the text, but rather to let the letter be, or better, to let it accomplish the purpose, illocutionary and perlocutionary, for which it was sent: "[My Word] will not return to me empty, but will accomplish what I desire and achieve the purpose for which I sent it" (Isa 55:11). In short, the Spirit convicts, illuminates, and sanctifies the reader in order better to minister the Word.[37]

How do we foster this ecclesial context in which a Spirit-inspired hermeneutic or reading of Scripture takes place? For Stephen Fowl, the answer includes not only reading *with* the Spirit but also learning to "read the Spirit." He writes:

> If Christians are to interpret with the Spirit, they will also need to learn how to interpret the Spirit. Further, our prospects for interpreting the Spirit are closely linked to our proficiency at testifying to the Spirit's work, particularly the Spirit's work in the lives of others. Such testimony depends on the forming and sustaining of friendships in which our lives are opened to others in ways that display the Spirit's working. Welcoming strangers and the extension of hospitality become building blocks for such friendships. Finally, building such friendships, becoming people of the Spirit, and recognizing and interpreting the work of the Spirit all take time and demand patience from us.[38]

The current chapter is an attempt to initiate the sort of ecclesial bonding called for by Fowl. Evangelicals who are good at operating in the first horizon—the retrospective aspects of hermeneutics—require communion and cooperation from Pentecostals who are good at operating in the second horizon—the active or prospective aspects of hermeneutics. As both traditions collaborate together around the Word, filled by the Spirit, we may achieve far more than if we huddle away in our respective ecclesial ghettos, and we may achieve a retroactive reading of Scripture that enriches our respective theologies.

DOCTRINAL ENRICHMENT

The final issue that deserves attention is the movement from Scripture through exegesis to doctrine. How do we speak of doctrinal development

---

37. Vanhoozer, *Is There a Meaning in This Text?*, 413.
38. Fowl, *Engaging Scripture*, 119.

when a retroactive hermeneutic is adopted? The correct development of doctrine is one involving a retroactive reading of the canon. Moltmann calls this a "reverse movement,"[39] while Pannenberg labels it "proleptic."[40] Or, for Donald Bloesch, it is a theology of "Word and Spirit."[41] When the two are kept together, theological construction emerges as both faithful and creative. But does it develop, change, or grow out of the original revelation preserved in Scripture? How do we articulate the relationship between exegesis and systematic theology when working within a retroactive hermeneutic?

The Synoptic evangelists unfold the apostolic preaching of Christ as they tell the life history of Jesus. In these histories the central event is Jesus' death on the cross and the experience of the presence of the risen One in the Spirit. Hence, we start with the past, with the "deposit of faith" left to us in the canon, and then in successive generations we attempt to penetrate its truth or reality. Under the guidance of the Holy Spirit, and with advances in science and technology, we implement every means of inquiry in order to unpack and interpret the canon, not develop or improve on it. But within these tools of inquiry, the determinative principle of interpretation will always be the indwelling Holy Spirit.[42]

---

39. Jürgen Moltmann, *The Way of Jesus Christ: Christology in Messianic Dimensions*, trans. M. Kohl (London: SCM, 1990), 75. In his work *The Crucified God: The Cross of Christ as the Foundation and Criticism of Christian Theology* (New York: Harper & Row, 1974), 112ff., Moltmann speaks similarly of holding together the reciprocal relationship between historical and eschatological method, the historical and eschatological history of Jesus.

40. Although Pannenberg's use of "proleptic" (derived, one would suppose, from the initial use by J. Weiss) includes a considerable amount of philosophical connotations that we do not include in our term "retroactive." See Wolfhart Pannenberg, *Systematic Theology*, trans. G. W. Bromiley (Grand Rapids: Eerdmans, 1988), 2:365, and *An Introduction to Systematic Theology* (Edinburgh: T. & T. Clark, 1991), 53-69.

41. See the pneumatic/christological exegesis of Donald G. Bloesch in *Holy Scripture: Revelation, Inspiration & Interpretation*, Christian Foundations 2 (Downers Grove, IL: InterVarsity, 1994), 181, 200, 206-8, and "A Christological Hermeneutic: Crisis and Conflict in Hermeneutics," in *The Use of the Bible in Theology: Evangelical Options*, ed. R. K. Johnson (Atlanta: John Knox, 1985), 78-102, and more fully worked out in *A Theology of Word and Spirit: Authority and Method in Theology*, Christian Foundations 1 (Downers Grove, IL: InterVarsity, 1992).

42. This would concur at many points with Peter Stuhlmacher's call for a "hermeneutic of consent." See his *Vom Verstehen Des Neuen Testaments: Eine Hermeneutik*, 2nd ed., NTDSup 6 (Gottingen: Vandenhoeck & Ruprecht, 1979), 205-25.

With Pinnock we assert that "God gives us freedom to operate within biblical boundaries by the Spirit, who inspired the witnesses and also opens the significance of scriptural words."[43] Or with Francis Watson we affirm that:

> It is crucially important to achieve a correct balance between the assertion that the disclosure of truth lies in the future and the assertion that it lies in the past. What lies in the future is a true apprehension of what has already happened in the past; and revelation is thereby tied irrevocably to the historicity and particularity of human existence within the world and prevented from drifting away into gnostic fantasy. Conversely, however, the meaning of what happened in the past cannot simply be read out of that past, conveyed by means of an authoritative tradition.[44]

Colin Gunton has provided an alternative to the idea of doctrinal *development* that accords with what has been presented here. He understands development to be more accurately that of "enrichment."[45] "Development" suggests a continuing process of change that could more accurately be termed "evolution." "Enrichment," in contrast, is a Spirit-inspired reading of the past from the vantage point of the future. It is a retroactive enterprise undertaken within the knowledge that we do not have the whole truth, but as the tradition passes through our hands, we seek to enrich it, and hence, it is not merely retrospective.[46] Utilizing Gunton's imagery of "enrichment" we may reject a view of an "evolutionary" development of doctrine in which its conclusions are patently different from its origins. Under this model of doctrinal development

---

43. Clark H. Pinnock, *Flame of Love: A Theology of the Holy Spirit* (Downers Grove, IL: InterVarsity, 1996), 230. See further among his earlier works, "The Work of the Holy Spirit in Hermeneutics," *Journal of Pentecostal Theology* 1 (1993) 3-23, and "Role of the Spirit in Interpretation," 491-97.

44. Francis Watson, *Text, Church, and World: Biblical Interpretation in Theological Perspective* (Edinburgh: T. & T. Clark, 1994), 260-61.

45. Colin Gunton, *Theology through the Theologians: Selected Essays 1972-1995* (Edinburgh: T. & T. Clark, 1996), 48-49. This is similar to what is termed "traditioning" by Gerard Kelly, "Spirit, Church and the Ecumenical Endeavour," in *Starting with the Spirit*, eds. Steven Pickard and Gordon Preece (Hindmarsh, South Australia: Australian Theological Forum, 2001), 175.

46. In this regard see the programmatic thesis of Vern S. Poythress, *Symphonic Theology: The Validity of Multiple Perspectives in Theology* (Grand Rapids: Zondervan, 1987).

the original message has been transformed into something different. It is no longer related to the original canon. One such example would be the suggested "development" from the earliest worship practices characterized as polytheism, to a developed monotheism of the later Hebrew and early Christian writers, to contemporary forms of panentheism and pantheism. The latter positions are of a different sort than the former from which they have moved away. The development model is a modernist one which claims that most teaching before the modern age is obsolete, so development involves being critical of it.

By contrast, Gunton's enrichment model or notion of "organic development" is intimately related to the canon. It is not another gospel but an enriched understanding of the original. The model of enrichment treats history as significant, but the original witness, the canon, remains supremely authoritative. An example of an organic development of doctrine would include the historical enrichment of the christological and Trinitarian doctrines. In the fourth century, Gregory Nazianzen moved beyond the words of Scripture to further articulate christological thought, using the term *perichoresis* to describe the intimate communion between the two natures of Christ. In the seventh century, Pseudo-Cyril used the same term to help illustrate the coinherence of the three persons of the Trinity.[47] In commenting on the theology enshrined in the orthodox creeds and definitions of Christendom such as Nicaea (AD 325), Constantinople (AD 381), and Chalcedon (AD 451), F. C. Grant writes, "these were not ventures in speculation, but, as their very language indicates, simply statements which *ruled out* various conceptions or attempted definitions which infringed or invalidated the language of Scripture and religious experience, especially of worship."[48] In this way, doctrine was enriched through the tradition and made relevant for a contemporary audience.

When we apply this hermeneutic to Christology, we see that while Jesus was misunderstood until after the resurrection and Pentecost, this very lack of understanding led to more reflection and deliberation on the actual life of Jesus, his words, and works (cf. John 16:4). Any rewriting of history in a quasi-mythological way would have devalued the benefit

---

47. On the use of *perichoresis* see John P. Egan, "Toward Trinitarian Perichoresis: Saint Gregory the Theologian (Oration) 31.14," *GOTR* 39 (1994) 83–93.

48. Frederick C. Grant, *An Introduction to New Testament Thought* (New York: Abingdon, 1950), 243.

of Christ's life for the Christian community rather than enriching it.[49] As such, the Gospels must be read in light of these eschatological events and the reinterpretation of them in light of the Spirit's illumination.[50] "As Christianity could properly claim to be a legitimate interpretation of the Old Testament in the light of Jesus, so the *kerygmatic* Christ can claim to be a legitimate interpretation of the historical Jesus in the light of Jesus' resurrection."[51] What the Gospels evince is the reinterpretation of Jesus, his identity and mission. It is a theological-biographical-historical account of the Messiah—the Christ—and a retroactive reading of his life and ministry.[52] As Cullmann summarizes,

> The problem of Jesus in its full theological scope was recognized only in the light of the new events of his death on the cross and the experience immediately following his resurrection. These events caused those momentary glimpses of recognition during Jesus' earthly life to stand out in the bright light of perception, and at least a few came to understand those indirect references of his which had found no open ears during his lifetime.[53]

Aspects of a retroactive hermeneutic, albeit couched in different terms and developed within quite a different context, have been adopted in recent ecumenical methodology as witnessed to by a recent Faith and Order paper on hermeneutics:

> The Holy Spirit inspires and leads the churches each to rethink and reinterpret their tradition in conversation with each other, always aiming to embody the one Tradition in the unity of God's church. The churches of God as living communities, constituted by faith in Jesus Christ and empowered by the Holy Spirit,

---

49. Edwyn Hoskyns and Noël Davey, eds., *The Riddle of the New Testament* (London: Faber and Faber, 1958), 170. Also see Pinnock, *Flame of Love*, 243 where he lists four points for evaluating claims to illumination and discernment.

50. What has been termed "a hermeneutic from within" by Royse G. Gruenler, *New Approaches to Jesus and the Gospels: A Phenomenological and Exegetical Study of Synoptic Christology* (Grand Rapids: Baker, 1982), 129.

51. James D. G. Dunn, *Unity and Diversity in the New Testament: An Inquiry into the Character of Earliest Christianity* (Philadelphia: Westminster, 1977), 216.

52. Colin Gunton, *Yesterday and Today: A Study of Continuities in Christology* (London: Dartman, Longman and Todd, 1983), 61, speaks of Jesus' "suprahistorical significance" for the evangelists.

53. Oscar Cullmann, *The Christology of the New Testament* (London: SCM, 1959), 319.

must always re-receive the Gospel in ways that relate to their present experience of life. It is in this process of re-reception that the minds of Christian communities are enlightened by the Holy Spirit to discern truth from falsehood and to acknowledge both the richness and the limitedness of the diverse geographical, historical, religious and social circumstances in which the Gospel is made manifest. Ecumenical hermeneutics is not an unaided human enterprise. It is an ecclesial act led by the Spirit and therefore it should be carried out in a setting of prayer.[54]

A retroactive hermeneutic is one in which the text of Scripture, the life of Christ, and the ongoing illumination of the Holy Spirit are equal participants in the church's ongoing task of understanding and articulating the Word of God for today. This hermeneutic and model of doctrinal enrichment offers a way beyond sectarian disputes toward a more united Christian thought and practice.

---

54 *A Treasure in Earthen Vessels: An Instrument for an Ecumenical Reflection on Hermeneutics*, Faith and Order Paper 182 (Geneva: WCC, 1998), n. 32.

Part Two

Constructing Theology *with the Spirit*

7

Eastern Promises: Remedying the Pneumatological Deficits of Western Theology

by Hugh Bowron

OF REVOLUTIONS AND THEOLOGY

As the Bolshevik revolution consolidated its grip on Russian society, increasing numbers of the intelligentsia got the message that it would be wise in terms of personal survival and career opportunities to join the general exodus into Western Europe. Between 1919 and 1922 something like three million Russians left the Rodina, moving first to Berlin where the collapse of the mark made refugee living cheap, and then to Paris, where a substantial *émigré* community would settle down, always hoping to return, but in fact were there for the rest of their lives.

Amongst this Russian diaspora were some fine theological minds that came together to form the Institute of St. Sergius, at first just some students and teachers huddled together in small draughty rooms, but which would later morph into a theological college and teaching faculty of considerable renown. Throughout the 20s, 30s, and 40s names such as

Sergei Bulgakov, Vladimir Lossky, Paul Evdokimov, Nicholas Arfanes'ev, and Georges Florovsky would come to the attention of a much wider theological public.

This was helped by a remarkable combination of favorable circumstances. It was often the case that the hosts of these Russian orthodox intellectuals were very receptive to what they had to say, and not just out of sympathy for their plight or the lure of Eastern *exotique*, but rather because they sensed that a fresh perspective on a number of key theological issues was in the offing. This encouragement came not just from Christian intellectuals in France, but also from members of the Church of England, an engagement that would later turn into a series of major theological conversations and then theological agreements.

The Institut Saint-Serge was also greatly favored by the considerable intellectual freedom it enjoyed in Paris. Tsarist Russia, since the time of Peter the Great, had imposed a tight control on the Russian Orthodox Church, including its seminaries. Now, for the first time, a tight-knit community of Russian theologians was free to teach, write, and publish what was on their mind without state interference. They were also free to appropriate the best of Western theological scholarship. Theology could move from reiteration and transmission to speculation and exploration.

It could be argued that Lenin had done the European theological world a backhanded favor by exporting to the West a Russian ginger group who would stir things up, particularly in the fields of pneumatology, Trinitarian theology, and soteriology. This blessing would soon extend to the Atlanticist world, as Georges Florovsky, uncomfortable with Bulgakov's speculative sophianity in his pneumatology, would move to America to join the emerging St. Vladimir's Orthodox Theological Seminary in Crestwood, New York. From this matrix would come the next generation of Western-engaging Orthodox theologians, such as John Meyendorff and Alexander Schmemann. In our own time the torch has passed to some extent to the Greeks with names such as John Zizioulas and Christos Yannaras coming to the fore. And of course Western converts are coming on stream such as Kallistos (Timothy) Ware, David Bentley Hart, and Andrew Louth.

In this chapter I want to look at the extent to which Western theology has heard, engaged with, and been prepared to shift ground arising out of the dialogue with these Orthodox voices. The title "Eastern Promises" is a nomenclature shamelessly expropriated from David Cronenburg's recent excellent film about the operations of the Russian Mafia in London.[1] I will be looking at the way the Russians and their successors tested and probed the pneumatological deficits of Western theology. Do we now think about the person and the mission of the Holy Spirit in a different way as a result of their arrival in the West?

What I propose to do is paint in broad-brush strokes the highlights of the engagement zones in pneumatology, and their knock-on consequences in Trinitarian theology. Then I will focus on the doctrine of *theosis* as a more examined test case of the two theological traditions closing with one another. Remember that the Orthodox discuss divinization in heavily pneumatological terms. For them salvation is a matter of "acquiring the Holy Spirit" to quote St. Seraphim of Sarov.[2] Purification, illumination, and then union are the stages the Holy Spirit takes the believer through in the journey back to the Father.[3] By contrast, in the West we have tended to lean heavily on the metaphor of incorporation into Christ, whose life-giving grace flows down to us from him as head as we are incorporated into his body the church.[4]

PNEUMATOLOGICAL DEFICITS OF THE WEST

So let us consider the charge sheet brought by the Russians against Western pneumatology. Vladimir Lossky alleged that Western theologians treated the Holy Spirit as the lieutenant of Christ, the subaltern who runs his errands and does his bidding, but who receives little attention or regard in his own right. Similarly, within the Triune life the role of the Spirit was reduced to being a kind of gopher who shuttles back and forth between the Father and the Son resourcing their life, and staying out of the limelight.[5] Who can wonder, they thought, that this

---

1. David Cronenberg, *Eastern Promises* (Focus Features, 2007).

2. Donald Nicholl, *Triumphs of the Spirit in Russia* (London: Darton, Longman and Todd, 1997), 51.

3. Norman Russell's *The Doctrine of Deification in the Greek Patristic Tradition* (Oxford: Oxford University Press, 2004), lays this out theologian by theologian.

4. Aidan Nichols, *Say It Is Pentecost: A Guide through Balthasar's Theo-logic* (Washington, DC: Catholic University of America Press, 2006), 150.

5. Vladimir Lossky, *The Mystical Theology of the Eastern Church* (London: J. Clarke, 1973), 169–70.

etiolated role is thrust upon it when Augustine of Hippo, the theologian that Orthodox theologians love to hate, got Western thinking about the Trinity focused first and foremost on the substance that unites the Trinity, without paying sufficient attention to the hypostases that differentiate the Divine persons?[6] And who can wonder that all this energy needs to go into preserving the unity of the Trinity when the *filioque* clause, a false teaching first cooked up by Tertullian and then accelerated in its development by Augustine, fails to honor the Father in his role as the origin of the Divine processions? Given Schleiermacher's apparent low priority for Trinitarian theology there was also wondering about how much it mattered to Western theology in general.[7]

Similarly the Holy Spirit is alleged to have a stilted and reduced role in the life of the church. John Zizioulas in *Being as Communion* claims that in Western thinking the church is an ecclesial structure brought into existence by Christ, to which is later added the ingredient Holy Spirit. But to Eastern Orthodoxy the church is first and foremost a charismatic community brought into existence by the action of the Spirit, and then assuming its essential and institutional form out of a process of organic development as the Holy Spirit vivifies it and adds depth and substance to its collective life.[8] The Eastern *émigrés* thought too that the church they were now in contact with seemed to lack a sense of living towards an eschatological horizon, that future zone from which the Holy Spirit tirelessly works to complete and perfect human salvation. Prayer seemed rarely to be thought of in terms of "appropriating by faith the powers of the age to come," to borrow from Hebrews 6:4–5. And a somewhat flat earth kind of eucharistic theology had little sense of each celebration of the liturgy making the kingdom present in that place for that brief period of time amongst a particular body of the baptized who were thereby constituted into Christ's collective presence. That in turn raised

---

6. Ibid., 57, and John Zizioulas, *Being as Communion: Studies in Personhood and the Church* (London: Darton, Longman and Todd, 2004), 88, make this charge against Augustine. For detailed references to the primary sources of Augustine's Trinitarian theology and a powerful defence of Augustine against the charge, see Lewis Ayres, *Nicaea and Its Legacy: An Approach to Fourth-Century Trinitarian Theology* (Oxford: Oxford University Press, 2007), 364–83.

7. For a balanced discussion of this claim see Francis S. Fiorenza, "Schleiermacher's Understanding of God as Triune," in *The Cambridge Companion to Friedrich Schleiermacher*, ed. J. Mariña (Cambridge: Cambridge University Press, 2005), 171–88.

8. Zizioulas, *Being as Communion*, 132.

an issue of underlying theological anthropology, because to their way of thinking human beings were surely relational beings rather than rational, autonomous subjects, so that what the Holy Spirit did in the church was to create *koinonia*, to engender that sense of Spirit-filled community in which human beings could fully realize their relational capacity.

So, starting with the Trinity, how was the state of play in Western theology? In fact, thanks to the two Karl's—Barth and Rahner—a renaissance of Western Trinitarian theology was under way, and pretty much under its own steam. In the *Church Dogmatics* Karl Barth would insist on placing the Trinity at the heart of his theological system.[9] But as one stood back to assess what he had made of the dyad within the triad, some odd features became apparent. What he had produced was out of balance because of its massive christocentrism, accompanied by a theology of the Holy Spirit that could be describe it as the interrupter, the overruler, and the contradictor. Assuming as he did that human beings could have no reliable natural knowledge of God, and that Divine revelation breaks into our world to make faith possible, the role of the Holy Spirit then is to overrule the rebellion of the confused human will, and to reconfigure it with the life-giving will of God. Since Divinity and humanity are such radically different orders of being, the role of the Spirit is to bind these disparate states together in a kind of force field that mediates the benefits of the incarnation—and thus to make possible that continuing miracle by which fickle human beings persist in their walk of faith. Only in this way could human fidelity be possible, because salvation could never be seen as the fruit of strengthened dispositions, infused virtues, and regenerated and enlarged capacities. Barth had read about divinization, and wouldn't have a bar of it.[10] His was an anthropology grounded in an Augustinian pessimism about the freedom of the human will, or rather the lack of it, in which the Holy Spirit was a kind of CRC®[11] spray-on agent to de-rust our severely wounded human nature and frozen will.

If this was a perspective that confirmed the wise men from the East in their low opinion of Western pneumatology and Trinitarian theology,

---

9. Karl Barth, *Church Dogmatics*, ed. G. W. Bromiley and T. F. Torrance, trans. G. W. Bromiley, 2nd ed. (Edinburgh: T. & T. Clark, 1975), I/1:301.

10. See George Hunsinger, "Karl Barth's Doctrine of the Holy Spirit," in *The Cambridge Companion to Karl Barth*, ed. J. B. Webster (Cambridge: Cambridge University Press, 2005), 182–83.

11. CRC® is a silicone spray-on lubricant and protectant.

something more promising was in the offing from Karl Rahner. He simply ignored the *filioque* clause, in contrast to Barth's staunch defense of it, and was similarly not keen on Augustine's psychological analogy of the relationship between the Divine persons, another Eastern Orthodox neuralgia point. But it was his coining of the relationship between the immanent Trinity and the economic Trinity that would open up a potential meeting point between East and West.[12] Here was a way of coming into dialogue around Gregory Palamas's distinction between the *energies* and the *essence* of God,[13] a concept that has caused much head shaking amongst Western theologians since it came into prominence thanks to Vladimir Lossky's influential book *The Mystical Theology of the Eastern Church*.[14] By and large Western theologians have thought that Rahner had the healthier and more effective way of equating the relationship between the two by stating that the immanent Trinity is the economic Trinity, and the economic Trinity is the immanent Trinity. Palamas's distinction has caused widespread concern that it creates the possibility of a God behind God, or that of a God beyond God. In other words, if we can only know God in his *energies* as they radiate out to his creatures then how can we be sure that it is the same God we are dealing with as he is in himself—what is the quality mark that ensures the continuity and contiguity between the God of revelation and the God to be known in the beatific vision?[15]

And that of course brings out into the open another key distinction where East and West still feel distinctly uneasy with one another. While Eastern theology has been more optimistic about the possibility of the Spirit bringing the believer into union with God in this life, it has been insistent that no human being can contemplate or behold the essence of God in the life of the world to come. Western theology sees this in reverse terms: in this life we are exiles and pilgrims, whereas in the heavenly country it is possible to behold the vision of God. Some ingenious explanations have been offered as to how it is possible to cross this great ontological divide—one thinks of Aquinas's insight that God

12. Karl Rahner, *The Trinity* (New York: Herder and Herder, 1970), 22.

13. Anna Williams, *The Ground of Union: Deification in Aquinas and Palamas* (New York: Oxford University Press, 1999), 137–56.

14. Lossky, *Mystical Theology*.

15. Thomas F. Torrance, *The Christian Doctrine of God: One Being Three Persons* (Edinburgh: T. & T. Clark, 1996), 186–88.

will permit the believer's intuition to share in God's intuitive awareness of his own being.[16]

If fundamental differences remain in this area it is interesting to note how some sections of Western theological and ecclesial opinion have been prepared to yield ground in the matter of the *filioque* clause. The 1978 Lambeth conference, the 1976 Moscow agreed statement between the Anglican and Orthodox churches, together with the 1984 Athens statement and the 2006 Cyprus report entitled "In the Church of the Triune God," have all agreed that the Anglican Church should drop the *filioque* clause from the creed in its public worship, so as to bring it back into its original form as devised by the Council of Constantinople in 381.[17] The trouble is, as it so often is with anything the Anglican Church agrees to, there is no mechanism to bring this about. Anglican prayer books have continued to be published with their *filioquist* versions of the creed, the creed has continued to be said or sung in public worship in its unamended form, simply because there is not the energy, interest, political will, disciplinary apparatus, or institutional means to change things.

But even if this change had come to pass it would not be the end of the matter, as that unabashed *filioquist* Hans Urs von Balthasar has pointed out. He argued that this would merely be a cosmetic change that wouldn't alter the fact that in his reading of history a pluralism of opinion and belief on the double procession of the Spirit had been permitted between the Eastern and Western wings of the church throughout the Patristic period, until opinion hardened in the East, with an increasingly intransigent position being taken from the time of Photius onwards. From then on Orthodoxy was pursuing a zero-sum game.[18] At a more

16. Williams, *Ground of Union*, 96–97.

17. For the 1978 Lambeth Conference see http://www.lambethconference.org/resolutions/1978/; "Moscow Agreed Statement 1976," in *Growth in Agreement: Reports and Agreed Statements of Ecumenical Conversations on a World Level*, H. Meyer and L. Vischer, eds., Faith and Order Paper 108 (Geneva: World Council of Churches, 1984), 41–49; "Agreed Statement, Anglican-Orthodox Dialogue 1976-1984," in *Growth in Agreement II: Reports and Agreed Statements of Ecumenical Conversations on a World Level, 1982–1998*, eds. J. Gros, H. Meyer, and W. G. Rusch, Faith and Order Paper 187 (Geneva: World Council of Churches, 2000), 81–102; and International Commission for Anglican-Orthodox Theological Dialogue, *The Church of the Triune God: The Cyprus Agreed Statement*, ed. M. Dyer and J. Zizioulas (London: Anglican Communion Office, 2006).

18. Hans Urs von Balthasar, "The Spirit of Truth," in *Theo-logic: Theological Logical Theory* (San Francisco: Ignatius, 2005), 3:207–18.

telling theological level Balthasar argued that a monopatrist version of the Trinity undermines the freedom and equality of the other Divine persons since all these "two hands" have to do is simply carry out his commands. It is a view of Christology and of pneumatology that verges on subordinationism.

This steadfast opposition is worth noting in a theologian who in other aspects of his writings is seen as something of a bridgehead to Orthodoxy, being one of the first of the Westerners to give attention in his writings to Maximus the Confessor, and who lays his multi-volume systematic theology on the foundations of the classical world's "transcendentals" of truth, beauty, and goodness. We might bear in mind also Balthasar's considerable influence on Pope Benedict XVI, who in 2008 convened a major theological conference in Rome whose agenda was the re-Hellenization of dogma. This could be seen as preparing the ground for a theological rapprochement with Eastern Orthodoxy at a fundamental level.

I want to refer in passing to Balthasar's pneumatology in two of its most intriguing *leitmotifs*. He sees the Spirit's work as interpreting the interpreter. God directs at us a steady stream of communicating energy that can be tuned in to by human beings at a level appropriate to their life experience. So the Son, the Divine Word, speaks to his earthly contemporaries in parables, earthed in the everyday life of Galilee. The Spirit then takes this enfleshed narrative, and interprets it and makes it accessible to those of us in later times and places, overcoming misunderstandings and miscommunications in this continuing work of explanation.[19] Then, in the second part of his work, the *Theo-drama*, he writes about the gospel as a play, a drama enacted before our eyes in which each one of us is being invited up on stage to take the role and the part that is uniquely ours, an acting role of mission and ministry that provides the fulfillment of our lives. The author of this gospel play is the Father, the principal actor is the Son, and the Holy Spirit is the director, our drama coach who encourages us and animates us into this role of a lifetime.[20]

If the Anglican agreement to drop the *filioque* clause was a cosmetic ecumenical gesture, we can note a much more powerful and enduring Orthodox contribution to ecumenical theology that is both surprising and

---

19. Nichols, *Say It Is Pentecost*, 135–38.

20. Aiden Nichols, *No Bloodless Myth: A Guide through Balthasar's Dramatics* (Washington, DC: Catholic University of America Press, 2000), 29–34.

pneumatological. This is the notion of reception as developed by Alexei S. Khomiakov, one of the principal theoreticians of the nineteenth-century lay Russian Orthodox movement known as Slavophilism.[21] Pivoting off a romantic and exalted notion of peasant society, it stressed the notion of *sobornost* or communality, which defined the church as the revelation of the Holy Spirit in the mutual love of Christians. This interior presence of the Spirit is superior to any external revelation. Through the Spirit, Christ leads the church interiorly into all truth, and he does this by means of the mutual love of the church's members. Coercion and external authority in this way of thinking cannot be the way the church makes up its mind in vital matters of Christian truth. Patriarchs, bishops, and ecumenical councils may propose agenda items for the church's belief, but these will have no binding or effectual force unless and until the general body of lay Christians receive, agree to, and interiorize these proposals for faith. Their reception of what the officers and decision-making councils of the church propose is the sign that the Spirit has assented to them. Despite this unlikely chauvinist source, the doctrine of reception has become a powerful and influential tool of twentieth-century ecumenical theology, and is widely used in both Catholic and Protestant ecclesiology.[22]

Earlier I stated that the Eastern critique has lamented the loss of an eschatological horizon in Western thinking. Many may want to respond that Moltmann, Pannenberg, and Jenson put that right in recent times, and have done so by inserting a more relational spin on their anthropology. While at the most immediate and obvious level this is true, the adjustment has been carried out in ways that Orthodox theologians find to be rather too accomodationist to current secular Western thinking. With due regard to Professor Badcock's perspective in chapter 2, perhaps their biggest objection is that all three of the aforementioned have got a bit too much Hegel in their Trinitarianism, so that God is perceived to be in a process of becoming and developing as he hauls human suffering into the core of his being via the cross of Christ, and then spreads

---

21. Aiden Nichols, *Light from the East: Authors and Themes in Orthodox Theology* (London: Sheen & Ward, 1999), 115-22.

22. See the Anglican–Roman Catholic International Commission documents, particularly "Mary: Grace and Hope in Christ," May 2005, online: http://www.anglicancommunion.org/ministry/ecumenical/dialogues/catholic/arcic/docs/mary_grace%20_and_hope.cfm; and also International Commission for Anglican-Orthodox Theological Dialogue, *Church of the Triune God*.

it around the Divine persons. In this way the sufferings of humankind become the grand narrative of the Divine persons drawing one another out to become fully known to one another. It is hard to overstate just how objectionable Orthodoxy finds this kind of Patripassionist thinking, and I think it is worth quoting David Bentley Hart at some length to see why this is:

> If God's identity is constituted in his triumph over evil, then evil belongs eternally to his identity, and his goodness is not goodness as such but a reaction, an activity that requires the goad of evil to come into full being. All of history is the horizon of this drama, and since no analogical interval is allowed to be introduced between God's eternal being as Trinity and God's act as trinity in time, all of history is this identity: every painful death of a child, every casual act of brutality, all war, famine, pestilence, disease, murder... all are moments in the identity of God, resonances within the event of his being, aspects of the occurrence of his essence: all of this is the crucible in which God comes into his own elected reality.... The collapse of the analogical interval between the immanent and economic Trinity, between timeless eternity and the time in which eternity shows itself, has not made God our companion in pain, but simply the truth of our pain and our only pathetic hope of rescue; his intimacy with us has not been affirmed at all: only a truly transcendent and "passionless" God can be the fullness of love dwelling within our very being, nearer to us than our inmost parts, but a dialectical Trinity is not transcendent—truly infinite—in this way at all, but only sublime, a metaphysical whole that can comprise us or change us extrinsically, but not transform our very being. ... Theology must, to remain faithful to what it knows of God's transcendence, reject any picture of God that so threatens to become at once both thoroughly mythological and thoroughly metaphysical, and insist upon the classical definition of impassibility, immutability, and nonsuccessive eternity.... God does not have to change or to suffer in order to love us or show us mercy—he loved us when we were not, and by this very "mercy" created us—and so, as love, he can overcome all suffering.[23]

---

23. David B. Hart, *The Beauty of the Infinite: The Aesthetics of Christian Truth* (Grand Rapids: Eerdmans, 2003), 165–66.

Of the three theologians under consideration I think Orthodoxy would be inclined to find Pannenberg and Robert Jenson the most sympathetic, particularly Jenson.

Pannenberg has a pneumatology that has been described as "an ontology of the future."[24] He thinks "the presence of God's Spirit in his creation can be described as a field of creative presence, a comprehensive field of force that releases event after event into finite existence."[25] He uses this scientific image to account for the Spirit's role in Trinitarian relations when he describes it as "the force field of their fellowship that is distinct from them both."[26] Is this a Christian existence that is living towards an eschatological horizon, or is it an eschatological horizon that is pulling all of Christian existence towards it? I wonder if the wise men from the East find that there is rather too much future eschatological horizon here even for their tastes?

Earlier I suggested that Robert Jenson is the most Byzantine of these three contemporary theologians. This is in part because he agrees with the criticism of Barth, who in his massive christocentrism sees the gift of the Spirit as merely one of the roll-out consequences of the resurrection of Christ. Jenson agrees with the Orthodox that the gift of the Spirit at Pentecost is a peer event with the resurrection, it matters as much, and it has equal significance. What is more, Jenson also agrees in large measure with the Orthodox in taking up a critical stance against the *filioque* clause. He is in sympathy with Orthodoxy's analysis of where this has taken Western Christianity's doctrine of the Spirit. As he writes, "The common factor in Western problems with the Spirit, one may suggest, is a tendency of the Spirit simply to disappear from theology's description of God's triune action just when he might be expected to have the leading role."[27] But he can see the point of the *filioque* clause, and considers the way Eastern theologians have tried to affirm it. He is prepared to go this far:

---

24. Veli-Matti Kärkkäinen, *The Trinity: Global Perspectives* (Louisville: Westminster John Knox, 2007), 127.

25. Wolfahrt Pannenberg, *Systematic Theology*, trans. G. W. Bromiley (Edinburgh: T. & T. Clark, 1991), 1:194.

26. Ibid., 1:383.

27. Robert W. Jenson, *Systematic Theology*, vol. 1, *The Triune God* (New York: Oxford University Press, 1997), 153.

> The Father is the source of the Spirit's being, of his sheer givenness as an other than the Father or the Son, but the Spirit's *energies*, his participation and agency in the triune life, come to him from the Father through the Son or, it can even be said, from the Father and the Son. For the whole divine life begins with the Father and is actual through the Son and is perfected in the Holy Spirit. The Spirit does not derive his being from the Son, but does derive his energy from the Son.[28]

He concurs with the analysis of the Cappadocian Fathers that "the Spirit receives his existence from the Father, but lives eternally with and in the Son."[29] He quotes several times with approval their view that the work of our salvation originates with the Father, is developed through the Son, and is completed and perfected by the Spirit. For Jenson the Spirit is, as it were, the future dimension of God, God coming to us from the future as the kingdom, and this also is the place from which the risen Christ came to the disciples after the resurrection, as it is the dimension from which risen Christ presides over the church. Augustine viewed the Spirit as the link point, the relational binder of the Father and the Son. Jenson seems to take it the other way around. The Father as the originator, and the Spirit as perfector and finisher are bound together by Christ, who holds both poles of this saving work in his person as the mediating link point.

There are, however, parts of Jenson's work that would make a Byzantine theologian squirm, particularly in its rejection of the influence of neoplatonic metaphysics on Christian theology, its rejection of the doctrine of Divine impassibility, and in its rejection of the Palamite *essence/energies* distinction.

THEOSIS AS A TEST CASE

I promised to conclude with a consideration of the doctrine of *theosis*, the Byzantine doctrine of salvation that, having been a minority interest in the West for many years, is now coming on like gangbusters in its popularity. Yet even in the years of its obscurity there were significant shifts of opinion going on. Paul Tillich, in his *Systematic Theology*,

---

28. Ibid., 158–59.
29. Ibid., 159.

questioned whether the Western quest for the justice of God as focused on by Augustine and the Reformers got to the heart of what salvation was about.[30] He wondered if justification by faith had reached its use-by date, overtaken by a more promising Eastern soteriology with its deep interest in the victory of God and life over death. There was a growing general uneasiness about the thinness of the description of salvation if all it amounted to was the forgiveness of sins, leading a moral life, and an inner emotional reassurance that one was right with God. The notion that it also involved God supplying fresh resources of being as the believer advanced in the process of salvation came to seem increasingly appealing.

Now, *theosis* studies has become something of a minor industry, with astonishing retrospective claims being made that the greats of Western theology such as Augustine, Luther, and Calvin really believed in divinization after all, if only one knew where to look in the primary sources, and if only one overlooked the forensic and staurological obsessions and distortions of their later disciples.[31] It is therefore something of a relief to see these inflated claims cut down to size in a recent essay by the Swedish Catholic theologian Gösta Hallonsten, in which he calls for clarity in distinguishing between the *theme* of *theosis* as it generally appears in the writings of many theologians, and the *doctrine* of *theosis*, a dense cluster of ideas circling around certain key motifs, as held by a relatively small number of mostly Byzantine theologians.[32] It simply will not do to say that because a theologian mentions union with God or participation in the Divine nature in a few places in his writings that he thereby is signed up a member of the *theosis* club, because, after all, in addressing key biblical themes such as *filiation*, adoption, and the indwelling of God, one is highly likely to use *theosis*-sounding language. And it is worth asking in what sort of writings these references occur. Augustine, for instance, uses this sort of language reasonably often in his sermons, but never in his treatises on grace. But then it could be argued that it is actually quite

---

30. Veli-Matti Kärkkäinen, *One with God: Salvation as Deification and Justification* (Collegeville, MN: Liturgical, 2004), 118.

31. Carl E. Braaten and Robert W. Jenson, eds., *Union with Christ: The New Finnish Interpretation of Luther* (Grand Rapids: Eerdmans, 1998).

32. Gösta Hallonsten, "Theosis in Recent Research: A Renewal of Interest and a Need for Clarity," in *Partakers of the Divine Nature: The History and Development of Deification in the Christian Traditions*, eds. Michael J. Christensen and Jeffrey A. Wittung (Grand Rapids: Baker, 2007), 281–93.

difficult to preach a Christmas sermon and to not use *theosis*-sounding terminology somewhere in it.

But the key issue in this debate is, what kind of anthropology does a theologian deploy? Does she believe in a relationship of image and likeness between God and humankind? As Hallonsten puts it, "The whole structure of this comprehensive doctrine is determined by a teleology that implies that creation and human beings from the very beginning are endowed with an affinity and likeness that potentially draws them to God."[33] He argues that the Greek Fathers have a fundamentally dynamic anthropology that assumes in humankind an inbuilt forward momentum towards God. To quote him again, "The meaning of the Christian life is to assimilate to God, to grow according to the prototype."[34] Of course this kind of dynamic anthropology draws on neoplatonic sources, wellsprings from which many Protestant theologians do not want to drink. And they in turn have been deeply influenced by a radical Augustinian pessimism about the scarring of human nature in the fall. It seems to me that if you believe in the doctrine of total depravity, if you reject an *analogia entis* between God and humankind, then you cannot hold the doctrine of *theosis*.

Andrew Louth raises the question of what kind of framework a theologian deploys in her doctrine of salvation in an even more interesting form in a recent essay on the place of *theosis* in Orthodox theology.[35] Reinforcing the point that you can't just jam *theosis*-sounding language on top of a conventional Western view of the subject, he writes that a theologian's cosmology is a key determinant in the way he sees the economy of salvation working. He asks us to imagine a great arch stretching from creation to deification in which we see God's loving design to fulfill his purposes for all the creation, to draw it back to himself so as to be all in all to it. Along that arch Adam fails to cooperate with God's purposes and falls away from these plans and intentions with grievous downwind consequences for all the creation. God therefore puts in place his redemption strategy to correct this fault, and to bring humankind back into its role as priests of all creation, the microcosm within which

33. Ibid., 284.

34. Ibid.

35. Andrew Louth, "The Place of Theosis in Orthodox Theology," in *Partakers of the Divine Nature: The History and Development of Deification in the Christian Traditions*, eds. Michael J. Christensen and Jeffrey A. Wittung (Grand Rapids: Baker, 2007), 32.

the creation is restored to its proper style of operations. This redemption strategy is a smaller arch, just below the bigger one, in which the focus is just on humankind in its journey from fall to fulfillment. But this is only part of the story of God's economy of salvation. And that is the problem with Western accounts of salvation—the relentless focus on redemption as though this was the entire content of salvation in which God is only interested in humankind. In this "moi, moi, moi" approach to the subject, the creation becomes merely stage scenery, a backdrop to the great drama of human salvation, and the purpose of the incarnation is reduced to merely that of human redemption. Humankind thereby loses its most glorious role as what Balthasar called the "cosmic liturgist," the microcosmic guardian and celebrator of the beauty of the creation.[36] The recapitulation of the creation ministry of Christ is also ours.

The intense debate about the value of the doctrine of *theosis* has also drawn Western theology into some fascinating places in the area of hermeneutics. Take for instance the 1989 Lutheran-Orthodox agreed statement on "The Canon and the Inspiration of the Holy Scripture."[37] Here is their novel solution to the knotty issue of biblical inspiration:

> Glorification is the transformation and renewal of the whole person (Romans 12:2). It empowered the authors of holy scripture to proclaim and write the word of God. Prophets, apostles and saints who have experienced God's glory and witnessed to it in holy scripture declare the truth of God and the ways of communion with him.... Those who have experienced the glory of God, which experience in itself cannot be expressed in words or conceived in thoughts, are yet inspired to use expressions and concepts of ordinary language in order to guide others to the same experience.... Within the life of the church Christians who become "a temple of the Holy Spirit" (1 Corinthians 6:19) and therefore are members of the body of Christ are led into all the truth in the experience of glorification, as the Lord prayed to the Father: "Father, I desire that they also, whom thou hast given me,

---

36. Nichols, *Say It Is Pentecost*, 96, and Hans Urs von Balthasar, *Kosmische Liturgie Maximus der Bekenner: Höhe und Krise des griechischen Weltbildes* (Freiburg: Herder, 1941).

37. "The Canon and Inspiration of Holy Scripture," in *Growth in Agreement II: Reports and Agreed Statements of Ecumenical Conversations on a World Level, 1982–1998*, eds. J. Gros, H. Meyer, and W. G. Rusch, Faith and Order Paper 187 (Geneva: World Council of Churches, 2000).

> may be with me where I am, to behold my glory which thou hast given me in thy love for me before the foundation of the world" (John 17:24).... Some books of the Bible were written by those authors who themselves have reached glorification, while other books were written about them or about historical events.[38]

Far from being just an adjunct of mystical theology, or a speculative aside in soteriology, deification has here acquired cash value in one of the most highly charged and contentious issues of contemporary church life. As I read it, the Lutheran and Orthodox theologians who framed this agreement are arguing that the biblical authors were in many cases glorified into union with God; were divinized individuals, who, irradiated by the divine *energies*, were inspired to write the book/s of the Bible that they did. Their transformation into close fellowship with God enabled them to put into words those classic narratives and other genres of sacred literature that make up the canon of Scripture.

Even more interesting to me is the work that Gregory Glazov has done in digging deep for the roots of the doctrine of *theosis* in Old Testament anthropology. He writes:

> In scripture keeping is normally a prerequisite for knowing. For the end of keeping God's words is entry into their life giving energies, into the joy of knowing and savouring their inner wisdom and goodness, gaining the ability to discriminate between things that lead to life and things that do not, and the capacity to bring peace-making judgement and to dispense life-sustaining counsel. Being ubiquitous in biblical wisdom, psalmody and salvation history, these patterns may be read back into the Garden of Eden story in Genesis 2–3 to help unravel the meaning of one of its multifold layers of wisdom.... Entry into life means transformation from lowly earth, that is, soil, into the full stature of an exalted tree of righteousness, a paradisal tree of life and knowledge, or a fragrant vine of understanding, thus becoming capable of yielding the fruit of righteousness, the fruit of knowledge and understanding of God.... Adam's failure to enter into life and preserve the status of an "oak of righteousness" derived not so much from a desire to "become like God," (God did, after all, create Adam in His own image and likeness), but, as in the case of the Pharaoh of Ezekiel 31, from the failure to become really like God by means of an inward, organic, transformative

---

38. Ibid., 228–29.

appropriation of godliness via holding onto God's words, opting instead, to try to attain this status via an act that severs any organic link between what one does and what one is, and thus to deny the ethically reflexive nature of human action. By means of this process, he would not have become less human, just as soil does not become any less material by entering into the life of a seed, that opens within it. But he would have become transhumanized—become more than he was—just as soil becomes more than it was, when it is transformed into a plant.[39]

Time has run out to take the *theosis* theme any further. I finish with the challenge that Patriarch Ignatius IV threw out to the 1968 meeting of the World Council of Churches, because it is the best summary I know of Orthodoxy's offering to the West in the area of pneumatology:

Without the Holy Spirit, God is far away
Christ stays in the past,
the Gospel is a dead letter,
the Church is simply an organisation,
authority is a matter of domination,mission is a matter of
    propaganda,the liturgy is no more than an evocation,
    Christian living a slave morality.

But in the Holy Spirit:
the cosmos is resurrected and groans with the birth pangs
    of the Kingdom,
the risen Christ is there,
the Gospel is the power of life,
the Church shows forth the power of the Trinity,
authority is a liberating service,mission is a Pentecost,
the liturgy is both memorial and anticipation,and human
    action is deified.[40]

---

39. Gregory Glazov, "Theosis, Judaism, and Old Testament Anthropology," in *Theosis: Deification in Christian Theology*, eds. S. Finlan and V. Kharlamov (Eugene, OR: Pickwick, 2006), 26–28.

40. Ignatius IV (Hazim), then the Orthodox Metropolitan of Latakia, delivered this statement at the WCC Fourth Assembly, Uppsala, Sweden, August 1968. Published in *Irenikon* 42 (1968) 344–59.

8

Theosis, Yes; Deification, No

by Myk Habets

THE RESURGENCE OF *THEOSIS* AND ITS HISTORICAL ANTECEDENTS[1]

Spirituality is a daunting instantiation of a term that has acquired such a range of meaning it threatens to collapse under the weight it has been asked to carry in contemporary thought. Coupled with the name *God* it is such a plastic term that one wonders how a concise definition of it may be offered, let alone using it as the focal point of a rigorous intellectual study. Be that as it may, the Christian tradition, East and West, has repeatedly appealed to the notion of spirituality as a way of representing the whole person (body, soul, spirit, and mind) before the Ultimate. When the whole person encounters God in a dynamic synthesis of faith, values, ethics, and duties, one's life is said to flourish through a form of divine communion. Eastern Christianity repeatedly refers to this as *theosis*. Western Christianity has been reluctant to incorporate the language

---

1. An earlier version of this chapter was originally read at the Calvin 500 Tribute Conference, Young Scholars Symposium, Geneva, July 8, 2009. My thanks to Dr. Gannon Murphy for comments made on a draft of this chapter.

or theology of *theosis* into its more forensic and extrinsicist understanding of salvation and spirituality, thus creating a certain hostility towards the East. Despite this, however, theology in the West is not immune to doctrines of *theosis* even if it is evinced, as Normal Russell remarks, in a "more muted way."[2]

As Bowron's contribution to this volume earlier affirmed, it has been variously observed that *theosis* is enjoying greater popularity today among Protestant theology than ever before. This may be so for various reasons, one of which is certainly the fact that patristic and Eastern Orthodox sources are now more readily available in English translation than ever before, occasioning a reconsideration of ancient soteriological metaphors and bringing these into dialogue with contemporary culture and concerns.[3] *Theosis* is perhaps the most popular of these ancient soteriological metaphors to receive sustained attention, initially amongst Lutherans[4] and latterly amongst a growing assemblage of Reformed

---

2. Norman Russell, *The Doctrine of Deification in the Greek Patristic Tradition* (Oxford: Oxford University Press, 2004), vii.

3. A notable example here includes Jules Gross, *La divinisation du chrétien d'après les pères grecs: Contribution historique à la doctrine de la grâce* (Paris: J. Gabalda, 1938), and Jules Gross, *The Divinization of the Christian According to the Greek Fathers*, translated by P. A. Onica (Anaheim, CA: A & C, 2002). On the recent reception of *theosis* in the West, consult Paul L. Gavrilyuk, "The Retrieval of Deification: How a Once-Despised Archaism Became an Ecumenical Desideratum," *Modern Theology* 25 (2009), 647–59.

4. On the Lutheran side the so-called Mannermaa School is the most fruitful. See Carl E. Braaten and Robert W. Jenson, eds., *Union with Christ: The New Finish Interpretation of Luther* (Grand Rapids: Eerdmans, 1998). For an essay on post-Reformation Lutheran theology of *theosis* see Rainer Hauke, *Gott-Haben—um Gottes Willen. Andreas Osanders Theosisgedanke und die Diskussion um die Grundlagen der evangelisch verstandenen Rechtfertigung. Versuch einer Neubewertung eines umstrittenen Gedankens* (Frankfurt: Peter Lang, 1999). This new Finnish interpretation has not gone unchallenged. Reformed theologian Bruce McCormack believes that "although Luther's tendency to prioritize regeneration over justification does open a door to the Finnish interpretation, it is my view that his new reading brings as much to Luther as it reads out of him." Bruce L. McCormack, "What's at Stake in Current Debates over Justification? The Crisis of Protestantism in the West," in *Justification: What's at Stake in the Current Debates*, ed. M. Husbands and D. J. Treier (Grand Rapids: InterVarsity, 2004), 95. Also critical of this thesis is Klas Schwarzwäller, "Verantwortung des Glaubens. Freiheit und Liebe nach der Deklogauslegung Martin Luthers," in *Freiheit als Liebe bei/Freedom as Love in Martin Luther*, eds. D. D. Biefeldt and K. Schwarzwäller (Frankfurt: P. Lang, 1995), 146–48. Schwarzwäller's critique of Mannermaa revolves around five areas: hermeneutics, history, logic, linguistics, and theology. See a brief

thinkers.⁵ In addition, several scholarly volumes on *theosis* have recently appeared and have clarified a number of central concepts regarding the history and development of *theosis* in the Christian traditions.⁶ One crucial factor these and other studies have highlighted is the distinction between *theosis* as a theme and *theosis* as a doctrine, also pointed out in the previous chapter by Bowron. This is a particular focus of Gösta Hallonsten's recent essay in which he argues that the presence of the *theme* of *theosis* in a thinker's work does not necessarily imply the presence of a *doctrine* of *theosis*.⁷ The distinction between *theosis* as a theme and as a doctrine is a useful one and Hallonsten is right to highlight the issue. Hallonsten defines a doctrine as "a rather well-defined complex of thought that centers on one or more technical terms,"⁸ while a theme is the

---

interaction with Mannermaa and Schwarzwäller in Robert Kolb, "Contemporary Lutheran Understandings of the Doctrine of Justification," in *Justification: What's at Stake*, 153–76.

5. See Carl Mosser, "The Greatest Possible Blessing: Calvin and Deification," *SJT* 55 (2002) 36–57; Julie Canlis, "Calvin, Osiander, and Participation in God," *International Journal of Systematic Theology* 6 (2004) 169–84; J. Todd Billings, "United to God through Christ: Assessing Calvin on the Question of Deification," *HTR* 98 (2005) 315–34; Myk Habets, "Reforming Theosis," in *Theosis: Deification in Christian Theology*, eds. S. Finlan and V. Kharlamov (Eugene, OR: Pickwick, 2006), 146–67; J. Todd Billings, *Calvin, Participation, and the Gift: The Activity of Believers in Union with Christ* (Oxford: Oxford University Press, 2007); Gannon Murphy, "Reformed Theosis?" *ThTo* 65 (2008) 191–212; Myk Habets, "'Reformed Theosis?' A Response to Gannon Murphy," *ThTo* 65 (2009) 489–98; and Myk Habets, *Theosis in the Theology of Thomas Torrance* (Surrey: Ashgate, 2009). A Reformed doctrine of *theosis* has not gone unchallenged. Bruce McCormack, for instance, argues that Reformed theology operates on a metaphysics which is incompatible with a doctrine of theosis. See Bruce McCormack, "Participation in God, Yes, Deification, No: Two Modern Protestant Responses to an Ancient Question," in *Denkwürdiges Geheimnis: Beiträge zur Gotteslehre. Festschrift für Eberhard Jüngel zum 70. Geburtstag*, ed. I. U. Dalferth, J. Fischer, and H-P. Großhans (Tübingen: Mohr-Siebeck, 2004), 347–74. McCormack pre-empted this conclusion in an earlier article, "For Us and Our Salvation: Incarnation and Atonement in the Reformed Tradition," *GOTR* 43 (1998) 281–316.

6. Three such works deserve special mention: Russell, *Doctrine of Deification*; Stephen Finlan and Vladimir Kharlamov, eds., *Theosis: Deification in Christian Theology* (Eugene, OR: Pickwick, 2006); and Michael J. Christensen and Jeffrey A. Wittung, eds., *Partakers of the Divine Nature: The History and Development of Deification in the Christian Traditions* (Grand Rapids: Baker, 2007).

7. Gösta Hallonsten, "Theosis in Recent Research: A Renewal of Interest and a Need for Clarity," in *Partakers of the Divine Nature*, 281–93.

8. Ibid., 283.

presence of a cluster of related terms around some central ideas. It is no wonder, Hallonsten stresses, that *theosis* can be found as a theme in such thinkers as Augustine, Aquinas, and Luther when it has a certain connection to biblical passages such as 2 Pet 1:4 and Ps 82:6, and to notions of union with Christ, indwelling, and beatific vision. "Yet employing the theme is not the same as making a doctrine out of it,"[9] argues Hallonsten. With these words of wisdom a good deal of the contemporary discussion regarding *theosis* may be clarified through an articulation of *theosis* as a theme or as a doctrine.

Hallonsten teases out the implications of this distinction by articulating what a doctrine of *theosis* consists of. Rejecting the notion that the central tenet of *theosis* is participation in divine life (!), Hallonsten's contention is that *theosis* is "a comprehensive doctrine encompassing the whole economy of salvation."[10] He goes on to stress what he considers to be the constituent features of a doctrine of *theosis*, namely:

> a certain view of creation, especially of human beings; a soteriology, including the meaning of the Incarnation; a view of Christian life as sanctification connected to the Church and sacraments; and the final goal of union with God. The whole structure of this comprehensive doctrine is determined by a teleology that implies that creation and human beings from the very beginning are endowed with an affinity and likeness that potentially draws them to God.[11]

Hallonsten and Bowron further argue that anthropology is the "fundamental feature" of a doctrine of *theosis*, especially in the distinction made in Genesis 1:26 between the "image and likeness" of humanity to God. It is this anthropological point that Hallonsten and Bowron find absent in most of what are touted as Western doctrines of *theosis*. Further, fundamental to a doctrine of *theosis* is an essentially Platonic (or in Bowron's case, neoplatonic) concept of Creator, creature, and participation, which works itself out into the categories of God's *essence* and *energies*. Hallonsten concludes his brief essay by saying "that the label 'doctrine of *theosis*' should preferentially be reserved for the integral doc-

---

9. Ibid.
10. Ibid., 284.
11. Ibid., 285.

trine of deification as presented by the Eastern tradition."[12] Bowron is in fundamental agreement with this claim in his essay.

Taking our cue from Hallonsten, I wish to build upon his distinction between *theosis* as a theme or as a doctrine and make the point that there is, in fact, no single *doctrine* (singular) of *theosis* at all; there are, rather, *doctrines* (plural) of *theosis* and in every instance one must discern what form each thinker gives to it. This applies as much to the East as it does to the West. This may appear to be a very basic claim and yet it is one that has escaped the common practice amongst contemporary theologians; both Hallonsten and Bowron fail to grasp this central point. All too often a thinker is judged upon their adoption or otherwise of a supposed definitive doctrine of *theosis* and is thereby accepted or rejected depending on the *a priori* stance of the critic. According to Hallonsten's and Bowron's analysis, the East has *the* doctrine of *theosis* and all other appeals to such a doctrine must be evaluated in light of this one. But this is problematic to say the least. Hallonsten points out that Gregory Palamas cannot simply be looked to for *the* representative Eastern doctrine of *theosis* given the largely polemical nature of his writings. (Yet it is Palamas, seemingly, that Bowron looks to for *the* Eastern doctrine of *theosis*.) But Hallonsten then offers no other viable candidate. The volume in which Hallonsten's essay appears is instructive at this point, given it examines *doctrines* of *theosis* within such figures as the Cappadocians, Athanasius, Maximus the Confessor, and Ephrem the Syrian, to name but a few, and in each instance what is highlighted is the idiosyncratic doctrine of *theosis* each thinker has in contradistinction to other thinkers—and even, on occasion, the different *doctrines* of *theosis* within the same author, as for instance in Athanasius and Gregory of Nazianzus![13] Thus to limit a definition of *theosis* to that of an Eastern Orthodox thinker, such as Palamas, with his distinction between the *essence* and *energies* of God (as Bowron seems to do), or to Eastern Orthodoxy more generally (as Hallonsten does), is erroneous and misleading today given the many varieties of *theosis* that exist. Rather, it needs to be recognized that there are themes and doctrines of *theosis* which require evaluation on their own merits not in relation to some perceived but fictitious doctrine that "rules them

---

12. Ibid., 287.

13. In this regard see Vladimir Kharlamov, "Rhetorical Application of Theosis in Greek Patristic Theology," in *Partakers of the Divine Nature*, 115–31.

all" in Tolkien-like fashion. I shall return to this point further below after establishing a context into which we may place Calvin's contribution or otherwise to doctrines of *theosis*.

THEOSIS IN WESTERN THEOLOGY

According to most Reformed scholars, union with Christ is at the heart of Reformed theology. While various theologians debate where exactly union with Christ fits into the *ordo salutis* (or at the least the sequencing in the *opera trinitatis ad extra*), it is certain that it is an integral component.[14] While union with God and *theosis* are not identical, they are closely related, such that Reformed doctrines of the "mystical union" (*unio mystica*) with Christ and the "wonderful exchange" (*mirifica commutatio*) are compatible with a doctrine of *theosis* if that doctrine is clearly articulated and distinguished from other competing doctrines. When a doctrine of *theosis* is examined on its own terms, not those of any predetermined Eastern formulation, one can clearly find it within the theology of John Calvin. That is, at least, the claim I hope to illustrate in the next section.

Calvin and Theosis

Contrary to some scholars, the concept of *theosis* is clearly present in Calvin.[15] For Calvin the concept of *theosis* comes closest to what is more commonly in Calvin and the West termed "union with Christ."[16] This is not to imply that union with Christ and *theosis* are equivalents, rather, it is a more modest claim that Calvin's construal of the *unio mystica*[17] is

---

14. See Robert Letham, *The Work of Christ* (Leicester: InterVarsity, 1993), 55–56.

15. Frederick W. Norris, "Deification: Consensual and Cogent," *SJT* 49 (1996) 420. Wendel also thinks this is the case given Calvin's radical distinction between the two natures of Christ; see François Wendel, *Calvin: Origins and Development of His Religious Thought*, trans. Philip Mairet (New York: Harper & Row, 1963), 235 and 259.

16. See Dennis E. Tamburello, *Union with Christ: John Calvin and the Mysticism of St. Bernard*, Columbia Series in Reformed Theology (Louisville: Westminster John Knox, 1994).

17. While we shall focus only on the *unio mystica* and the *mirifica commutatio*, other aspects of Calvin's theology also merit attention, especially his doctrines of the sacraments, his christological anthropology, and the *duplex gratia*, all of which are beyond the limited scope of the present study.

compatible with the way in which he utilizes the concept of *theosis*.[18] It has been argued that the *unio mystica* is Calvin's central dogma.[19] If this is true, and there is good evidence that it is, then in a derived fashion the doctrine of *theosis* is also of importance to Calvin's theology.[20] In one of his rare uses of the word "deification" Calvin writes, in reference to 2 Pet 1:4, "We should notice that it is the purpose of the Gospel to make us sooner or later like God; indeed it is, so to speak, a kind of deification."[21] Calvin, when writing about the thought of us partaking of the divine "nature" makes it plain that this does not mean we partake of the divine essence but what he calls "kind." "The apostles," writes Calvin "were simply concerned to say that when we have put off all the vices of the flesh we shall be partakers of divine immortality and the glory of blessedness, and thus we shall be in a way with God so far as our capacity allows."[22] Calvin thus shows a willingness to utilize the concept of *theosis* in his work but not in any preconceived, and even less in any Eastern Orthodox sense.[23] Thus his implicit doctrine of *theosis* is not equivalent to Eastern doctrines of deification/divinization *simpliciter*.

18. Charles Partee, *The Theology of John Calvin* (Louisville: Westminster John Knox, 2008), 176, has misunderstood comments I have made to this effect in an earlier essay, Myk Habets, "Reforming Theosis," in *Theosis: Deification in Christian Theology*, 146–67. I trust my comments here clarify this misunderstanding.

19. See Wilhelm Kolfhaus, *Christusgemeinschaft bei Calvin* (Neukirchen, Ger.: Buchhandlung des Erziehungsvereins, 1939); Tamburello, *Union with Christ*; Wilhelm Niesel, *Reformed Symbolics: A Comparison of Catholicism, Orthodoxy, and Porotestantism*, trans. David Lewis (Edinburgh: Oliver & Boyd, 1962), 184; and Charles Partee, "Calvin's Central Dogma Again," *Sixteenth Century Journal* 18 (1987) 191–99. Partee's latest work, *The Theology of John Calvin* (Louisville: Westminster John Knox, 2008), successfully shows how one of Calvin's central theological ideas is that of union with Christ, and yet this does not occupy an integrative motif or formal principle of correlation for Calvin or his supposed theological system. According to Partee, "union with Christ is the basic confession of Calvin and a basic doctrine of the Reformed churches." Ibid., 167n95.

20. See for example John Calvin, *Calvin's New Testament Commentaries*, vol. 12, *Hebrews and 1 and 2 Peter*, eds. D. W. and T. F. Torrance, trans. W. B. Johnston (Grand Rapids: Eerdmans, 1963), 330; and John Calvin, *Institutes of the Christian Religion*, ed. John T. McNeill, trans. Ford L. Battles, LCC 20–21 (Philadelphia: Westminster, 1960), 1.13.14; 2.7.1; 3.2.24; 3.11.10; 3.25.10; 4.17.2, 4, 11. Hereafter *Institutes*.

21. Calvin, *Hebrews and 1 and 2 Peter*, 330. Cf. Calvin, *Institutes*, 4.17.9.

22. Ibid.

23. This is explained by Billings, *Calvin, Participation and the Gift*, 55, who argues for a distinctly Western construal of *theosis* in Calvin's work. While Eastern Orthodoxy

For Calvin a doctrine of *theosis* was initiated in our election for salvation, is effected in our union with Christ, and is made possible in two unified ways. First, *theosis* is made possible by the incarnation of the Son, thus divinizing humanity through the humanizing of divinity. Calvin speaks of partaking of the divine nature in terms of the *mirifica commutatio* or

> wonderful exchange which, out of his measureless benevolence, he has made with us; that, becoming Son of man with us, he has made us sons of God with him; that, by his descent to earth, he has prepared an ascent to heaven for us; that, by taking on our mortality, he has conferred his immortality upon us; that, accepting our weakness, he has strengthened us by his power; that, receiving our poverty unto himself, he has transferred his wealth to us; that, taking the weight of our iniquity upon himself (which oppressed us), he has clothed us with his righteousness.[24]

Second, *theosis* is made possible through the work of the Holy Spirit. This partaking of the divine nature, or more specifically of Christ, is then experienced and further developed through the sacraments and the life of piety lived out in the Spirit's power.

Behind Calvin's treatment of *theosis* the doctrine of the Trinity provides a control and a context into which to understand the doctrine. Like classical formulations, Calvin's doctrine of *theosis* is built around the hypostatic union. *Theosis* is only possible because human nature has been "deified" in the one person of the Mediator. As men and women are united to Christ his divinization deifies them.[25] *Theosis* is only possible by the unique work of the incarnate Son who unites us to himself so that through the Holy Spirit we may know and worship the Father. In Mosser's summation of Calvin's doctrine of *theosis* we read, "The believer's union with Christ and the Father, the indwelling presence of the Spirit in our hearts, restoration of the divine image, being made like Jesus and our eventual glorification are each important themes in Calvin's soteriology

---

does not have a single doctrine of *theosis*, all Eastern Orthodox theologies of *theosis* do share the same constitutive points.

24. Calvin, *Institutes*, 4.17.2.

25. See David Willis-Watkins, "The Unio Mystica and the Assurance of Faith According to Calvin," in *Calvin: Erbe und Auftrag*, edited by W. van 't Spijker (Kampen: Kok Pharos, 1991), 78.

and eschatology. They are all pervaded by the language of *theosis*."[26] This provides a suitable overview and summary of the place of *theosis* within Calvin's theology from which we may further examine his doctrines of mystical union and wonderful exchange.

Calvin and the Unio Mystica

There is a disturbing reticence on behalf of many Reformed scholars to any notion of participation, let alone *theosis*. It would appear that much of this reticence is due to a one-sided application of certain arguments utilized by Calvin against the erroneous views of Osiander.[27] Trevor Hart presents the issue in its wider context:

> The problem with both Catholic and Protestant formulations of the doctrine of grace would seem to be not so much that which each seeks to affirm (for which both can provide considerable biblical warrant) but rather the framework within which they both operate, a framework which tends in practice to separate the person of Christ from his work, and to define salvation as humanity's direct and immediate participation in certain "benefits" procured by the latter.[28]

From this deficient framework both sides, in Hart's estimation, are unable to adequately affirm the truth that the human person reconciled to God in Jesus Christ is *simul iustus et peccator*. Hart provocatively writes, "Do we really possess *iustitia* as Christians, or is the grace which we proclaim to be understood in terms of a cloak which covers a corpse? Is the church a Society of Saints or a School for sinners?"[29] Hart concludes that "both points of view may be described as 'extrinsicist': one makes grace something external to our being, and the other tears it away from

---

26. Mosser, "Greatest Possible Blessing," 55.

27. See the analysis in Canlis, "Calvin, Osiander, and Participation in God," 169–84.

28. Trevor A. Hart, "Humankind in Christ and Christ in Humankind: Salvation as Participation in Our Substitute in the Theology of John Calvin," *SJT* 42 (1989) 69. "It is not uncommon," writes Canlis, "Calvin, Osiander, and Participation in God," 177, "to observe 'union' depreciated as merely a method of appropriation—as that which brings us the benefits of Christ." She then cites a passage from T. H. L. Parker, "Calvin's Doctrine of Justification," *EvQ* 24 (1952) 106: "by faith we are made one with Christ, therefore *partakers in the properties* of Christ" (italics added).

29. Hart is not suggesting by the use of this phrase that Lutheran soteriology is any better! Hart, "Humankind in Christ and Christ in Humankind," 69.

its ontological moorings in the humanity of the Saviour; they both ultimately rob his humanness of its true *mediatorial* significance."[30] Thomas Torrance levels the same critique at his own Reformed tradition, and with good cause. For Hart as for Torrance, the solution is found within the heart of Calvin's soteriology—we need to consider the questions of grace and justification again from a strictly *christological* perspective, asking ourselves, "who am I in Christ?"[31] The basis for this is in the doctrine of the *unio mystica* or *unio cum Christo*.[32]

Not only is union with Christ central to Calvin's theology, it is also central to Reformed theology more generally, so much so that many consider this to be *the* hallmark of Reformed theology.[33] According to Calvin, the roots of the *unio mystica* lie in the pre-temporal electing will of the Father whereby in time the elect will come into a relationship with God through Christ by the Spirit of adoption. Believers then become by grace "sons" of the Father as they participate in the Son's eternal relation with his Father, which is a sonship by nature. The formula "his by nature ours by grace" is of course a familiar patristic phrase adopted by Calvin.[34] By presenting the doctrine in this way God the Father is both the first cause and final end of our union with Christ,[35] and in union with Christ

30. Ibid.

31. Ibid., 70.

32. See Kolfhaus, *Christusgemeinschaft bei Johannes Calvin*, 80.

33. See Canlis, "Calvin, Osiander, and Participation in God," 172. Emil Brunner, *Vom Werk des Hiligen Geist* (Tübingen, 1935), 38, considers union with Christ to be "the center of all Calvinistic thinking"; cited in Lewis B. Smedes, *Union with Christ: A Biblical View of New Life in Jesus Christ*, 2nd ed. (Grand Rapids: Eerdmans, 1983), 31. See Thomas F. Torrance, "The Distinctive Character of the Reformed Tradition," in *Incarnational Ministry: The Presence of Christ in Church, Society, and Family. Essays in Honor of Ray S. Anderson*, ed. C. D. Kettler and T. H. Speidell (Colorado Springs: Helmers and Howard, 1990), 6, 7; and Paul M. Achtemeier, "The Union with Christ Doctrine in Renewal: Movements of the Presbyterian Church (USA)," in *Reformed Theology: Identity and Ecumenicity*, edited by W. M. Alston and M. Welker (Grand Rapids: Eerdmans, 2003), 336–50.

34. Calvin, *Institutes*, 1.18.3; 2.12.2; and John Calvin, *Commentary on the First Epistle of John* (4.16), in *The Comprehensive John Calvin Collection* (CD-ROM; Albany, OR: AGES Software, 1998).

35. Calvin, *Institutes*, 2.14.3. The fact that union with Christ is initiated in the pre-temporal electing will of the Father does not imply that for Calvin an *ordo salutis* must start with the *pactum salutis* and work its linear way from there in a logico-causal fashion, such as was evident in post-Reformation Reformed dogmatics. Rather, it is the necessary reminder that salvation is by grace alone.

we receive the whole Christ including his obedient life as the beloved Son. We do not simply receive the benefits of *an* obedient life in terms of merit, but rather we have the whole *beneficia Christi* imputed to us which consists in the life, death, and resurrection of the *beloved Son* who has given us intimate union and communion with the Father by the Spirit.

This is far from the application many, especially in the Reformed tradition, have made of Melanchthon's dictum, "to know Christ is to know his benefits," as if this were some mechanistic, extrinsic transaction wedded to a forensic imputation of righteousness.[36] What Calvin does here is to place union with Christ before justification in his *ordo salutis* so that righteousness is considered a benefit of salvation, along with justification and sanctification. Alister McGrath claims that "Calvin understands both justification and sanctification to be the chief *beneficia Christi*, bestowed simultaneously and inseparably upon the believer as a consequence of his *insitio in Christum* . . . Calvin is actually concerned not so much with justification, as with incorporation into Christ."[37] Any attempt at a strictly chronological construction of the *ordo salutis* is dismissed by Calvin as is evident throughout his *Institutes*, for instance, when he famously treats sanctification first, then justification, and only at the end of book 3 does he deal with predestination.[38]

---

36. See Canlis, "Calvin, Osiander, and Participation in God," 178–82; and McCormack, "For Us and Our Salvation, 281–316.

37. Alister E. McGrath, *Iustitia Dei: A History of the Christian Doctrine of Justification*, 2nd ed. (Cambridge: Cambridge University Press, 1998), 225. Earlier McGrath compared Bucer and Calvin on the *ordo salutis* as follows (224):

> Bucer: electio → *iustoficatio impii* → *iustificatio pii* → *glorificatio*
> Calvin: electio → *unio mystica* → *iustificatio/sanctificatio* → *glorificatio*

Subsequent to Calvin Reformed scholars tended to adopt a chronological *ordo salutis* in which union with God was made subsequent to certain soteriological steps. This move has been pointed out by Canlis, "Calvin, Osiander, and Participation in God," 173, where she directs the reader to a recent Reformed reappropriation of union over against this traditional *ordo salutis* in Richard Gaffin, *Resurrection and Redemption: A Study in Paul's Soteriology* (Phillipsburg, NJ: Presbyterian and Reformed, 1987). Lutheran scholarship also separated sanctification from justification, making it a secondary feature. See Ross Aden, "Justification and Sanctification: A Conversation between Lutheranism and Orthodoxy," *SVTQ* 38 (1994) 87–109.

38. It is the adoption of a chronological ordering of the *ordo salutis* that most distinguishes Reformed scholasticism from Calvin's own theology. This is chronicled in McGrath, *Iustitia Dei*, 226–31. For a history of the term within Reformed theology see Otto Weber, *Foundations of Dogmatics*, trans. D. L. Guder (1955; reprint, Grand

The incarnation is the way in which union with Christ is achieved. Union with Christ is the soteriological correlate to the christological notion of the hypostatic union.[39] This makes the hypostatic union coextensive with *unio mystica*; while distinct it is nonetheless inseparable. The object of our *unio mystica* is the Mediator, Jesus Christ. Calvin is insistent at this point:

> How do we receive those benefits which the Father bestowed on his only-begotten Son—not for Christ's own private use, but that he might enrich poor and needy men? First, we must understand that as long as Christ remains outside of us, and we are separated from him, all that he has suffered and done for the salvation of the human race remains useless and of no value for us. Therefore, to share with us what he has received from the Father, he had to become ours and to dwell within us.[40]

It is only by means of the incarnation that God joins believers to the Son in order for men and women to enjoy the benefits of salvation in Christ. The sole access to the Father is through Christ the Son, made possible by faith, which is the operation of the Spirit.[41] Calvin viewed this as a product of the priestly activity of the incarnate Son (and Spirit), an activity that does not cease to exist into eternity.[42] Calvin cuts out any extrinsicist notions of justification or reconciliation by positing justification as a benefit of union with Christ.[43] In our participation in Christ we receive all the benefits of salvation including Christ's righteousness. This righteousness equates to the filial life, Christ's sonship is now shared by

---

Rapids: Eerdmans, 1983), 2:336–38, cf. Karl Barth, *Church Dogmatics* (Edinburgh: T. & T. Clark, 1956–75), IV/2:505ff.; and Thomas F. Torrance, *Scottish Theology from John Knox to John McLeod Campbell* (Edinburgh: T. & T. Clark, 1996), 128.

39. Seng-Kong Tan, "Calvin's Doctrine of Our Union with Christ," *Quodlibet Journal* 5 (2003), online: http://www.quodlibet.net/tan-union.shtml.

40. Calvin, *Institutes*, 3.1.1. There is a sustained polemic at the back of Calvin's thought here in which he seeks to distinguish his own theology from that of Osiander, who argued that the divine Logos, stripped of his humanity, is the indwelling and transforming Christ within. Cf. ibid., 3.11.5–10.

41. We shall not investigate the relationship between faith and *unio mystica* here. For a brief study see S. P. Dee's comments cited in Kolfhaus, *Christusgemeinschaft bei Johannes Calvin*, 16; McGrath, *Iustitia Dei*, 224–26; and Achtemeier, "Union with Christ Doctrine in Renewal," 336.

42. Tan, "Calvin's Doctrine of Our Union with Christ."

43. Thomas F. Torrance, "Distinctive Character of the Reformed Tradition," 5–9.

his Body, the church. Calvin insists on the forensic nature of justification but insists we are justified based upon our union with Christ.[44] This is affirmed when he writes, "You see that our righteousness is not in us but in Christ, that we possess it only because we are partakers in Christ; indeed, with him we possess all its riches."[45]

Integral to an understanding of Calvin's doctrine of the *unio mystica* is the role of the Trinity, as previously highlighted. "This understanding of the Christian life, as grounded in the believer's union with Christ, is deeply trinitarian," writes Paul Achtemeier. "Through our engrafting into Christ by the power of the Spirit, believers enter into communion with the Father, indeed, become partakers and participants in the trinitarian life of God."[46] Calvin follows Augustine's trinitarian axiom closely here, *opera trinitatis ad extra indivisa sunt*, but nevertheless correctly posits legitimate "distinctions" or appropriations between the three persons.[47] According to Calvin the *unio mystica* is a personal union as men and women participate in a real way in Christ. Christ is thus the *mediating* bond of union. This union is not without the Spirit, however, and so the Spirit functions as the *unitive* bond of union with Christ.[48] Calvin appropriates aspects of the Augustinian notion of the Spirit as the "bond of love" (*vinculum caritatis*) between Father and Son and equally applies it to the bond of union between Christ and the believer.[49] This enables Calvin to state that "the Holy Spirit is the bond by which Christ effectu-

---

44. The forensic nature of justification is explicit in all editions of the *Institutes*; see McGrath, *Iustitia Dei*, 223, 462n31–33. McGrath sees Calvin adopting certain essential features of Melanchthon's doctrine here on forensic imputation, but also preserving an important aspect of Luther's standing on justification as the personal union of Christ and the believer in justification. As a result of his stress on union with Christ, Calvin was able to affirm both imputation and impartation of righteousness, understood christologically of course.

45. Calvin, *Institutes*, 3.11.23.

46. Achtemeier, "Union with Christ Doctrine in Renewal," 337. Torrance makes this same point in "Distinctive Character of the Reformed Tradition," 5–9.

47. Calvin, *Institutes*, 1.13.18, 25.

48. I am grateful to the study of Tan, "Calvin's Doctrine of Our Union with Christ," for these distinctions.

49. Calvin, *Institutes*, 3.1.1. Calvin does not use this Augustinian idea to limit the Trinity however, as Bowron in the previous chapter correctly notes others have done.

ally unites us to himself."⁵⁰ Seng-Kong Tan summarizes Calvin's position well when he writes:

> Through the unitive operation of the Holy Spirit, Christ and the elect are brought into reciprocal relationship. The one is the humanward trajectory—Christ's participation in us—where "he had to become ours and to dwell within us"; the other is the Christward movement—our participation in Christ—where we are said to be "engrafted into hi" [Rom 11:17], and "to put on Christ" [*Institutes* 3.1.1].⁵¹

A final feature of Calvin's *unio mystica* we note here is the organic union it creates not only between Christ and the believer but between believers in the Body of Christ. Again Tan is helpful in his summary statement that "the inseparable corollary of communion with Christ is 'the communion of saints.' Although salvation has an intensely personal dimension, *viz.* an individual person's relation to God, nonetheless, it is not a private affair, since its context is ecclesiologically framed [*Institutes* 4.1.3]. Hence, a proper understanding of the reality of *unio mystica*, which recognizes the Spirit's function as its *vinculum*, demands that righteousness and holiness be interpreted communally."⁵²

When Calvin speaks more directly of how the Spirit unites us to Christ at the start of Book Three of the *Institutes* he asks, "How do we receive those benefits which the Father bestowed on his only-begotten Son—not for Christ's own private use, but that he might enrich poor and needy men?" Calvin replies, "We also, in turn, are said to be 'engrafted into him' [Rom 11:17], and to 'put on Christ' [Gal 3:27]; for, as I have said, all that he possesses is nothing to us until we grow into one body with him. It is true that we obtain this by faith."⁵³ This is the fundamental basis of *unio mystica* for Calvin, to "put on Christ" and to be "engrafted into him." In his monograph on the topic Dennis Tamburello includes a detailed appendix of references to union with Christ in selected Calvin texts and includes as cognates the following: engrafting, communion, fellowship, in the Spirit, mysterious/incomprehensible, one flesh/marriage, spiritual union, mystical union, growing together/becoming one,

---

50. Ibid.
51. Tan, "Calvin's Doctrine of Our Union with Christ."
52. Ibid.
53. Calvin, *Institutes*, 3.1.1.

union with God, adoption, regeneration, and partakers of Christ.[54] This is important as it shows that within Calvin's theology, a theology which exerted an immense influence over Reformed and subsequent western theology more generally, the ideas behind the classical formulations of *theosis* are already present and indeed become central to an understanding of Reformed soteriology.[55]

The most concise definition Calvin gives to the *unio mystica* is found in the *Institutes* 3.11.10:

> Therefore, that joining together of Head and members, that indwelling of Christ in our hearts—in short, that mystical union—are accorded by us the highest degree of importance, so that Christ, having been made ours, makes us sharers with him in the gifts with which he has been endowed. We do not, therefore, contemplate him outside ourselves from afar in order that his righteousness may be imputed to us but because we put on Christ and are engrafted into his body—in short, because he deigns to make us one with him. For this reason, we glory that we have fellowship of righteousness with him.

Once again the themes of "putting on Christ" and "engrafted" are developed. According to Tan's reading, the former metaphor works within Calvin's theology to represent the imputed righteousness received by the believer in justification. The latter metaphor stands for the imparted holiness of Christ received by the believer in sanctification. While both are distinct concepts they are not separate and they are both the benefits received in faith through the *unio mystica*. "Thus, the distinction between the once-for-all 'alien' righteousness of Christ freely imputed on [*sic*] a sinner (justification) and the progressive holiness imparted through the indwelling Spirit in the regenerated person (sanctification) is obtained without separation, since they are simultaneous realities within *unio mystica*."[56]

---

54. Tamburello, *Union with Christ*, 111–13.

55. The Reformed theologian Thomas Torrance adopts many of these same cognates into his own soteriology in order to present his doctrine of salvation with a concept of *theosis* at its heart. See Myk Habets, *Theosis in the Theology of Thomas Torrance* (Surrey: Ashgate, 2009). Barth does the same, although he is careful not to use the term *theosis* and he is as reticent as Torrance to use the actual term *unio mystica*. See Barth, *Church Dogmatics*, IV/2:538–49; and Myk Habets, "T. F. Torrance: Mystical Theologian Sui Generis," *Princeton Theological Review* 14 (Fall 2008) 91–104.

56. Tan, "Calvin's Doctrine of Our Union with Christ."

An external transaction between Christ and the Father applied to the believer as imputed righteousness is not wrong *per se* but it is insufficient if it is made to represent the entire doctrine of salvation. When this happens exclusively juridical categories of atonement are adopted and salvation becomes something less than evangelical. This is not a rejection of the Reformational doctrine of imputation but rather a relocation of the doctrine into the context of participation. Imputation can only rightly be understood "not just in terms of imputed righteousness but in terms of a participation in the righteousness of Christ which is transferred to us through union with him."[57] When we see salvation in relation to the *unio mystica*, or as a personal participation in Christ, then we see that *all* the benefits he won for us are actually imputed *and* imparted to us simply because we are *in Christ* and *in the Spirit*.[58] Participation also may be seen as an aspect of the broader theological vision of *theosis*. What a Western doctrine of *unio mystica* achieves is a more dynamic understanding of salvation whereby Christ becomes ours and we become Christ's through an organic, vital, spiritual, eternal, and mystical union[59] in which justification and sanctification are no longer separated, since they are simultaneous realities of the *unio mystica*.

The final goal of salvation is not only to be united to Christ by the Spirit but to commune with the Father through the incarnate Son in or by the Holy Spirit. Union with Christ is thus understood to be participation in the Divine life. In his commentary on 2 Pet 1:4, the key patristic text on *theosis*, Calvin rejects at once any Platonic idea of imitation or Manichean emanationism, or neoplatonic mysticism by which human being and divine being are blurred or mixed. Rather, he argues that the biblical text asserts that the end of justification and sanctification is that we may become "partakers of divine and blessed immortality and glory,

---

57. Torrance, "Distinctive Character of the Reformed Tradition," 6.

58. This is not to imply, of course, that all the benefits of Christ are imparted to the believer at any given point, such as at the point of conversion.

59. For these categories and definitions see Augustus H. Strong, *Systematic Theology* (Philadelphia: Judson, 1907), 800–802. Strong also provides a concise overview of what *unio mystica* is not: a natural union (rationalists); a moral union (Socinians and Arminians); an essential union (mystics, pantheists); or a sacramental union (Romanists, Lutherans). Ibid., 799–800. Of course these terms are all culturally conditioned and so cannot be taken as abiding categories, however they are still useful to note.

so as to be as it were one with God as far as our capacities will allow."[60] In unequivocal terms Calvin affirms the theme of *theosis* when he concludes, "Let us then mark, that the end of the gospel is, to render us eventually conformable to God, and, if we may so speak, to deify us."[61] But does Calvin raise the use of *theosis* to the level of a doctrine? It appears he does. In arguing against the views of Servetus[62] and Osiander,[63] Calvin contends that in our union with Christ the divine essence is not mixed with our own but an energetic or spiritual union is achieved through "the secret power of his Spirit."[64] To be a partaker of the Divine nature means a participation not of "essence but of quality," and so it is not strictly speaking a substantial union but is, nevertheless, an ontic participation in the divine nature, for it involves a sharing in the properties of the essence or what we may term "nature."[65] Calvin is not implying that our participa-

---

60. John Calvin, *Commentary on the Second Epistle of Peter* (1:4), in *The Comprehensive John Calvin Collection*.

61. Ibid.

62. Calvin accused Servetus of an emanationistic theological anthropology by which believers participate in the actual substance (essence) of God. Calvin, *Institutes*, 1.15.5.

63. According to Calvin, Osiander was trying to equate the bond of union between the divine Persons with the bond of union between believers and Christ. For Calvin, as for the traditional concept of *theosis* more generally, the two were not symmetrical. Calvin, *Institutes*, 3.11. Compare *Institutes*, 3.11.5 with John Calvin, *Commentary on the Gospel According to John* (17:21), in *The Comprehensive John Calvin Collection* (CD-ROM; Albany, OR: AGES Software, 1998).

64. See John Calvin, *Sermons on the Epistle to the Ephesians*, sermon 42 on Eph 5:31–33 (1562; reprint, Edinburgh: Banner of Truth Trust, 1973), 614: "I have told you briefly already how we are bone of our Lord Jesus Christ's bone, and how we are his flesh. It is not that we are taken out of his body, for we come of the lineage of Adam, but because we live of his own substance, according to this saying that his flesh is our meat and his blood our drink, by which he means that we live in him—spiritually, however."

65. Partee, "Calvin's Central Dogma Again," 198, suggests that Calvin does not go this far in his use of "union" for it is not "mystical," nor "substantial" but merely "real" in a general but unspecificable sense. Partee's reticence and even withdrawal from Calvin's clear affirmation of *theosis* as involving an ontic element is understandable but not defensible. Calvin does allow in his theology of the *unio mystica* an echo of the Platonic idea of imitation, however he guards it from Platonic mysticism. See his comments on Plato in his *Commentary on the Second Epistle of Peter* (1:4). Tan, "Calvin's Doctrine of Our Union with Christ," agrees with Partee that Calvin does not speak of an essential participation, "and yet it must be affirmed that *unio mystica* is not idealistic, but ontic." See Tamburello, *Union with Christ*, 88–89, for evidences of this spiritual union

tion in the Divine nature is the same as the hypostatic union. There is only one hypostatic union and that is found within the God-man Jesus Christ. We participate through *his* humanity and so our *unio mystica* is formulated within an asymmetrical relationship to Christ's *unio* with the Father.[66] Like classical formations of *theosis*, this upholds Christ as God and Son by nature and believers as "gods" and "sons/children" by grace.

While the *unio mystica* has a certain beginning point in our history —the point of personal faith in Jesus Christ—union is not a static state but a dynamic process that is only begun by the "engrafting." Seen in relation to justification, our engrafting is complete in Christ; in relation to sanctification, our union is partial and grows. In a passage on our assurance being built on the fact that Christ is one with us, not standing far off because he "makes us, ingrafted into his body, participants not only in all his benefits but also in himself,"[67] we read that "Not only does [Christ] cleave to us by an indivisible bond of fellowship, but with a wonderful communion, day by day, he grows more and more into one body with us, until he becomes completely one with us."[68] Ultimate participation will not be realized until the eschaton. Until then, Christ draws nearer to us by the Spirit as we draw nearer to him by the same Spirit. At the final resurrection ultimate union with God shall be realized as resurrection includes both body and soul.[69]

In Calvin's presentation of the believer's participation in the divine nature through union with Christ, understood within a strictly Trinitarian context, an implicit doctrine of *theosis* is clearly in view. More recent Reformed scholarship has identified Calvin's commitment to *theosis* and thus the possibility for a thoroughly Reformed construal of the doctrine.[70] Not only is participation in the divine nature a thoroughly Reformed notion, it is a significant feature of Eastern Orthodox doctrine.

---

throughout Calvin's works. Canlis, "Calvin, Osiander, and Participation in God," also supports the notion that it is right to speak of "participation in God" but within Calvin this participation is of a non-substantialist type.

66. The fact that union with Christ is with his human nature is discussed in Tamburello, *Union with Christ*, 91–93. If believers were united with Christ's divine nature this would constitute a hypostatic union thus making them divine as Christ is.

67. Calvin, *Institutes*, 3.2.24.

68. Ibid.

69. Ibid., 3.25.

70. See especially Mosser, "Greatest Possible Blessing," and Canlis, "Calvin, Osiander, and Participation in God."

> Reformed understandings of the believer's union with Christ involve an understanding of Christian existence as participation in the divine life. Such recognition could provide at least a starting point for significant dialogue with Eastern Orthodox understandings of salvation in terms of *theosis*, or "deification." The importance of these concepts to the two traditions surely provides the basis for conversation and exploration.[71]

It is this distinctively Western and Reformed construction of *unio mystica* which allows Calvin to speak of *theosis*, the believer's real participation with God or partaking of the divine nature, and not just fellowship with God.

CALVIN AND CRITICS OF *THEOSIS*

This all too brief survey of aspects of Calvin's theology illustrates how a doctrine of *theosis* is both evident within Calvin's thought and is compatible with Reformed theology generally conceived. This is a contested claim, as we have already highlighted, with various scholars arguing for the incompatibility of *theosis* on Reformed soil.[72] One such detractor is worth interacting with for illustrative purposes, namely Charles Partee, who judges Calvin's position regarding *theosis* on the basis of an *a priori* standard, that of Eastern Orthodoxy, and thus rejects *theosis* as a valid doctrine for the Reformed faith.[73]

In his excellent study *The Theology of John Calvin*, Partee includes an excursus entitled "Mysticism and Deification: Two Disavowals,"[74] in

---

71. Achtemeier, "Union with Christ Doctrine in Renewal," 345.

72. I also note that Bowron considers any Western construal of *theosis* inappropriate given his commitment to the Orthodox *essence/energies* distinction coupled with a rejection of Western theologies of original sin, total depravity, and an *analogia entis*.

73. A second Reformed scholar arguing against any form of *theosis* on Reformed soil is Bruce McCormack. Over a series of articles McCormack has registered his objections to *theosis*. See especially "For Us and Our Salvation: Incarnation and Atonement in the Reformed Tradition"; "The End of Reformed Theology? The Voice of Karl Barth in the Doctrinal Chaos of the Present," in *Reformed Theology: Identity and Ecumenicity*, eds. W. M. Alston and M. Welker (Grand Rapids: Eerdmans, 2003), 46–64; "Participation in God, Yes, Deification, No"; "What's at Stake in Current Debates over Justification?"; and "Union with Christ in Calvin's Theology: Grounds for a Divinisation Theory?" in *Tributes to Calvin*, ed. D. Hall (Phillipsburg, NJ: Prebyterian and Reformed, 2009). A projected essay is planed to interact with McCormack's arguments.

74. Partee, *Theology of John Calvin*, 167–79.

which he concludes that Calvin's theology can be said to contain aspects of mysticism, but only under specific controls, and in no way can one legitimately read a doctrine of *theosis* out of Calvin's theology. Partee claims:

> The concept of deification applied to Calvin might have some plausibility if the reality of Father, Son, and Holy Spirit is understood in a Sabellian direction. However, since Calvin's hope is located in Christ, the goal is participation in him, not divinization. In other words, a sharply focussed Christology precludes a blurry deification.[75]

Taking Partee seriously, I could not agree more with a central aspect of this claim. If a doctrine of deification consists of the blurring of human and Divine natures then Calvin will have nothing of it. If a doctrine of deification is not centered in Christ and the believer's christification, or participation in Christ, then Calvin can in no way be seen as a sponsor of it. And so Partee is right that for Calvin the goal is participation in Christ, not divinization, if by divinization is meant some ontological participation in the Godhead so that humans literally become divine.

But the question has to be asked, what is the doctrine of *theosis* Partee assumes and adopts as a standard by which to evaluate Calvin's theology? On close examination it is a Palamite doctrine of *divinization*, with its Platonic notion of participation, the *essence-energies* distinction as central to its Trinitarianism, and an anthropology that overly distinguishes between the image and likeness of God in humanity.[76] The *deification* envisaged by Partee is one in which the Creator-creature distinction is radically blurred if not completely collapsed.[77] Under these conditions

---

75. Ibid., 167.

76. This is why the next chapter by Stuart Print becomes so important as he reconsiders the *imago Dei* from the vantage point of the *Pneuma* in tandem with that of the *Logos*. Print shows how a Western anthropology can be dynamic and make space for a doctrine of *theosis* while still being Western, and in the process provides an alternative to Bowron's earlier claims regarding Western deficiencies, particularly in its anthropology.

77. In his construal of deification Partee is only partially correct as his highly selective citations suggest. It is a basic tenet of Orthodox doctrines of *theosis*, including that of Gregory Palamas, that far from our ascent to something more than human our destiny is that we will at last become truly human through Christ by the Holy Spirit. See Russell, *Doctrine of Deification*, 312–13, for an articulation of this principle, where he makes a convincing case that the key to a satisfactory modern approach to *theosis* is

Calvin's theology patently does not make any claims to a doctrine of *deification*. But what of a doctrine of *theosis*?[78]

In an earlier citation Hallonsten suggested certain constituent features of a doctrine of *theosis*, namely:

> a certain view of creation, especially of human beings; a soteriology, including the meaning of the Incarnation; a view of Christian life as sanctification connected to the Church and sacraments; and the final goal of union with God. The whole structure of this comprehensive doctrine is determined by a teleology that implies that creation and human beings from the very beginning are endowed with an affinity and likeness that potentially draws them to God.[79]

If one starts with the central rudiments of a concept of *theosis* such as this and reads Calvin in this light, then the results are quite different and Calvin can be seen to advocate an implicit doctrine of *theosis*. That is to say, when the Eastern Orthodox hegemony on doctrines of *theosis* is broken, one is able to discern *doctrines* of *theosis* in their own right and not impose upon the doctrine any *adiaphora* such as Palamitism.[80] Calvin's theology can then be seen to adopt and utilize a doctrine of *theosis*, but one that Calvin defines himself. From this perspective Partee seems to me to be entirely correct when he states:

> The truth is we are "united with Christ by the secret power of his Spirit" (III.11.5). I take this comment to affirm a "Trinitarian indwelling" understood and confessed christologically. In my judgement, mystical union and deification in Calvin are not two

---

found in understanding that to become partakers of the Divine nature is to share fully in the relationship of love between the Father and the Son made possible through the incarnation and realized in a human way.

78. "Deification" and "divinization" are synonymous terms and they are legitimate translations of *theosis*. The point made here is that the theological meanings of these terms is often different so that *theosis* is the wider term than the more specific deification/divinization, often understood in a Neoplatonic sense. I have no objection to these terms given the etymology (as my thesis 5c below will highlight), but only if certain notions in currency today are not associated with such terms.

79. Hallonsten, "Theosis in Recent Research," 285.

80. Partee, *Theology of John Calvin*, 172, defines deification as "the believer's reception by grace of what the Christ is by nature," and then traces the idea back to Plato's *Theatetus*, and through to Gregory Palamas and his *essence-energies* distinction.

doctrines but one. Union with Christ alone permits and defines the discussion of theosis.[81]

On the basis of such logic I derive the title of this chapter, "*Theosis, Yes; Deification, No.*" As Partee himself affirms, "This doctrine can be called deification if deification is defined *not* as becoming God but becoming like God *as far as possible.*"[82] It would be better to speak of a doctrine of *theosis* and not of divinization/deification, despite the semantic equivalents of the terms, so as to distinguish between what one theologian does or does not assert as opposed to some static dogma imposed upon a thinker from without. In this light Calvin's theology does exhibit an implicit doctrine of *theosis* when understood on its own terms.

TEN THESES ON A WESTERN DOCTRINE OF *THEOSIS*

What may a doctrine of *theosis* look like that builds upon the insights of Calvin and yet moves beyond some of the perceived limitations in his own work? This is a question which demands a lengthy and complex reply, one that is beyond the scope of this final section. What is possible here is an initial attempt to sketch what the contours of such a doctrine may look like. Paul Gavrilyuk concluded his survey of *theosis* in recent thought with the rather ominous warning:

> If I may venture a conditional forecast, deification, provided that its full implications are realized, will work like a time-bomb in due course producing a "creative destruction" of the soteriological visions developed by the Churches of the Reformation.[83]

In order to forestall such a forecast I suggest the following constituent features of a doctrine of *theosis*, understood from within an orthodox, Western, Reformed theological context.

1. *We must think from a center in God rather than from a center in ourselves. As a result we move from the economic Trinity to the ontological Trinity.*
    a. This follows the hermeneutics of a scientific theology in which the method of knowledge must correspond to the nature

---

81. Ibid., 168.
82. Ibid., 178.
83. Gavrilyuk, "Retrieval of Deification," 657.

of the object. This is the basic *kata-physic*, or "descending," structure to revealed theology.[84]

    b. The stratification of truth and knowledge in all sciences applies equally to theological science. Through our experience of the triune God we come to know God as he wishes to be known, in his freedom to be God for us. We then develop theological heuristics to further indwell this revealed mystery and then settle on certain scientific beliefs that govern our thought and experience of God.

    c. The key heuristics we have are the doctrines of the *homoousios* of the Father, Son, and Holy Spirit, and the doctrine of Trinitarian *perichoresis*, correctly understood.

2. *The doctrine of the ontological Trinity recognizes, upholds, and respects God's freedom.*

    a. All theological science must be *a posteriori* and as such must continue to rely on the Word of God and the Spirit of God for communion with God.

    b. This entails an utter rejection of the Orthodox distinction between the Divine *essence* and the Divine *energies*.

3. *God is always Father, not always Creator. Therefore, there is no necessary relation between God and the world, which he has freely created.*

    a. There is and ever remains an ontological distinction between God and human creatures.

    b. Platonic and neoplatonic philosophy should not exert an influence over a Christian use of *theosis*.

    c. Neoplatonic notions of essential participation are rejected.

4. *We cannot know the triune God by somehow going behind the back of the Word incarnate, Jesus Christ. Also, we cannot know Jesus Christ by going behind the back of the Holy Spirit.*

    a. God meets us in our experiences; but the object of Trinitarian communion is and remains God and never becomes our experiences of faith and hope.

    b. The Word of God written remains our authoritative standard for faith and practice until the *Parousia*, but only in so far as it

---

84. See Habets, *Theosis in the Theology of Thomas Torrance*.

points us behind the words of Scripture to the eternal Word, and his Father, by the Spirit.
   c. Platonic notions of mystical contemplation are ruled out as valid paths to *theosis*.

5. *Jesus Christ is the* Imago Dei, *the one human who perfectly images God and has full communion with God.*
   a. Human beings are created with a *telos*—to image *the* Image— Jesus Christ. This is only possible through union with Christ by the Holy Spirit.
   b. The hypostatic union of Jesus Christ ensures his uniqueness as the one Mediator between God and humanity. He who is the Son of God by nature became a son of man so that we who are the humans by nature might become the sons and daughters of God by the grace of adoption.
   c. The hypostatic union applies uniquely to the incarnate Son of God, and thus in him humanity is divinized and divinity is humanized.

6. *By his life, death, resurrection, and ascension Jesus Christ perfectly, fully, and finally unites humanity to divinity.*
   a. Without ceasing to be God, the eternal Word takes to himself a human nature, healing and restoring this nature to its intended *telos*: communion with the triune God. In this way God becomes what we are and enables humans to become like he is when united to him.
   b. By means of the Holy Spirit, the Word incarnate lives a life of perfect obedience to the Father, dies a sinner's death in our place, and then defeats sin and death through his resurrection. At Pentecost the Spirit of Christ is given to believers to recreate within them the life and mind of Christ.
   c. *Theosis* is thus christologically conditioned from beginning to end as humans are united to the humanity of Christ and in that union they participate in the Divine life and love.

7. *Believers are united with the risen and ascended Lord Jesus Christ and thus participate in his continuing mediation and ministry for us and on our behalf.*
   a. In our union with Christ we are justified and sanctified, declared righteous and made holy.

    b. Through participation in the humanity of Christ believers commune with the triune God in worship, ministry, and mission.
8. *Through the church, the one Body of Christ on earth, the Holy Spirit unites us to Christ and to one another by Word, sacrament, and communal life.*
    a. By these means the Christlike life is recreated in us.
    b. Our responses to Christ constitute our participation in Christ's present ministry at the right hand of the Father in his ascended humanity.
    c. The sacraments instituted by Christ are the means by which believers commune with God and progress in *theosis* as they participate in Christ's worship, which moves from the Spirit through the Son to the Father.
9. *Worship and mission are understood as the act in which believers participate through the Holy Spirit in the incarnate Son's communion with the Father and the Son's mission from the Father, with the Spirit, to the world.*
    a. The vicarious humanity of Jesus Christ is salvific for all humanity.
    b. Those united to Christ participate in his ministry, his worship, and his communion with the Father by the Spirit.c. Christ's continuing life of vicarious worship becomes the spiritual locus of *theosis*.
10. *At the resurrection the believer is given a new body like that of the risen Lord Jesus Christ and enabled to more fully participate in the incarnate Son's communion with the Father by the Spirit.*
    a. With the sin nature removed the believer is enabled to see God more fully, to know God more clearly, and to participate in the Triune communion more completely.
    b. As we partake of the humanity of the incarnate Son by the Spirit unencumbered by sin, we are now able, for the first time in our existence, to perfectly experience the love of the Father for the Son as love for us in the Son by the Spirit in such a way that we can return this love to the Father, through the Son by the Spirit with utter thanks and love and obedience.

c. The communicable attributes of God are now able to be experienced by resurrected believers in such a way that perfect communion between God, humanity, and creation (the new heavens and new earth) is realized, without collapsing any one into the others.

d. According to Paul faith, hope, and love remain for all eternity (1 Cor 13:13), thus the believer can expect the resurrected life to be a dynamic existence, in constant reliance on the Son and the Spirit, focused on the worship of the Father, in which we work, play, and rest in God. In this dynamic nexus of activity and rest the believer experiences the eternal realization of *theosis*—Trinitarian communion in which the Father is glorified through the Son by the Holy Spirit, but never apart from the ongoing presence of Jesus Christ, the one to whom believers are eternally united.

9

Teleology as the Key to Pneumatological Anthropology

by Stuart Print

LOOKING BEYOND THE *IMAGO DEI*

Throughout the ages humanity has been seeking an answer in regard to the meaning or purpose of life. The worldwide religions have attempted to answer this in various ways, often concluding that we have a desire to become a part of, or like God.[1]

Christianity has always maintained that human life is distinct to that of other creatures. The first creation story of the Bible recorded in Genesis 1:3—2:4a presents God creating humanity in his "image" and "likeness." Both male and female are created in the "image of God" (*imago Dei*) in Genesis 1:27. A tremendous amount of theological discussion and thought has developed regarding the status of humanity in

---

1. An example is how the Upanishads see the goal of humanity as becoming one with Brahman. See E. Leslie Stevenson, *The Study of Human Nature, from the Upanishads* (Oxford: Oxford University Press, 1991), 16.

relation to the *imago Dei*. The church fathers laid the foundation for the *substantive* view of the *imago Dei*. This proposed that the Divine image in humankind is something of substance that we possess.[2] The Reformer's developed a *relational* view of the *imago Dei*, with Calvin often referring to the image in terms of a reflection in a mirror.[3] Barth further developed this view by proposing that "the image consists in man's reflecting the internal communion and encounter present within God."[4] A third and more recent view has developed which considers both the substantive and relational views and develops an eschatological purpose for humanity. This *teleological* view reasons that persons are created with the *telos* or purpose of becoming like *the* image of God, *Jesus Christ* (Col 1:15). Christians will be conformed to the image of the incarnate Son (Rom 8:29) so that we can in a human and limited way "mirror the functioning of the divine persons."[5]

While Trinitarian in its theological method, this view of the *imago Dei* is quite rightly focused on the second person of the Godhead, Jesus Christ. Christ is the Son of God in whose image we are created, with the *telos* of becoming like him as we are perfected by the Holy Spirit in union with him.

If the first creation story focuses on the relationship of the *Logos* with humanity, then I propose that the second creation story focuses on the relationship of the third person, the Holy Spirit, with us. The second creation story in Genesis 2:4b–25 distinguishes humanity's worth above other creatures because God "breathed into his nostrils the breath [*nephesh*] of life; and the man became a living being" (2:7, NASB). While it is *nephesh* that the first human received, we shall discover that it is the Breath (*Ruach*)[6] of God in Scripture, the Holy Spirit, who gives life.

---

2. See Paul Ramsey, *Basic Christian Ethics*, Library of Theological Ethics (Louisville: Westminster John Knox, 1993), 254.

3. See Stanley J. Grenz, *The Social God and the Relational Self: A Trinitarian Theology of the Imago Dei* (Louisville: Westminster John Knox, 2001), 166.

4. Millard J. Erickson, *Christian Theology* (Grand Rapids: Baker Academic, 1985), 507.

5. Thomas A. Smail, "In the Image of the Triune God," *IJST* 5 (2003) 27.

6. While "breath" in Genesis 2:7 is translated from the word *naphach*, the Holy Spirit is identified as the breath, usually *ruach*, which also means "wind" or some type of air movement. See online: http://www.blueletterbible.org/cgi-bin/c.pl?book=Gen&chapter=2&verse=7&version=KJV#7.

Calvin perceived life as the "immediate action" of the Holy Spirit.[7] In fact, "Man would cease to exist if God were . . . to withdraw his Spirit from him."[8]

The methodology of a Spirit Christology attempts to view theology from a pneumatological perspective without letting go of *Logos* Christology.[9] For every aspect of theology that is christologically focused, there will be a parallel pneumatological perspective. The two creation stories provide a rich illustration of how "Word and Spirit go out from the Father in a mutual, co-inhering relationship with each other."[10] So while it remains appropriate to consider the role of the Spirit in regard to the *imago Dei*, I want to consider tracing the Breath of Life towards its *telos*, which, while different from the goal of the *imago Dei*, should track in perfect relationship to it.

In this chapter I will show why the teleological view of the Breath of Life is to experience the divine *koinonia* of God. The way humanity responds to the Spirit mediating the Father's love for the Son in *koinonia*-relationship illustrates the drama of redemptive history through four key movements: first, the Good in creation, as we walk with God; second, the Bad in the fall, as we attempt to live for self; third, the New in Christ, as we are united to him; and finally, the Perfect, as we experience communion in the Trinity most fully in the *eschaton*.[11]

WITH THE SPIRIT THROUGH THE DRAMA OF REDEMPTION

The Good—Walking with God

Orthodox Christianity believes in a triune God who created everything from nothing (*creatio ex nihilo*). In considering the role of the Holy Spirit

---

7. See Thomas F. Torrance, *Theology in Reconstruction* (London: SCM, 1965), 104.

8. Ibid., 103.

9. For a comprehensive introduction to and definition of Spirit Christology, see Myk Habets, *The Anointed Son: A Trinitarian Spirit Christology* (Eugene, OR: Pickwick, 2010); and idem, "Spirit Christology: Seeing in Stereo," *JPT* 11 (2003) 199–235.

10. Habets, "Spirit Christology," 235.

11. I am grateful to Paul Windsor, past principal of Carey Baptist College, for his articulation of the four tarditional movements of creation, fall, redemption, and renewal as the Good, the Bad, the New, and the Perfect; a creative development of an idea first articualted in John R. W. Stott, *Issues Facing Christians Today* (Grand Rapids: Zondervan, 2006) 62–64.

we must first consider what God is like, as our theology of the Trinity will have implications for the rest of our theology.

In his book *Flame of Love: A Theology of the Holy Spirit*, Clark Pinnock proposes that we consider God as a social Trinity, a communion of loving persons who are involved in the Divine dance (*perichoresis*).[12] Founded on the theology of the Cappadocian Fathers, *perichoresis* presents the Trinity as one being or essence of three persons bound in a *koinonia*-relationship of love. George Hunsinger defines a *koinonia*-relation as two identities mutually indwelling each other without either losing their distinction.[13] We see this *koinonia*-relationship on display as the Father eternally loves the Son by the Holy Spirit. The Son eternally responds to the Father's love by loving the Father by the Holy Spirit. Throughout eternity, the Spirit constantly mediates the divine love between the Father and the Son.

Frank Macchia criticizes Pinnock for upholding tradition by choosing to define God as three persons—one being rather than one person.[14] Macchia believes that God's dance is the dance of "One"![15] Apart from being unorthodox and heretical, this model has been criticized amongst Macchia's own Pentecostal community. Based on the work of David Coffey,[16] Steven Studebaker suggests a "mutual love" model that presents the Holy Spirit as the mutual love that is eternally generated between the Father and Son.[17] Studebaker believes that the person of the Spirit is given greater distinction in this model.[18] While his mutual love model, where the Holy Spirit is eternally generated as the mutual love between Father and Son, may be adequate in order to trace the Breath of Life, it still subordinates the Spirit to an expression of emotion between the First and Second Persons of the Trinity. A better way to conceive of the

---

12. Clark H. Pinnock, *Flame of Love: A Theology of the Holy Spirit* (Downers Grove, IL: InterVarsity, 1996).

13. George Hunsinger, "Baptism and the Soteriology of Forgiveness," *IJST* 2 (2000) 247–69.

14. Frank Macchia, "Tradition and the Novum of the Spirit: A Review of Clark Pinnock's Flame of Love," *JPT* 6 (1998) 35.

15. Ibid., 36.

16. For more information on Coffey's mutual love model see David M. Coffey, "The Holy Spirit as the Mutual Love of the Father and the Son," *TS* 51 (1990) 193–229.

17. Steven M. Studebaker, "Integrating Pneumatology and Christology: A Trinitarian Modification of Clark H. Pinnock's Spirit Christology," *Pneuma* 28 (2006) 11.

18. Ibid., 11–12.

relations is to return to the traditionally rich concept of *perichoresis* which does distinguish personhood: the person of the Holy Spirit mediates the divine love between the persons of the Father and the Son for each other. What is essential for our task at hand is the fact that the Holy Spirit is the mediator of *koinonia*, or the communion of love within the triune Godhead.[19]

Pinnock proposes that the communion of love is so great that God desires to create in order to share his love with creation. Creation arises from an "abundant interpersonal love" within the Divine nature.[20] Colin Gunton reminds us of the Trinitarian aspect of creation and rightly shows God's Word and Breath working in tandem.[21] The Father creates the world through his Son, the Word, by his Breath, the Holy Spirit.[22] Humanity is formed from dust in the image of the Son, while life is given and sustained by the Holy Spirit as the Father breathes into the nostrils of the first human, Adam. Humanity thus comes to possess life.[23]

Many scholars have incorrectly assumed that God breathed an immortal soul (based on the semantics of Platonic substance metaphysics) into Adam, therefore distinguishing him from the animals.[24] However, to understand the Breath of Life we must consider the Hebrew usage of both *ruach* and *nephesh*. While *ruach* translates into "wind" or "breath" and is the term used for the Holy Spirit in the Old Testament, it is *nephesh* —which also translates as "breath"—which Adam received. *Nephesh* is not what distinguishes humanity from animals, but what distinguishes breathing creatures from plants.[25] Everything that breathes on this planet is considered to have the *nephesh* of life.[26]

---

19. Veli-Matti Kärkkäinen, *Toward a Pneumatological Theology: Pentecostal and Ecumenical Perspectives on Ecclesiology, Soteriology, and Theology of Mission* (New York: University Press of America, 2002), 100.

20. Pinnock, *Flame of Love*, 55.

21. Ps33:6. Colin Gunton, "The Spirit Moved over the Face of the Waters: The Holy Spirit and the Created Order," *IJST* 4 (2002) 192.

22. Pinnock, *Flame of Love*, 60.

23. Ibid., 73.

24. See Claus Westermann, *Genesis 1–11: A Commentary* (Minneapolis: Augsburg, 1974), 207.

25. Christopher J. H. Wright, *Knowing the Holy Spirit through the Old Testament* (Downers Grove, IL: InterVarsity Academic, 2006), 27.

26. Gen1:20, 24, 28, 30; 6:17; 7:4.

Yet Job, in a closely related passage, declares that "as long as life [*nephesh*] is in me... the breath [*ruach*] of God is in my nostrils..." (Job 27:3, NASB). Therefore, Gunton, along with Pinnock and the Creed's characterization, present the Spirit as the "Lord, the giver of life."[27] Life is a gift, given and maintained by the Holy Spirit. It is not that humanity is immortal because God breathed into us an immortal soul. What Genesis 2 highlights is the intimacy of the original relationship between God and humanity.[28] When God, by his *Ruach*, bestows life upon humanity, he does so with a kiss. By intimately breathing into his nostrils, the Spirit has initiated *koinonia* by way of the "Kiss of Life." God has created an image-bearing creature, which not only has the ability to receive the love of the Father for the incarnate Son, mediated by the Spirit, but also has the ability to respond to the love of the Father, through the incarnate Son, by the Spirit. Just as the Son responds to the Father's love, the Father desires that human persons will reflect the incarnate Son's image by responding to the same love. Humanity's destiny is to experience the *koinonia* of love from the Father to the Son, mediated by the Holy Spirit, as we are united to the real Image of God, the incarnate Son.[29] Put simply, *summum bonum* of human life is the ability to experience communion with God in Christ by the Holy Spirit.

In critiquing the role of *theosis* in Thomas Torrance's theology, Myk Habets reminds us that Torrance viewed the human spirit as an "essential and dynamic correlate of... the divine Spirit."[30] Human persons are "creatures of God's Spirit," writes Pinnock.[31] Humanity is endowed with a "transcendental determination" according to Torrance, giving it the "capacity to think and act in accordance with nature of what is other than himself."[32] The Breath of Life gives us the ability to respond by an act of free will to an outside agent—ultimately God. The biblical accounts of creation present humanity as living creatures. They live in a Divinely-designed environment which God declares is "very good" (Gen 1:31). We

---

27. Gunton, "Spirit Moved over the Face of the Waters," 192.
28. Wright, *Knowing the Holy Spirit through the Old Testament*, 28.
29. Pinnock, *Flame of Love*, 73.
30. Myk Habets, *Theosis in the Theology of Thomas Torrance* (Surrey: Ashgate, 2009), 37.
31. Pinnock, *Flame of Love*, 73.
32. Habets, *Theosis in the Theology of Thomas Torrnace*, 37.

find God "walking" in the garden (Gen 3:8), implying that a relationship is developing between the Creator and his creation. While human persons are "very good," they are yet to be ultimately fulfilled. Humanity was to find fulfillment in life by walking with or towards God. Gunton rightly acknowledges that for creation to achieve what it was created to realize, there must be obedient human activity.[33] In fully appreciating the Father's love, we should have realized the full meaning of life. By growing in its loving response, humanity was to experience ecstasy (*ek-stasis*) as it gave of itself to the Other. Humanity should have grown in its response to the Father's love of the Son through the empowering of the Spirit, by obediently reflecting the response of the Son to the Father by the Holy Spirit.

The Breath of Life—the Holy Spirit—mediates the communion that exists between the Father and the Son to human persons in the economy in the same way the Spirit mediates the communion that exists between Father and Son *in se*. However, this *koinonia* of love is not only a vertical relationship between God and humanity, but should also be a horizontal relationship that exists between human persons and extends to other aspects of creation itself.

The Bad—Living for Self

According to Pinnock, God took a risk in creating creatures capable of responding freely as it allowed them the chance to say no to the Spirit mediating the Father's love for the Son to them.[34] He perceives freedom to be the liberty to love, or not to love.[35] The narrative of the garden presents humanity using this freedom by saying no to God (Gen 3:1–24). Instead of being fulfilled in the *koinonia*-relationship that they were experiencing in the garden, they chose to seek fulfillment by determining their own destiny. Instead of experiencing the relationship of responsive love towards God, they chose to respond to their own desires. Humanity takes the overabundant love of the Father for the Son that the Spirit mediates to them, and instead of allowing this *koinonia* of love to flow through them back to the Father, and to each other, and towards creation as a whole, they chose to retain this love for self-seeking purposes. So

---

33. Gunton, "Spirit Moved over the Face of the Waters," 192. Cf. Ps 33:6.
34. Ibid., 75.
35. Ibid., 74.

the love of God becomes stagnant within. Humanity has broken their fellowship with the Trinity. Their fear has separated them "from their evening communion with God."[36] By saying no to God, as he offered his love, instead of moving towards his *koinonia*, humanity broke away from God, placing its faith in itself resulting in a path to self-destruction.[37]

God told Adam and Eve that if they disobeyed they would surely die (Gen 3:3). But death is not a punishment by God; it is a consequence of our own actions. Human persons die because they have rejected the *koinonia* of the Father, mediated by the Spirit. They have broken the communion of love that actually sustains life. The Spirit's sustaining power is rejected as we seek to find the source of fulfillment in life from within ourselves. Elihu proclaims to Job that all humanity would perish and return to dust if God were to remove his *ruach* and *nephesh* (Job 34:14–15). Ecclesiastes describes death as God's *ruach* returning to him and the body of dust returning to the earth (Eccl 12:7). So although all of God's creation is essentially good, and although the human creature was "very good," left to their own devices, humanity will return to the state of nothing from which they were created.[38] The Breath of Life is God's gift to humanity, but when the Holy Spirit leaves us, we die.[39]

Yet while the fall had a catastrophic effect on humanity's relationship with the Breath of Life, the Holy Spirit does not abandon us, or we would cease to exist. Pinnock states that God doesn't forsake his creatures even though they are enslaved in loving themselves.[40] However, humanity is left in a precarious state that is seemingly hopeless. For while the human person is alive the *telos* intended by the *Ruach* of God remains possible. We continue to have a transcendental determination to experience *koinonia* with God. The Father continues to love us in the Son. The Holy Spirit continues to graciously mediate the Father's love for the Son to us. But we are left in bondage as we continue to say no to God's initiative. We are addicted to the attempts to fulfill our own destiny through our own self-determination, rather than by the transforming and life-sustaining power of the Holy Spirit.

36. Edith Humphrey, *Ecstasy and Intimacy: When the Holy Spirit Meets the Human Spirit* (Grand Rapids: Eerdmans, 2006), 34.
37. Pinnock, *Flame of Love*, 76.
38. Gunton, "The Spirit Moved over the Face of the Waters," 194.
39. Wright, *Knowing the Holy Spirit through the Old Testament*, 30.
40. Pinnock, *Flame of Love*, 75.

Although we have rejected the *Ruach* of Life, faithfully, the Spirit persists in his mission of freeing us from our self-determination.[41] Gunton suggests that the Spirit has begun to work amidst this context of opposition.[42] So although the Spirit continually mediates the love of the Father for the Son to us, we oppose this by constantly breaking the *koinonia*-relationship. We are hostile to the prompting of the Spirit to experience God, by seeking self-fulfillment as we attempt to become gods in our own way.

The narrative of the flood describes how precarious our situation has become. God declares to Noah that he is about to destroy all flesh that has the *Ruach* of Life (Gen 6:17). But in this moment of hopelessness, God reveals hope as he declares that he will establish a covenant with Noah and his family. Covenants are a type of *koinonia*-relationship. We see God choosing a person, or a people, or in Noah's case "all flesh." He chooses them as his own and bestows a grace upon them, and loves them. These *koinonia*-relationships have an expectation that the love that people receive within the covenant will be passed on to be a blessing and reveal who God is. The Spirit is now mediating the intimate love of the Father for the Son to chosen people, in the hope that they will say yes and return God's love in a gracious response. But these covenants still seem to be a pale imitation of the *telos* that humanity was created to one day realize.

There is hope though. The covenants are pointing towards a time when *koinonia* will be renewed. The prophet Ezekiel describes the *Ruach* of God breathing new life into a valley full of dry bones (Ezek 37). The Holy Spirit will begin a renewal, resuscitation, even a resurrection of humanity. Kärkkäinen, while alluding to the work of Hans Urs von Balthasar, reminds us that there is a groaning of the Spirit in creation, as it seeks restoration (Rom 8:20–22).[43] But how can God save humanity? In fact, how can he restore all of creation from this precarious state that it finds itself in? Habets rightly answers that, by the mediation of the Spirit, God the Son unites creatureliness to himself in order to save it.[44]

---

41. Ibid., 76.

42. Gunton, "Spirit Moved over the Face of the Waters," 194.

43. Kärkkäinen, *Toward a Pneumatological Theology*, 221.

44. Habets, *Theosis in the Theology of Thomas Torrance*, 26.

The New—Union with Christ

If the *Ruach* of Life has a destiny in the human person, then adopting a Spirit Christology should produce exciting insights regarding this breath of the Spirit in the life of the Image of God, Jesus Christ. Pinnock views Jesus Christ's life on earth "as an aspect of the Spirit's mission."[45] The Spirit is so dominant in Christ's life that "Jesus was conceived, anointed, empowered, commissioned, directed (to his passion) and raised up" by the Spirit.[46] In this mission, Christ by his absolute dependence on the Spirit, recapitulates the destiny of humanity.[47]

We see the Spirit hovering over Mary (Luke 1:35) just as it brooded over the waters in the beginning.[48] God is re-creating. Gunton suggests that "the Father through the Spirit . . . [forms] a body of flesh for his eternal Son."[49] The Divine and human have once again entered a *koinonia*-relationship, mediated by the *Ruach* of God. The hypostatic union is united in a *koinonia*-relationship. The divine and human natures interpenetrate each other in the one person of Jesus Christ. Ross Hastings, in analyzing the Spirit in the works of Jonathan Edwards, concludes that "by *perichoresis* . . . [Christ] is constituted as one human-divine communion."[50] The Second Person of the Trinity has taken on human flesh, and in so doing has entered a relationship of human dependence on the Third Person to live a human life. The *Ruach* of Life is once more able to mediate the fulfilling love of the Father to his one and only Son, the human Image of God, Jesus Christ.

Pinnock seriously undermines the role of the Spirit in the hypostatic union. He places an unusually strong emphasis on the anointing at Jesus' baptism, declaring that it is the anointing that makes him the Christ rather than the incarnation by means of the hypostatic union.[51] Studebaker correctly challenges Pinnock in this regard and highlights the importance of the Spirit's work in "uniting the divine Son with the humanity of Jesus

---

45. Pinnock, *Flame of Love*, 80.
46. Ibid., 81–82.
47. Ibid., 81.
48. Ibid., 82.
49. Gunton, "Spirit Moved over the Face of the Waters," 197.
50. W. Ross Hastings, "'Honouring the Spirit': Analysis and Evaluation of Jonathan Edwards' Pneumatological Doctrine of the Incarnation," *IJST* 7 (2005) 292.
51. Pinnock, *Flame of Love*, 80.

Christ."⁵² Pinnock's overemphasis on the anointing actually subordinates the Spirit to the Son.⁵³ The Synoptic conception accounts show that the Spirit actualizes the incarnation while John presents the *Logos* assuming human flesh. Studebaker rightly states that both these events refer to the same reality; the Holy Spirit creates a *koinonia*-relationship of love from the Father that unites the Word to humanity.⁵⁴ Hastings agrees by maintaining that the hypostatic union was immediate.⁵⁵ As we consider the destiny of humanity, the Spirit's role as the *Ruach* of Life in the hypostatic union is essential.⁵⁶

While Pinnock incorrectly places a higher significance on Jesus' anointing at his baptism over and above the hypostatic union, the baptism experience of Jesus still has high significance as we see the true human Jesus experience the fullness of *koinonia* from the Father by the Holy Spirit. Throughout his life Jesus grew in grace and wisdom, yet at his baptism we see the Father offer his love for the Son and the Spirit descends upon Jesus like a dove.⁵⁷ The rest of Jesus earthly mission shows him being directed by the Spirit from the temptation narrative to the passion. Jesus ministers by the power of the Spirit performing signs and teaching with authority. Ultimately, Jesus Christ realizes what all humanity was destined to experience, "the communion of God and humanity."⁵⁸

Pinnock suggests that the power of the cross was in essence a *koinonia* event. The love of the Trinity is seen when, "Through the Spirit, the Son offered himself to the Father, and on the cross the Father's forgiving love and the Son's suffering love were brought together by the Spirit."⁵⁹ The Father hands his beloved Son over to die out of love for his creation.⁶⁰ The incarnate Son dies as humanity's representative, bearing our sin and pain, and thereby creating a new status for humanity before God.⁶¹ The

---

52. Studebaker, "Integrating Pneumatology and Christology," 6.
53. Ibid.
54. Ibid., 16.
55. Hastings, "'Honouring the Spirit,'" 293.
56. Ibid., 281–82.
57. Pinnock, *Flame of Love*, 85.
58. Ibid., 81.
59. Ibid., 104.
60. Ibid.
61. Ibid., 105.

Son offers himself through the Holy Spirit (Heb 9:14), in obedient love to the Father.[62] The cross is therefore not just an act of propitiation before an angry God, but also an act of recapitulation by a loving God. This aspect of recapitulation in Christ's death shows *koinonia*, although this has often been overlooked.

While he agrees with Pinnock that it may not be God's anger that needs appeasement, Terry Cross reminds us that a penalty still needed to be paid.[63] I believe that both propitiation and recapitulation needed to be realized. A penalty was paid for by Christ. Humanity in the person of Jesus Christ received what we all deserved; abandonment by the Spirit. While on the cross, Jesus the God-man for the first time experienced lack of *koinonia*, or the absence of God. For the first and only time in eternity, the Holy Spirit withheld the love that the Father had for his Son. This caused Jesus to cry out, "My God, My God, Why have you forsaken me?" (Mark 15:34). The Johannine account is perhaps more clear. The disciple whom Jesus loved often used water as a metaphor for the Spirit (John 7:39). Jesus offered the Samaritan woman "living water" so that she would never thirst (John 4:10). The water he offered the woman would become a "spring of water gushing up to eternal life" (John 4:14). At the Festival of Booths, Jesus invites anyone who is thirsty to come to him and drink, for "out of the believer's heart will flow rivers of living water" (John 7:37–39). So how can the person who has the ability to give overabundantly of this water suddenly cry out on the cross, "I am thirsty?" (John 19:28). The One who gives the Spirit excessively, is suddenly experiencing our punishment, the absence of the Spirit. Jesus experienced being outside the eternal *koinonia*-relationship, and he dies. The cross is the climax of God's love towards humanity in his Son, and while the Father's love never ceased, the Son experienced what humanity's punishment should have been: the absence of the Father's love, mediated by the Holy Spirit.

If the *Ruach* of Life began the restoration of humanity in the garden, then the resurrection of the God-man is the second great act of renewal. Pinnock notes that if death was humanity's problem, then life has to be its answer.[64] The promise of Ezekiel is realized. The Spirit, the *Ruach* of Life

---

62. Pinnock, *Flame of Love*, 105.

63. Terry Cross, "A Critical Review of Clark Pinnock's: *Flame of Love: A Theology of the Holy Spirit*," JPT 6 (1998) 19.

64. Pinnock, *Flame of Love*, 99.

and the power of creation, makes the dead live again through the power of the resurrection.[65] The *Ruach* of Life made the first humans become living beings; but *the* human, Jesus Christ, became a life-giving Spirit (1 Cor 15:45). Neill Hamilton says that "In the same way God breathed the breath of life into the man of dust so that that breath and man's life became synonymous, so also at Christ's resurrection the Father breathed the Holy Spirit into his dead Son so that He lived and so that the Spirit and the life of the resurrected Christ became synonymous."[66]

Lyle Dabney declares that the image of God "has become nothing less than the model of our own redemption."[67] Pinnock agrees and suggests that Christ went on a representative journey for humanity from death to life.[68] Jesus Christ, the incarnate Son of God, was raised from the dead by the Holy Spirit out of the Father's love for him. We see Jesus changing from glory to glory in his resurrection appearances until his ascension to the right hand of the Father (John 20:17). The *Ruach* of Life breathed life into Christ so that we can be united to him and become adopted children of the Father. The Spirit creates a *koinonia*-relationship between us and the incarnate Son as we are baptized into his own death, burial, and resurrection. The same communion that unites the Trinity, the same power that created the hypostatic union, now recreates human beings in order that they may be able to experience the love of the Father for the Son by the Spirit, as they are united to the incarnate Son. Through the total journey of Jesus, from incarnation to glorification, something has happened that opens the door for humanity to be united to God.[69] Christ the real human has objectively realized perfect *koinonia* with God for us. What still remains is a subjective human response, enabled, not surprisingly, by the Breath of Life.[70]

When Jesus appears in the Johannine Gospel, he breathes *Pneuma* (the Greek equivalent of *Ruach*) on the disciples and says, "Receive the Holy Spirit" (John 20:22). This is an obvious allusion back to creation in

---

65. Ezek 37:1–10; Rom 1:4. See Pinnock, *Flame of Love*, 90.

66. Neill Q. Hamilton, *The Holy Spirit and Eschatology in Paul* (Edinburgh: Oliver and Boyd, 1957), 14–15.

67. D. Lyle Dabney, "'Justified by the Spirit': Soteriological Reflections on the Resurrection," *IJST* 3 (2001) 50.

68. Pinnock, *Flame of Love*, 100.

69. Ibid., 93.

70. Ibid., 96.

Gen 2:7 and the valley of dry bones in Ezekiel 37.[71] To be saved means to be born again (or from above) (John 3:3), or born (baptized) of the Spirit (John 3:5–6). Luke's account of Pentecost in Acts tells how the Holy Spirit came in power on people of faith (Acts 2:1–4). God has begun his work of recreating life in people of faith by placing the Holy Spirit in their hearts, uniting them to the incarnate Christ that they may once again experience a *koinonia*-relationship with God (2 Cor 1:21–22). Salvation involves both the grace of God mediated by the Spirit and the free response of the human will.[72] Freedom remains essential. What has occurred in Jesus is that we are no longer bound to our self-determination, but once again have the ability to respond with a yes to the Father's loving approaches. Pinnock describes this *koinonia*-relationship as humanity having an "ember of the *Imago Dei* . . . [which the] Spirit blows on" to bring life.[73] He refers to being saved more in terms of falling in love with God, and describes the Spirit as wooing people home to their destiny.[74]

As human persons living in the church age, the Spirit comes to individuals and mediates the Father's love to them. When we initially respond in faith, we are justified and are baptized by the Spirit and united as believers into the church and into the death and resurrected life of the Son. The Spirit continues to mediate the love of the Father to us through the incarnate Son, and as we respond by the Spirit in obedient love (worship) we become transformed into the likeness of the incarnate Son and love the Father through the mediation of the Spirit.

Renewal is a gradual process,[75] but *koinonia*-relationships should be visible in two tangible organisms: the church, which is the body of Christ; and the marriage relationship, which is meant as an image of Christ and his church. In both contexts the Spirit mediates the Father's love to the incarnate Son. There is such an abundance of love that it overflows so that the Spirit mediates the same love to those united to his Son. Not only does the Father desire that we respond in love back to him in worship so that the Spirit in turn mediates our love back to the Father through the Son, but there is so much Divine love that it should overflow to our

71. Ibid., 163.
72. Ibid., 160.
73. Ibid.
74. Ibid., 156–57.
75. Ibid., 168.

relationships with other persons created in the *imago Dei*, and to the rest of creation. In regard to the church, we are united to other believers through the same *koinonia*-relationship that unites us to Christ. This is why unity in the church is essential as it should reflect the diversity-in-unity of the fellowship of God. God's love is so abundant that it should overflow into the world which is yet to believe. By loving the world, it too may experience God's *koinonia* and enter into a relationship with him.

In the marriage relationship, a man and a woman are also united to each other in a *koinonia*-relationship that makes unity-in-diversity visible. Physically, emotionally, and spiritually two persons become one. The love with which God loves us should also be mediated by the Spirit between a husband and a wife. But God's love is so excessive that he allows us to reproduce life so that we may love our children with his love. The *koinonia* of love that exists in the Godhead should be made visible in the family, and through the family to society, and through society to the entire world.

People of God are people within whom the *Ruach* of Life dwells. They will find fulfillment in life as they, by faith, understand and experience the unconditional love of the Father, mediated by the indwelling Spirit through the incarnate Son they are united to. They will have truly "ecstatic" experiences when they respond in love to God and other persons as the Spirit produces his fruit within them (Gal 5:22–23). The *koinonia*-relationship created by the *Ruach* of Life, while incomplete, is a seal guaranteeing redemption leading to a resurrected and perfect *koinonia*-relationship (Eph 1:13–14).

The Perfect—Experiencing Communion within the Trinity

In Kärkkäinen's search for ecumenical agreement he sees one defining motif between both the Eastern and Western traditions (and possibly many of the world's religions): union with God.[76] Pinnock believes that the Spirit is leading us to union with God.[77] This form of *theosis* or deification is a "transforming personal intimate relationship with the triune God."[78] It will be ultimately realized in the *eschaton* and will mean that we

---

76. Kärkkäinen, *One with God*, 119.
77. Pinnock, *Flame of Love*, 149.
78. Ibid. Cf. John 17:3.

will be like Christ, realizing the *telos* of the *imago Dei* (1 John 3:1–2). It will also mean sharing in the glory of the "divine sphere of life," realizing the *telos* of the *Ruach* of Life.[79]

Kärkkäinen appreciates the perspectives of Pinnock, Rybarczyk, and aspects of Roman Catholicism on the goal of human life. From Pinnock he specifically notices the perspective that the goal of salvation consists of "glorification and union with God, the Spirit."[80] In considering the thesis of Edmund Rybarczyk, Kärkkäinen appreciates that both Orthodoxy and Pentecostalism believe that it is within the "mystical human core that the Spirit of Christ seeks to have communion with human persons and thereby transform them into his image."[81] This describes what I believe the *Ruach* of Life causes us to seek; as Rybarczyk suggests, the human person was "created for a transforming fellowship with God."[82] From the Roman Catholic tradition Kärkkäinen agrees that that Christian life may be defined as "fullness of life in the Spirit."[83] From each account Kärkkäinen is clear that what is essential to notice is the active role of the Holy Spirit in the transformation of human persons from self-centered individuals to those in harmonious *koinonia*-relations with God, one another, and all of creation.

We cannot experience *koinonia* in all its fullness yet, but we wait for the *Parousia* where the *Ruach* of Life will achieve its *telos* in us. God's desire will be realized as believers receive the love of the Father, through the Son, by the Spirit, and respond by loving God in return. Habets states that the "end and perfection is union with the humanity of Christ and through that union a communion with the Father through the Son in the Holy Spirit."[84] God's salvation of willing humanity will be complete. This echoes familiar themes found within the theology of the Greek patristic theologians, most notably Athanasius, the doctrine of *theosis* espoused by the Eastern Orthodox tradition, and more recent claims by such thinkers as Kärkkäinen that "God became human without ceasing to be God in

---

79. Pinnock, *Flame of Love*, 181.

80. Kärkkäinen, *One with God*, 84.

81. Edmund J. Rybarczyk, "Beyond Salvation: An Analysis of the Doctrine of Christian Transformation Comparing Eastern Orthodox with Classic Pentecostalism," PhD diss., Fuller Theological Seminary, 1999, 3; cited in Kärkkäinen, *One with God*, 110.

82. Rybarczyk, "Beyond Salvation," 313; cited in Kärkkäinen, *One with God*, 113.

83. Ibid., 114.

84. Habets, *Theosis in the Theology of Thomas Torrance*, 148.

order to enable believers to participate in the divine nature without ceasing to be human."[85] The Father's love is so vast that as we experience God's *koinonia*, that love will overflow from us so that we can also respond by loving other human beings. In doing so, we will share *koinonia* with other people reflecting the divine nature as we image the Son.

Pinnock expresses the experience of *koinonia* as being so intimate that he defines it along with Scripture in sexualized terms.[86] The church becomes the Bride of Christ,[87] the beloved of the Song of Songs. The *Ruach* of Life will continue to mediate the love of the Father to the Son with whom we are united to in a *koinonia*-relationship of love. United to the *imago Dei*, as individual believers, we will respond in love through the Son, back to the Father. As the church, together we will also respond to the Father's love in perfect communion with each other bound together by the *Ruach* of Life. This is life. Humanity will experience eternal life lived in the *koinonia* of the divine dance. Jesus said, "I have come that they may have life, and have it abundantly" (John 10:10).

CONCLUSION

In this chapter I have shown that there is a teleological view of the *Ruach* of Life which, while distinct from the teleological view of the *imago Dei*, walks along the same path. Word and Spirit are walking hand in hand towards the human destiny of union with God. Christologically, it means to be conformed to the likeness of the Son. Pneumatologically, it means to experience the *koinonia* of the Divine nature.

God is a social Trinity where the Father loves the Son by the Holy Spirit and the Son returns the love of the Father by the same Spirit. God has so much to give that he creates the cosmos, including humanity, created in the image and likeness of God, and God breathes the *Ruach* of Life into Adam's nostrils. Humanity has a created "transcendental determination" towards becoming like God, towards experiencing communion with God, but in the fall chooses a self-determined destruction of trying to become like God in their own way, through sin.

---

85. Ibid., 142.
86. Pinnock, *Flame of Love*, 152.
87. See Rev 19:9; 21:2; and 22:17.

The *Ruach* of Life re-creates human persons by uniting the Son to humanity in the hypostatic union. Jesus Christ experiences God's *koinonia* at his baptism and is directed by and ministers in the power of the Holy Spirit. We see this communion of the Spirit between Father and Son throughout the Gospel narratives until the Son experiences our deserved destiny, the absence of the *Ruach* of Life, on the cross. The *Ruach* of Life continues to re-create by resurrecting Christ from the dead, and continues to transform him until his ascension back to the Father. The Son's journey from incarnation to glorification is a vicarious one where human persons can follow his path, from death to life, by the Father adopting us as "sons" and the Spirit uniting us to the Son. We can once again respond to the Father's love.

The *Ruach* of Life once again mediates the Father's love to us. By faith, we respond and are justified through the baptism of the Holy Spirit who unites us to the Son, and to his body the church. We look forward to the *Parousia* when our *telos* will be realized and believers in the Father's Son will experience the fulfillment of the divine *koinonia* by the Holy Spirit. This thesis presents the *telos* of humanity in a truly Trinitarian way. The goal is Life—God's Life.

> Then an angel showed me the river of the water of life, bright as crystal, flowing from the throne of God and of the Lamb. ... The Spirit and the Bride say, "Come." And let everyone who hears say, "Come." And let everyone who is thirsty come. (Rev 22:1, 17)

10

"When Groans and Mumblings Are Not Enough": Investigating Being "Slain in the Spirit" in Acts

by Darren Ayling

SPIRIT, SLAYING, AND OTHER ECSTATIC PHENOMENA

Aimee sat at the back of the church watching the proceedings before her with interest. She had been a Christian for six months and her faith had turned her life around. She had been invited by a friend to a service at her church for "an experience of the Holy Spirit." Aimee struggled to make sense of the scene in the church. Most of the seats had been stacked hurriedly at the sides of the auditorium, leaving a large space immediately in front of the platform. Off to one side the worship band was playing upbeat, loud music. The music almost, but not quite, drowned out the voices of the prayer team who were moving amongst the people, most assuming the same posture of one hand toward the sky and the other on the forehead of the person they were praying for. In response to the prayers people were falling backwards at an alarming rate, being supported by "catchers" and lowered gently to the ground, where some lay still, others were laughing or sobbing, and still others were trembling as members of the prayer team knelt beside them praying fervently. Aimee's friend leant towards her and said, "How about you? Do you want to go and get slain in the Spirit?" Aimee fidgeted nervously in her chair not sure whether to head for the door or the floor.

Aimee's experience is not unfamiliar to many Christians, who at some stage in their faith journey have experienced or have been encouraged to experience physical phenomena associated with the presence of the Holy Spirit. This chapter examines the phenomena of being "slain in the Spirit" with particular reference to the experience of the Spirit in the Book of Acts.

Being slain in the Spirit, also referred to as "'resting in the Spirit" or "going under the power,"[1] or colloquially as "carpet time with God,"[2] has been defined as "The power of the Holy Spirit so filling a person with a heightened inner awareness that the body's energy fades away and the person collapses to the floor."[3]

In its most typical form a person, usually after being prayed for by others, often accompanied by the laying on of hands, is seen to fall backwards and is, ideally, lowered to the ground by one or more "catchers." Despite a raised awareness of the phenomena associated with the Toronto Blessing movement of the mid-1990s, the experience of being slain in the Spirit is not a recent phenomenon.

Some of the earliest dialogue in regard to "ecstatic" physical manifestation of the "power of the Holy Spirit" is in relation to the Montanist movement initiated by Montanus around AD 155.[4] Although the nature

---

1. Brian F. Pendleton and Margaret M. Poloma, "Religious Experiences, Evangelism and Institutional Growth within the Assemblies of God," *JSSR* 28 (1989) 421.

2. Maryn Percy, "Adventure and Atrophy in a Charismatic Movement: Returning to the 'Toronto Blessing,'" *Journal of Contemporary Religion* 20 (2005) 71, reporting on the Toronto Airport Fellowship, indicated that the leaders of the movement referred to being slain in the Spirit with this phrase.

3. Pendleton and Poloma, "Religious Experiences," 421.

4. The limitations of this chapter prohibit an exhaustive survey of the historical evidence of the phenomena of being slain in the Spirit. Kydd, for example, lists other occurrences associated with, among others, St. Barnard, the radical reformation in Switzerland and Germany, Les convulsinoairs de St. Medard in Paris in the 1720s. Ronald Kydd, "A Retrospectus/Prospectus on Physical Phenomena Centered on the 'Toronto Blessing,'" *JPT* 6 (1998) 75.

of the physical manifestations associated with the movement is unclear,[5] an anonymous opponent claimed that Montanus "lost control of himself, falling into 'a sort of frenzy and ecstasy.'"[6] Tertullian, who was a convert to Montanism, reported on a woman who "fell into ecstasy" during the course of a service but "did not communicate her revelation until the congregation had departed."[7]

The experience of Perpetua when she was martyred, in AD 203 according to P. H. Alexander, has been interpreted as an example of being slain in the Spirit.[8] Alexander also suggests that an account of a fourteenth-century monk likewise alludes to being slain in the Spirit.[9]

Adrian Chatfield in his study on Anabaptist spirituality cites the *Anonymous Biography of David Joris*, written about 1540. Joris, in apparent solitude, had the experience whereby

> There came to him the power of an almighty, divine, heavenly being, just like a Spiritual burden. It entered the top of his head in a perception of or sensitivity to the resurrection. It pressed inward through his head and all his members, moving down into his legs so that he had to sit down and could no longer remain on his knees because of the weight of the heavy burden. And behold, he felt the power touching forcefully upon him

---

5. Christine Trevett notes an absence of descriptions of "roarings, states of collapse, and wild bodily movements," but observes that Gregory of Nazianzus makes reference to "Montanist Bacchic Ravings," in *Montanism: Gender, Authority, and the New Prophecy* (Cambridge: Cambridge University Press, 1996), 89.

6. Stanley M. Burgess, "Montanism," in *The New International Dictionary of Pentecostal and Charismatic Movements*, eds. S. M. Burgess and E. M. van der Maas (Grand Rapids: Zondervan, 2002), 903. Herafter *NIDPCM*.

7. Ibid., 904.

8. Paul H. Alexander, "Slain in the Spirit," in *NIDPCM*, 1073. Perpetua was taken into an amphitheatre with her friend and fellow martyr, Felicity and "If they trembled it was for joy and not for fear. Perpetua was the first to be thrown down, and she fell prostrate. She got up and, seeing that Felicity was prostrate, went over and reached out her hand to her and lifted her up. Both stood up together. Rousing herself as if from sleep (so deeply had she been in spiritual ecstasy), she began to look around. To everyone's amazement she said, 'When are we going to be led to the beasts?' When she heard that it had already happened she did not at first believe it until she saw the marks of violence on her body and her clothing." T. Jones, "Patron Saints Index: Saint Perpetua," online: http://saints.sqpn.com/saintp14.htm.

9. Alexander, "Slain in the Spirit," 1073.

before it fell upon his head. While it moved about or circulated, he perceived in this power five new senses from God.[10]

Although these are clearly references to ecstatic experiences with obvious physical manifestations, the clearest references to regular occurrences of being slain in the Spirit are associated with the Protestant revivals of the eighteenth century.

John Wesley, the founder of Methodism, reported in his journals regular occurrences of people falling over in the power of the Spirit during services. He describes an incident involving fellow revivalist George Whitefield, in July 1739:

> I had an opportunity to talk with [Whitefield] of those outward signs which had so often accompanied the inward work of God. I found his objections were chiefly grounded on gross misinterpretations of matter of fact. But the next day he had an opportunity of informing himself better: for no sooner had he begun (in the application of his sermon) to invite all sinners to believe in Christ, than four persons sank down close to him, almost in the same moment. One of them lay without either sense or motion. A second trembled exceedingly. The third had strong convulsions all over his body, but made no noise unless by groans. The fourth, equally convulsed, called upon God, with strong cries and tears.[11]

Jonathan Edwards, who Wesley described as "that very sensible man," was leading a similar revivalist movement to Wesley at around the same time in the American Colonies. Iain Murray reports that there were "cases of sudden physical collapse, of outcries, and of swoonings which were witnessed in many congregations from the summer of 1741 onwards."[12] It would seem that these manifestations were the cause of

---

10. Cited in Adrian Chatfield, "Zealous for the Lord: Enthusiasm and Dissent, Lovers and the Beloved: Brides of Christ," *JPT* 5 (1997) 106–7. Joris describes his new understanding as "a spiritual understanding in the form of a divine-human being, desirable and sweet, just as if God had revealed and manifested together both human and divine natures in an overlapping taste and desire." Joris goes on to experience the ability to "speak in new tongues." Chatfield suggests that "the reference to tongues is rare if not unique in the period." Ibid., 107.

11. John Wesley, *John Wesley's Journal*, eds. R. Backhouse and P. L. Parker (London: Hodder & Stoughton, 1993), 67.

12. Iain H. Murray, *Jonathan Edwards: A New Biography* (Edinburgh: Banner of Truth Trust, 1987), 217.

great debate, with one observer suggesting, "There is a great work in this town, but more of the footsteps of Satan than in any place I have yet been in: the zeal of some too furious: they tell of many visions, revelations and many strong impressions upon the imagination."[13]

Edwards did not encourage the physical responses; in fact he encouraged people to "refrain from such outward manifestations"[14] during services. Clearly the phenomena became divisive, with Edwards himself observing that "A great deal of caution and pains were found to be necessary to keep the people, many of them, from running wild."[15]

Into the nineteenth century the revivals associated with Charles Finney also seem to have episodes of people being slain in the Spirit. His *Autobiography* details occasions in which people "could not move or speak, in one instance for [sixteen] hours."[16] Finney describes one such occurrence in Antwerp, New York, in which large numbers of people fell to the ground as he preached: "If I had had a sword in each hand, I could not have cut them down as fast as they fell. I was obliged to stop preaching."[17]

Toward the end of the nineteenth century Maria Woodworth-Etter held evangelistic meetings at which being slain in the Spirit was a frequent occurrence. A meeting in Indiana in 1885 was reported in the local paper: "Dozens lying around pale and unconscious, rigid and lifeless as though in death."[18]

The Azusa Street revival at the start of the twentieth century, to which "nearly every Pentecostal denomination in the U.S. traces its roots,"[19] was known for its "free expression" of the Spirit. Roberts reports that the services at Azusa Street were "long" and "spontaneous": "Many shouted. Others were 'slain in the Spirit' or 'fell under the power'. Sometimes there were periods of extended silence or of singing in tongues."[20]

13. Eleazer Wheelock, after attending a meeting in Voluntown, Connecticut, October 21, 1741. Cited in ibid.

14. Ibid., 218.

15. Ibid., 219.

16. Cited in Alexander, "Slain in the Spirit," 1073.

17. Cited in Charles Finney, *Finney on Revivals: Selected Lectures*, ed. W. H. Harding (London: Oliphants, n.d.), 5.

18. Cited in Alexander, "Slain in the Spirit," 1073.

19. Cecil M. Robeck Jr., "Azusa Street Revival," in *NIDPCM*, 348.

20. Ibid., 346.

The ministry of Kathryn Kuhlman in the USA during the 1960s and 70s is also known for its phenomena associated with the Spirit. Kuhlman was the "world's most widely known female evangelist."[21] For a ten-year period commencing in the early 1960s Kuhlman ran services at the Los Angeles Shrine auditorium, where, according to D. J. Wilson, "she regularly filled the 7,000 seats."[22] Wilson reports:

> Apart from the well-documented healings, the most sensational phenomenon associated with Kuhlman was people "going under the power" (sometimes referred to as "slain in the Spirit"), or falling, when she prayed for them. This sometimes happened to dozens at a time and occasionally hundreds.[23]

Rodney Howard-Browne moved from South Africa to the United States in 1987. He began an itinerant preaching ministry and eventually went on to establish churches in various cities in the States. He describes how in 1989 the nature of his ministry changed:

> While I was preaching, the power of God began to fall. Many people began to fall out of their seats. It looked like someone was shooting them and in some places whole rows at a time would go down. They were laughing and crying and falling all over the place and looked like drunken people.[24]

Associated with people being slain in the Spirit at Howard-Browne's meetings were reports of physical healings, and this led to Howard-Browne being invited to speak regularly at rallies around the USA. A pastor who attended one meeting and was significantly impacted, Randy Clark, was subsequently invited to speak at the Vineyard Church next to Toronto Airport. Clark spoke at a series of meetings in January 1994. Again there were significant physical phenomena associated with the meetings.

> Laughter, prostration, "drunkenness" and other physical phenomena are the initial hallmark of the renewal, but it soon becomes apparent that people are having profound experiences

---

21. Dwight J. Wilson, "Kathryn Kuhlman," in *NIDPCM*, 826.
22. Ibid.
23. Ibid., 827.
24. Cited in D. Roberts, *The "Toronto" Blessing* (Eastbourne: Kingsway, 1994), 85.

while on the carpet—including visions—that are bringing internal change as well as outward excitement.[25]

The phenomena occurring at Toronto developed to include people roaring and making other animal noises as well as reports of gold fillings appearing in people's dentition and fine gold dust in people's hair.[26] The movement became well-known in churches around the world, including New Zealand, with many people experiencing the physical phenomena associated with the start of the "Blessing."

In December 1996, the Toronto Airport Congregation was excommunicated by its parent body the Association of Vineyard Churches. The then leader of the Vineyard movement, John Wimber, described what was happening as too "exotic."[27]

> We cannot at any time endorse, encourage, offer theological justification or biblical proof-texting for any exotic practices that are extra-biblical—whether in Toronto or elsewhere.... Though we understand that when the [Holy Spirit] is manifest among us there may be phenomena that we do not understand, it is our conviction that these manifestations should not be promoted, placed on stage, nor used as the basis for theologizing that leads to new teaching.[28]

The claim that much of this behavior is "extra-biblical" is difficult to refute, as the next section will show.

25. Ibid., 21.

26. Percy, "Adventure and Atrophy in a Charismatic Movement," 72. Percy indicates that despite numerous claims regarding gold and gold dust on various Web sites, the evidence remains "circumstantial and uncorroborated." Ibid., 74. Toronto Airport Vineyard Church have suggested that the animal sounds are related to prophecy citing Amos 3:8, "When the lion roars who will not fear; when God speaks who cannot but prophesy," and Hosea 11:10, "They will follow the Lord; he will roar like a lion. When he roars his children will come trembling from the west." Dave Roberts reports that "The phenomenon is regarded therefore as a prophetic symbol and Airport Vineyard leaders will urge those involved to prophesy in their own language following the symbolic action." *The "Toronto" Blessing*, 135.

27. "Toronto Blessing Too 'Exotic,'" *Christian Century*, January 3, 1996, 5.

28. Cited in ibid. It was not just the Vineyard movement that faced this level of controversy. The Southern Baptist Convention Foreign Missionary Board (FMB) fired two veteran missionaries in December 1996 for allowing congregants in their Singapore Church to be slain in the Spirit. The couple were fired when they failed to stop the practice despite the FMB deeming the practice as having no "sound biblical justification." See "Charismatic Missionaries Dismissed," *Christianity Today*, February 5, 1996, 102.

SPIRIT, SLAYING, AND SCRIPTURE

There does not seem to be a cohesive biblical defense of being slain in the Spirit in the literature.[29] Alexander suggests that a number of prooftexts are used to defend the practice. From the Old Testament, Gen 15:12–21, in which Abraham is described to have been overcome by a "deep sleep"; Num 24:4, which describes a person "who falls prostrate, and whose eyes are opened";[30] Ezekiel's experience when he "fell facedown" in Ezek 1:28 and where he is told to "stand up on your feet" in Ezek 2:1; have all been used to support the experience.[31]

The New Testament is also used to support the practice, particularly the Book of Acts. Most commonly highlighted are the references to Paul falling down at his conversion on the road to Damascus (Acts 9:4, 6, and recounted in 22:7 and 26:14) and Peter falling into a trance on the roof

---

29. At this juncture it is important to distinguish between the terminology of being "slain in the Spirit" and "baptism of the Spirit." The latter has been the subject of much debate in the literature. The nature of the debate is centered around the Pentecostal view of a "second baptism" being an essential feature of Christian fullness—in classic Pentecostal theology evidenced by the gift of speaking in tongues. In Pentecostal theology a clear differentiation is made between "conversion to Christ and the post-conversion experience of 'Spirit-baptism', the latter often defined as the cardinal doctrine of 'subsequence.'" Martin W. Mittelstadt, *The Spirit and Suffering in Luke-Acts* (London: T. & T. Clark, 2004), 1. The experience of the early church in the Book of Acts is used to defend this position, particularly the experience of Pentecost in Acts 2. Charles Parham, for example, argues that the experience of the contemporary church "should tally exactly with the Bible . . . with the 2nd Chapter of Acts." Cited in ibid. A response to this view has been most clearly articulated by James D. G. Dunn and, more recently, Max M. B. Turner. In assessing Dunn's view Mittlestadt suggests, "for Dunn, reception of the Spirit is soteriological, thus initiatory in character, bringing the recipient into the salvation experience." Ibid., 2. Max Turner suggests that the experience in Acts 2:38, 39 is paradigmatic in associating "the gift of the Spirit with conversional faith and baptism." *The Holy Spirit and Spiritual Gifts* (Peabody: Hendrickson, 1996), 45. In relation to being slain in the Spirit, an exhaustive literature review is outside the constraints of this chapter, however Mark Cartledge in his assessment of the physical phenomena associated with the Toronto Blessing, comments that "the Biblical approaches used to support the blessing are far from satisfactory." "Interpreting Charismatic Experience: Hypnosis, Altered States of Consciousness and the Holy Spirit?," *JPT* 6 (1998) 118.

30. Alexander, "Slain in the Spirit," 1073. Other Old Testament references used to support the phenomena include Saul laying "all day and night" (1 Sam 19:23–24) and Daniel falling in the presence of Gabriel (Dan 8:17; 10:9). See Eric E. Wright, *Strange Fire?: Assessing the Vineyard Movement and the Toronto Blessing* (Durham: Evangelical, 1996), 81.

31. Alexander, "Slain in the Spirit," 1073.

of Simon the Tanner's house (10:10).³² However these are tenuous links on which to build a case for a widespread practice. It is noteworthy that most commentators on the passages in question fail to address in any detail the nature of "falling" in either of the events.³³ Prooftexting of this nature misses the point of the passage; in the case of Paul's experience, a life-changing point of conversion, and an encounter with the resurrected Jesus. To focus on the act of falling seems at best misguided. Following this approach to the extreme, one could argue that it was the *location* that was important, leading, as Stott alludes to, mass pilgrimages to likely locations on various roads into Damascus.³⁴

One aspect of Lukan pneumatology in the Book of Acts relating to the practice of being slain in the Spirit, particularly in corporate situations such as Toronto, deserves comment. Mittelstadt suggests that suffering is a constant in Lukan theology; every "Spirit-led character" in the narrative of Luke-Acts faces rejection.³⁵ In the lives of Peter, John, Paul, and the other apostles in Acts there is great opposition, rejection, and persecution (Acts 3–4; 7:2–53; 9:15–16). It is in this context that Stephen, for example, is "full of the Holy Spirit" (Acts 6:3, 5, 10).³⁶ Mittelstadt implies that it is in this context of opposition that the signs and wonders occur.

NATURE VS. GRACE

Mittelstadt, writing from a Pentecostal perspective, observes that particularly in Western Pentecostal movements there is a rejection of the

---

32. Wright, *Strange Fire?* 81. Other New Testament references include the disciples falling at the transfiguration (Matt 17:6), Paul's vision (2 Cor 12:1–4), and John falling at Jesus' feet (Rev 1:17). Ibid., 81. Alexander suggests that the passage "foremost in support of the phenomenon" is John 18:1–6. In this narrative the chief priests and Pharisees who are attempting to seize Jesus "draw back and fall to the ground." As Alexander rightly observes there is no mention of the Spirit in the narrative, and clearly there was no conversion experience or development in character as they proceeded to arrest Jesus. Alexander, "Slain in the Spirit," 1074.

33. See for example Frederick F. Bruce, *The Book of the Acts*, NICNT (Grand Rapids: Eerdmans, 1988); Charles K. Barrett, *Acts: A Shorter Commentary* (London: T. & T. Clark, 2002); Ajith Fernando, *Acts*, NIVAC (Grand Rapids: Zondervan, 1998); I. Howard Marshall, *Acts*, TNTC (Leicester: InterVarsity, 1980); and John R. W. Stott, *The Message of Acts* (Leicester: InterVarsity, 1990).

34. Stott, *Message of Acts*, 166.

35. Mittelstadt, *Spirit and Suffering in Luke-Acts*, 8.

36. Ibid., 132.

notion of suffering. Pentecostal Christians expect "the blessing of God"; suffering seems to infringe on this right to happiness.[37] In this context then there is a risk that the "contemporary pursuit of the Spirit is often relegated to a personal, self-empowering experience . . ."[38]

That there are physical manifestations associated with the Spirit cannot be denied—this is clear in the Book of Acts. But if being slain in the Spirit is not backed up by Scripture or by the implied pneumatology of the Book of Acts, how can its proliferation be explained? Eric Wright suggests that "when the historical and doctrinal basis for the current 'renewal' proves shaky, its proponents inevitably turn to experience."[39] The process follows then, in the case of being slain in the Spirit, that the experience occurs, which then produces faith. Faith then produces an expectation that the experience will occur again, and when it does faith is strengthened and the experience becomes normative. This repeated experience provides proof and, *following* this, Scripture and history are engaged in the manner described above to support the experience.[40]

Although this may explain how an experience becomes normative for an individual or a group it does not explain the initiation of the experience. John White has suggested four potential reasons for the initiation of phenomena such as being slain in the Spirit. First, people do it to themselves. That is to say the manifestations have a psychological explanation, or are consciously or unconsciously self-induced. Second, preachers do it to suggestible listeners—producing a so-called mass hysteria or mass hypnosis. Third, the devil does it—the phenomena representing some form of demonic control. Finally, God does it.[41]

However, this seems an oversimplification of the issue, and the phenomena of being slain in the Spirit, at least in a corporate setting, does not fit tidily into one of White's categories. The human experience of the Spirit cannot be separated from the physical or psychological. Wright observes that "the physiology of the human body, the constitution of the brain, the individual's psychology, will all be ingredients in the religious

---

37. Ibid., 136.
38. Ibid., 137.
39. Wright, *Strange Fire?*, 167.
40. Ibid.
41. John White, cited in David Middlemiss, *Interpreting Charismatic Experience* (London: SCM, 1996), 216.

experiences that we have."[42] We may add to this the elements of group psychology that influence behavior. The phenomenon of being slain in the Spirit is susceptible, in a corporate setting, to be manipulated by charismatic (in the exuberant sense of the word) leaders and the pressure that comes from group expectations.[43] Turner wisely observes, "Although the Spirit gives the capacity to experience and respond to God, the identity of the Spirit must not be blurred with the human expressions offered through the idioms of culture."[44]

What becomes the default practice, it would seem, is that the physical phenomena become the focus; the desire is to maintain a phenomenon such as being slain in Spirit because it becomes highly valued by a group. Kydd observes that although the phenomena eventually tend to disappear, the behavior remains in corporate memory as a kind of icon pointing to a time of perceived religious purity and authenticity.[45]

This is the great risk of the proliferation of a phenomenon such as being slain in the Spirit. One person may well respond to the power of the Holy Spirit by falling over, but that physical act should not and cannot be seen as a measure of spirituality, or worse, normative for Christian living. When this occurs spirituality deteriorates to "more psychic self-grooming than engagement with the Holy Spirit of God."[46]

Although well documented in history, the evidence in Scripture for the phenomenon of being slain in the Spirit is at best limited. Further, it is not in keeping with a Lukan understanding of the work of the Spirit in Acts, and is clearly susceptible to human manipulation.

What, then, for our friend Aimee? I am forced to conclude that she would be wise to head for the door. John Wesley in 1759 suggested that a phenomenon such as being slain in the Spirit is a case of "nature mixed with grace."[47] It would seem that its recent practice in Western Christianity tends more towards nature than it does grace.

---

42. Thomas Smail, Andrew Walker, and Nigel Wright, *Charismatic Renewal: The Search for a Theology* (London: SPCK, 1995), 82.

43. Kydd, "A Retrospectus/Prospectus on Physical Phenomena," 78.

44. William Turner, "Preaching the Spirit: The Liberation of Preaching," *JPT* 14 (2005) 6.

45. Ibid., 78.

46. Luke T. Johnson, "Keeping Spirituality Sane," *Commonweal*, November 17, 2006, 30.

47. Wesley, *John Wesley's Journal*, 173.

11

Taking the Spirit to Work

by Peter McGhee

SPIRIT AND WORK

Since the beginning of the twentieth century, there has been an increasing focus on the S/spirit, spirituality, and spiritual phenomenon in Western society. Lately, this focus has shifted to the modern workplace with numerous articles and books, both popular and academic, championing the role of the S/spirit/spirituality in improving organizations, markets, and economies. Evidence of this exists simultaneously in the expanding academic[1] and practitioner literature.[2] Moreover, the introduc-

---

1. See for example: Ian I. Mitroff and Elizabeth A. Denton, *A Spiritual Audi of Corporate America: A Hard Look at Spirituality, Religion & Values in the Workplace* (San Francisco: Jossey-Bass, 1999); Donde P. Ashmos and Dennis Duchon, "Spirituality at Work: A Conceptualization and Measure," *Journal of Management Inquiry* 9 (2000) 134–45; Robert A. Giacalone and Carole L. Jurkiewicz, "Toward a Science of Workplace Spirituality," in *Handbook of Workplace Spirituality*, eds. R. A. Giacalone and C. Jurkiewicz (Armonk, NY: ME, Sharpe, 2003), 3–28; and *Spirituality in Business: Theory, Practice, & Future Directions*, eds. Jerry Biberman and Len Tischler (New York: Palgrave Macmillan, 2008).

2. See for example: Jennifer Labbs, "Downshifters," *Personnel Journal*, March, 1996,

tion of courses on management and spirituality in universities, special issues of peer-reviewed journals, and the development of interest groups among the academy (e.g., Academy of Management's (AOM) Spirituality and Religion (MSR) Group) are additional signs of this awareness. Indeed, Neal and Biberman contend that AOM's endorsement provides substantial "legitimacy and support for research and teaching in this newly emerging field."[3]

From a Christian perspective, this new interest in the S/spirit and spirituality in the workplace is both beneficial and alarming. It is beneficial because it is preferred over the scientific materialism that governs the modern workplace. It is also valuable when it acts against the sense of meaninglessness that afflicts many of today's employees, most of whom have been viewed as impersonal instruments to achieve material ends.[4] It is frightening because "spirituality" has become such an amorphous term that it covers all kinds of phenomena earlier generations of Christians would have dismissed as error. Indeed, Carson has called today's "spirituality" an applause word—that is, the kind of word that is no sooner uttered than everyone breaks out in applause.[5] In this sense, the modern understanding of the term depends on whoever is using it.

Whether spirituality in the workplace is a response to industrialization and the laws of economic rationality, a reaction to the individualism so prevalent in modern organizations, or simply a desire to see work as more than a means to an end, its literature and subsequent practices are questionable and have limited association with Christian pneumatology.

62–76; Sue Howard and David Welbourn, *The Spirit at Work Phenomenon* (London: Azure, 2004); Margaret Benefiel, *Soul at Work: Spiritual Leadership in Organizations* (New York: Seabury, 2005); and Joan Marques, Satinder Dhiman, and Richard King, *Spirituality in the Workplace: What It Is, Why It Matters, How to Make It Work for You* (Fawnskin, CA: Personhood Press, 2007).

3. Judi Neal and Jerry Biberman, "Introduction: The Leading Edge in Research on Spirituality and Organizations," *Journal of Organizational Change Management* 16 (2003) 363.

4. For a succinct analysis of the modern context of work and its current transformation, see the chapter entitled "The Transformation of Work" in Catherine Casey, *Work, Self & Society: After Industrialism* (London: Routledge, 1995), 26–49. Both Miroslav Volf in *Work in the Spirit: Toward a Theology of Work* (Eugene, OR: Wipf & Stock, 2001), 35–42; and David Jensen in *Responsive Labor* (Louisville: Westminster John Knox, 2006), 1–21, provide good critiques of modern work from a Christian perspective.

5. Donald A. Carson, "When Is Spirituality Spiritual? Reflections on Some Problems of Definitions," *JETS* 37 (1994) 381.

The purpose of this chapter is to evaluate contemporary understandings of spirituality in the workplace, both Christian and secular, and offer a constructive advancement of the concept from a pneumatological perspective. To this end, Miroslav Volf's pneumatological theology of work will act as a critical framework from which to comment on and further appreciate the role of the Spirit in the workplace.

A PNEUMATOLOGICAL THEOLOGY OF WORK

Miroslav Volf begins part two of his seminal study, *Work in the Spirit: Toward a Theology of Work*, by noting the distinct lack of theological focus on work historically.[6] This he attributes to "an illegitimate intrusion of Greek anthropology into Christian theology."[7] Citing the example of Thomas Aquinas, Volf notes the dualistic nature of his *vita activa* and *vita contemplativa*. In such a theology, work provides the necessities of life "without which human beings would not be apt for contemplation."[8] Apart from this practical use, work is detrimental to human beings since "it is impossible for one to be busy with external action and at the same time give oneself to Divine contemplation."[9] Therefore, if work exists as a means to a higher end then there is little point in reflecting on it extensively; it is but accidental to the real meaning of human life. Volf rightly rejects any view that subordinates *via activa* to *via contemplativa*. At the same time, he does not wish to elevate work over spirituality, which he refers to as the modern problem; rather, he proposes that "we treat them as two basic, alternating aspects of the Christian life that may differ in importance but that cannot be reduced to one another, and that form an inseparable unity."[10] Only with this view in mind can reflection on work be fundamental to the task of theology.

The doctrine of sanctification has traditionally been the basis for theological discussion on work.[11] Against the Greek view of labor as

---

6. Volf, *Work in the Spirit*, 69.

7. Ibid., 70.

8. Thomas Aquinas, *Summa Theologica* IIaIIae.182.3–4, cited in Volf, *Work in the Spirit*, 70.

9. Thomas Aquinas, *Summa Theologica* IIaIIae.182.3.

10. Volf, *Work in the Spirit*, 70.

11. Ibid., 71

demeaning and disgraceful,[12] believers now joined in union with Christ through the Spirit (Rom 6:5–11; Gal 2:20) were to discern how this new life influenced their daily work[13] and, perhaps more importantly, how work, in turn, shaped their new Christian character.[14] In this way, work took on an overtly ethical nature; we labor for Christ (Col 3:23) in a manner that honors God while we "muzzle the evil and disobedient flesh."[15] Unfortunately, the danger of this ascetic/ethical view is that it tends to lessen the intrinsic value of work, the workers themselves, and God's call on all humanity regardless of their station in life.[16] While sanctification is an indispensible aspect of a Christian ethic of work, it is not broad enough to be completely faithful to the biblical narrative nor is it necessarily compatible with our modern industrial age.

Rather than contribute to Christian ethical writings, Volf seeks to develop a "*new—pneumatological—theology of work*" (his italics), a "theological framework for understanding human work and to elucidate the implicit ethical principles that should guide our efforts to assess and restructure the world of work."[17] The foundational concept on which Volf

---

12. See Ivor J. Davidson, *The Birth of the Church: From Jesus to Constantine (A.D. 30–312)* (Oxford: Monarch, 2005), 30–36.

13. Volf, *Work in the Spirit*, 72, notes that the early church fathers affirmed the nobility of work and espoused an obligation to labor diligently while condemning excessive work and an overreliance on the results of human endeavor.

14. Jensen refers to this as "the ascetic view of work since it restrains the passions, calms unease, and soothes the soul . . . [or to put it] most bluntly, work prevents us from getting into further trouble." Jensen, *Responsive Labor*, 30.

15. Volf, *Work in the Spirit*, 72. While Col 3:23 is directed at Christian slaves, the context of the chapter implies that the whole of life, both thought and conduct, is to be submitted to the Lord, thus there is no gap between the sacred and the secular. See Peter T. O'Brien, *Colossians-Philemon*, WBC 44 (Dallas: Word, 2002), 44.

16. Jensen, *Responsive Labor*, 33. Indeed history supports this concern. Principe notes that under the influence of Scholasticism in the eleventh–twelfth centuries, the term "spiritual" begun to take on a different tone. That is, it no longer simply referred to two ways of life—the spiritual and the canal (1 Cor 2:6–15). Instead, it now distinguished the material from the incorporeal. By opposing *spiritualitas* to *corporalitas*, "this new use of the word changed its Pauline moral sense to a psychological sense. In this shift, one can foresee the confusion of spirituality with disdain for the body and matter [and consequently non-spiritual work] that was to mark many later movements dealing with spiritual life." Walter Principe, "Toward Defining Spirituality," in *Exploring Christian Spirituality: An Ecumenical Reader*, ed. Kenneth J. Collins (Grand Rapids: Baker, 2000), 45.

17. Walter Principe, "Toward Defining Spirituality," 76.

constructs his theology of work is the new creation. Building on Jürgen Moltmann's insight that Christianity is essentially eschatological,[18] Volf contends that "Christian life is life in the Spirit of the new creation or it is not Christian at all. And the Spirit of God should determine the whole life, spiritual as well as secular, of a Christian."[19] Consequently, all Christian work is under the inspiration of the Spirit and with a view towards the coming new creation. Such a specifically soteriological and eschatological theology, according to Volf, must exemplify a hope of the future completion of God's working in history.[20] Human work must reflect whatever God desires for his new creation (as opposed to how individuals may characterize work). This truth implies certain normative principles that should guide Christian behavior "in structuring the reality of human work."[21] Given these normative implications, theology's job is not to just pass comment on the world of work but to participate in its "promised and hoped for transformation in the new creation."[22] As Niebuhr noted, Jesus Christ, whose incarnation, sacrifice, and resurrection inaugurated this new creation, was no social or cultural commentator, rather he was a transformer of culture bringing God's kingdom to earth and indeed transforming this world into his kingdom.[23]

We find scriptural support for this in such passages as 2 Cor 5:17 and Col 1:13–14. According to 2 Cor 5:17, in Christ there is a new way of "seeing," as God has made all things new. It is less than correct to interpret this as an individual change or conversion. Rather, the accent of the verses falls on a person entering the new order in Christ, thus making the new creation an eschatological term for God's age of salvation based on Isa 51:9 and 54:9.[24] In Col 1:13–14, God has delivered us from darkness into the light under the rule of his beloved Son. The vivid description given here by Paul ensures that the Colossians (and other Christians) categorically understand they are now "children of light" and must behave

---

18. For a succinct summary of Moltmann's eschatology see Richard Bauckham, "Jürgen Moltmann," in *The Modern Theologians: An Introduction to Christian Theology Since 1918*, ed. David F. Ford (Malden, MA: Blackwell, 2005), 151–52.

19. Volf, *Work in the Spirit*, 79.

20. Ibid., 79.

21. Ibid., 81.

22. Ibid., 83.

23. H. Richard Niebuhr, *Christ and Culture* (New York: Harper, 1951), 190–96.

24. See Ralph P. Martin, *2 Corinthians*, WBC 40 (Dallas: Word, 2002), 40.

appropriately. In the kingdom of the Son, redemption signifies freedom from the imprisonment of sin, and is not simply a future hope but an existing reality, a present possession bound up with the person of Jesus. If we possess him, we are in the kingdom of Christ now and, therefore, must act in accordance with being a citizen of that kingdom.[25] We who are in Christ should acquit ourselves correspondingly. Finally, a theology of work should be comprehensive; it needs to "answer the question of how human work is related to all of reality: to God, human beings, and their non-human environment."[26]

Before specifying further details of his theology of work, Volf first rejects any view that holds to a radical discontinuity between the present and future states of the world.[27] Such a view postulates that at the final consummation, the utter annihilation of this present world will occur and a brand new world is created. This eschatological perspective has proven popular throughout Christian history and there is some biblical support for it.[28] Volf, however, argues that annihilating this world and creating a new one *ex nihilo* ensures our work only has earthly (temporal) value—for the worker's well-being, their community, and posterity—in other words, human work has no ultimate meaning, no eschatological significance.[29] While it is logically possible to believe the world will cease at some future point and yet still work in the present so as to please God and be socially responsible, it is theologically inconsistent since it runs counter to the intrinsic value and goodness of creation. The first chapter of Genesis resounds with goodness of God's creation (see vv. 4, 10, 12, 18, 21, 25). In Genesis 1:31, however, that appreciation changes in three ways

25 SeeO'Brien, *Colossians-Philemon*, 44.

26. Volf, *Work in the Spirit*, 84–85.

27. Ibid., 89.

28. After the New Testament period, attention focused less on Christ's second coming and more what would happen after death. Beginning in the Middle Ages with scholasticism, and peaking in the period of the Reformation, the doctrine of the last things reached its classic expression: heaven is a place where the righteous in Christ go (Heb 12:22–24), while hell is for the eternally damned (Rev 20:11–15). The world as we know it will cease to exist. This view survives today in various theologies and churches. A contemporary, if somewhat fanciful, exposition of it occurs in the recently published and very popular Dispensational theology of the *Left Behind* series by Tim LaHaye and Jerry B. Jenkins. For biblical support, see for example Isa 65:17; 66:22; Matt 24:35; 2 Pet 3:10; and Rev 21:1.

29. Volf, *Work in the Spirit*, 89.

that ensure the reader understands how good this creation is. First, it is applied to the whole creation, "all that he had made," instead of just two individual items. Second, instead of the usual word in Hebrew for "that," used earlier (*kî*, v. 4), "that . . . really" is used (*hinnēh*, v. 31), suggesting God's enthusiasm as he contemplated his handiwork. Third, the finished whole is said to be "very good."[30] Volf puts it succinctly: "what God will annihilate must either be so bad that it is not possible to be redeemed or so insignificant that it is not worth being redeemed."[31]

Taking the opposite stance to earthly-material annihilation, eschatological transformation assures that human work has intrinsic value and ultimate meaning via its relation, indirectly through sanctification and directly through what humans create, to the new creation.[32] In other words, whatever is good is transformed and perfected to become part of God's new creation. To belay any fears, Volf assures that human work cannot create or replace heaven. Rather, through divine eschatological transformation, our work integrates into the new heavens and new earth. This expectation invests our work with ultimate meaning. In our own limited and flawed way, our work contributes to God's new creation. Such is the grace of the triune God.[33]

How does human work contribute to God's new creation? After all, the entire world is currently under the power of sin (Rom 3:23) and the devil (Eph 2:2; 1 John 4:4). Furthermore, Scripture teaches that God through Jesus Christ is the source of this new creation (2 Cor 5: 17–20; Rev 21:2)—not human beings. Therefore, how is it possible that we can cooperate (or perhaps co-create) with God in this? The answer lies in understanding the difference between "God's eschatological action *in* history and his eschatological action *at the end* of history."[34] By the Spirit,

---

30. See Gordon J. Wenham, *Genesis 1–15*, WBC 1 (Dallas: Word, 2002), 1.

31. Volf, *Work in the Spirit*, 90–91.

32. Ibid., 91.

33. Ibid., 92. Volf provides several arguments for this eschatological transformation, including the earthly location of the kingdom of God in both the OT (Isa 11:6–10; 65:17–25) and the NT (Matt 6:10, 33), the liberation, not destruction, of creation from sin (Rom 8:21; 1 Tim 4:4), and the Judeo-Christian belief in the goodness of creation. We could add to this list the fact of physical resurrection. See in this regard Myk Habets, "Naked but Not Disembodied: A Case for Anthropological Duality," *Pacific Journal of Baptist Research* 4 (2008) 33–50.

34. Volf, *Work in the Spirit*, 100.

God works in history "using human actions to create provisional states of affairs that anticipate the new creation in a real way."[35] The Spirit of God is essential to any discussion about the new creation. The Spirit is the "firstfruits" or the "guarantee" of the future creation (Rom 8:23; 2 Cor 1:22), and the present means of eschatological transformation. Without the Holy Spirit, there is no new creation, either now or in the future, and there is certainly no transformation of the present. Any theology that wishes to interpret human work as an active anticipation of the new creation must therefore be a pneumatological theology of work.[36]

The Holy Spirit's transformative work is not limited to the inner salvation of humanity alone but rather extends to all of creation. Unfortunately, this internal salvific view has been central in much Protestant theology.[37] Badcock sources this belief from the period of the Protestant Reformation at which time controversy arose between Roman Catholics emphasizing the mediating role of the church in the gift of the Spirit and various radical Reformers arguing for a minimal role of the Word in the sanctification of mature Christians.[38] In response to this, Badcock contends the Reformers saw

> The link between the work of the Spirit and the Gift of faith, seen as a response to the Word of the gospel, is fundamental. The point is that faith, by which we appropriate the promises of God, is the gift of the Spirit. Because of the centrality of faith, however, the implication is that the main work of the Spirit must be to create faith in or give faith to those who believe.[39]

---

35. Volf differentiates his eschatological framework from a protological one (i.e., one based on the doctrine of creation) in which human beings cooperate with God to preserve the world. Such theologies complement an eschatological view but when existing alone face several difficulties. For example, a protological view denies the ultimate significance of human work, argues for the restoration as opposed to the renewal of creation, lacks application to modern work with its transformational technologies, and tends to justify the status quo. Ibid., 100–102.

36. Ibid., 102.

37. Examples of works that associate the role of the Spirit primarily with the spiritual, psychological, and moral life of the individual include: Alasdair I. C. Heron, *The Holy Spirit* (Philadelphia: Westminster, 1983); Robert C. Sproul, *The Mystery of the Holy Spirit* (Wheaton: Tyndale, 1990); and Graham A. Cole, *He Who Gives Life: The Doctrine of the Holy Spirit* (Wheaton: Crossway, 2007).

38. Gary D. Badcock, *Light of Truth & Fire of Love: A Theology of the Holy Spirit* (Grand Rapids: Eerdmans, 1997), 89–95.

39. Ibid., 89

The Spirit, however, is not limited to the inner person, but is operating in all of creation. The Holy Spirit engages with the world and is not limited to human "spiritual" experiences. Interestingly, in the New Testament, faith in Christ results in regeneration through the Spirit and a new creation begins (2 Cor 5:17). However, the Greek word for regeneration (*palingenesia*) occurs only twice in the New Testament. In Matthew 19:28 it refers to the renewal of all things (not just humanity), and in Titus 3:5 it is used where Paul refers to Jesus saving us "not because of righteous things we had done, but because of his mercy. He saved us through the washing of rebirth and renewal by the Holy Spirit" (NIV). Ferguson labels this verse a *hendiadys* and suggests a connection between the regeneration of the individual and the beginning of the new age. He notes that Paul's other use of the word "renewal" (*anakainōsis*) in Rom 12:2 implies a contrast between this world and the age to come.[40] Paul sees the present renewal as part of a larger eschatological renewal. Regeneration does not merely signify

> the phenomenon of spiritual change from within, from below as it were, but transformation from without and from above, caused by participation in the new age and more specifically by fellowship through the Spirit with the resurrected Christ as the second man, its firstfruits, the eschatological Adam.[41]

If we understand the Spirit of God as being active in all of creation, and not just with one's inner salvation, then it is not difficult to connect the Holy Spirit with human work. Our work, redeemed by the Spirit, contributes to this new age and is a foretaste of what is to come.

Building on this notion, Volf expands his theology of work by making a case that all functions and tasks of a Christian, including their work, are *charismata*, that is, concrete instantiations of gifts of the Spirit.[42] Providing a selection of verses from the Old Testament as evidence,[43] Volf contends that as the Spirit anointed selected individuals in the Old

---

40 Sinclair B. Ferguson, *The Holy Spirit* (Downers Grove, IL: InterVarsity, 1996), 117–18.

41 Ibid., 118.

42. Volf, *Work in the Spirit*, 113.

43. See for example Exod 35:2–3; 1 Chron 28:11–12; Judg 3:10; 1 Sam 16:13; 23:2; and Prov 16:10.

Testaments for special tasks, we who live under the new covenant are all gifted and called to various tasks by the same Spirit. In this way,

> All human work, however, complicated or simple, is made possible by the operation of the Spirit of God in the working person; and all work whose nature and results reflects the values of the new creation is accomplished under the instruction and inspiration of the Spirit of God (Isa. 28:24–29).[44]

If Christian work is in the Spirit then it must be in cooperation with God, since it is God who inspires and gifts humans to complete their tasks.[45] Even work that utilizes the natural abilities of Christians is nonetheless empowered by the Spirit, and it is impossible to separate the gift of the Spirit from the enabling power of the Spirit. Volf cites the New Testament in support for this. Paul writes in Gal 2:20, "I have been crucified with Christ and I no longer live, but Christ lives in me. The life I live in the body, I live by the faith of the Son of God, who loved me and gave himself for me."[46] What does this verse mean except that the Christian life is one of cooperation with God through Christ by the power of the Spirit? This must include our daily labors as much as our "spiritual" ones.[47] While I work as lecturer in ethics at a business school, the Spirit of Christ works through me. Therefore, "the Spirit who imparts gifts and acts through them is a 'guarantee' of the realization of the eschatological new creation, cooperation with God in work is proleptic cooperation with God in God's eschatological *transformatio mundi*."[48] Mundane human labor, empowered by the Spirit, permits a cooperation with the triune God in his kingdom that completes creation and renews heaven and earth.

Not all work participates in this redemptive act of the triune God. God will not arbitrarily renew everything from the present world into the new creation. The Day of Judgment precursors the full realization of the new creation and this is when all that is negative (sin) in the present creation ceases. What measure determines whether our work is acceptable

---

44. Volf, *Work in the Spirit*, 114.

45. Ibid.

46. In departure from the NIV, I have favored the subjective genitive here as it fits the context of Galatians better, but even if we were to take the objective genitive the point remains valid.

47 Volf, *Work in the Spirit*, 115.

48. Ibid.

in this new creation? Volf suggests such criteria exist in 1 Cor 3:12–15. Under the test of "fire," work that has ultimate significance, work that cooperates with God, will survive purified. However, insignificant work, work done in cooperation with the powers that wish to ruin God's good creation, will be unable to be part of the New Jerusalem (Rev 21:27).

A PNEUMATOLOGICAL CRITIQUE OF CHRISTIAN THEOLOGIES OF WORK

The Protestant Reformation, and two of its leading advocates, Martin Luther and John Calvin, offered a view of work as a *calling* or *vocation*. Responding to a spirituality that emphasized metaphysical speculation and a sharp distinction between clergy and laity, Martin Luther challenged the notion in medieval thought that the highest form of Christian life was only a possibility for those who had taken the cowl. Using his doctrine of justification by faith, Luther argued that all Christians had a double calling: a spiritual and an external vocation. The spiritual vocation was God's call on each individual believer's life. The external vocation was a call to serve God in the world through whatever profession one has in life.[49] John Calvin extended Luther's notion of vocation to all actions that occupy human existence. He wrote, "The Lord enjoins every one of us, in all the actions of life, to have respect to our own calling. . . . This, too, will afford admirable consolation, that in following your proper calling, no work will be so mean and sordid as not to have a splendour and value in the eye of God."[50] For Calvin, work in and of itself had no value except by the One who has entrusted it to us. Work has worth because God has called us to it.[51]

Understanding work from a vocational perspective has proved popular in this century, at least within Protestant circles.[52] This is not

49. Ibid., 105–6.

50 John Calvin, *Institutes of the Christian Religion* (1559), trans. Henry Beveridge (London: Clarke, 1953), 3.10.6.

51. Both Luther and Calvin rejected any notion that human labor, no matter how noble or "spiritual" they were thought to be, could save or make righteous. God through his gracious actions and Christ's obedient sacrifice on the cross saves and renders one righteous before God (Eph 2:8–10). Works (if they are good) contribute to the ongoing process of sanctification; they have no relevance to justification. For a good summary of this view, see Steve Jeffrey, Mike Ovey, and Andrew Sach, *Pierced for Our Transgressions: Rediscovering the Glory of Penal Substitution* (Nottingham: InterVarsity, 2007).

52. See Darrell Cosden, *Theology of Work: Work and the New Creation* (Eugene,

surprising given its natural affinity with the ascetic view of work found in early church writings.[53] Work is good for an individual (as long as it is legal); it is part of the sanctification process. No matter what one does, God has called them and they must labor as if serving the Lord himself.

Unfortunately, from a pneumatological perspective this theology of work has significant limitations. Volf identifies several of these.[54] First, it allows any type of work, no matter how dehumanizing, to be a vocation (providing one does not break God's law). Work that is dehumanizing contradicts the Spirit of God as *Spiritus redemptor* and *Spiritus recreator*. As redeemer, the Spirit liberates from enslavement to hostile forces. His presence gives freedom—the ability to reject sin and choose God's will (2 Cor 3:17),[55] not to be instigators or active practitioners of degrading or debasing work either for ourselves or others (one immediately thinks of slavery, sweatshops, or child labor). As Re-creator, the Spirit makes all things new. By joining us with Christ, the Spirit humanizes (in the fullest sense)[56] our labors in the new creation as we strive to participate in its completion.

Second, there is ambiguity between one's spiritual and external call when the two conflict. This can lead to a compromising synthesis whereby one's external vocation becomes their spiritual one. Anecdotally, a significant number of managers in financial firms causing the recent economic crisis would consider themselves Christian, as would many of

---

OR: Wipf & Stock, 2004), 39–42, for a succinct discussion on differing takes on the vocation/calling theme.

53 See Volf, *Work in the Spirit*, 71–73, for a discussion of these.

54. Ibid., 107–9.

55. Paul's use of the term "freedom" is only found only here in 2 Corinthians. It is linked with "boldness" in v. 12, and is the conclusion of Paul's argument that we should be bold because of our heritage as God's children (Rom 8:14–17), and as part of his new creation (Rom 8:19–25), proclaiming the message of "freedom in Christ" (Gal 5:1; Rom 8:2). See Martin, *2 Corinthians*, WBC (Dallas: Word, 2002), 40. This freedom in Christ is not limited to spiritual freedom alone since Christ renews all of creation.

56. This is not to be confused with a secular humanistic view of work. Such a view stems from a basic confidence in the power of human intellectual and cultural achievement and an underlying belief that "Man is the sum of all things." A Christian humanism is sourced in Jesus Christ. He is "the incarnate Word of God, as the complete person, the *imago Dei* in perfection and the one into whom men and women are being transformed, from glory to glory." Myk Habets, *Theosis in the Theology of Thomas Torrance*, Ashgate New Critical Thinking in Religion, Theology and Biblical Studies (Surrey: Ashgate, 2009), 31.

their counterparts in other multinational corporations that participate in practices that hardly contribute to the renewal of creation or anticipate the future. A pneumatological theology of work avoids such dichotomies. All Christian work empowered by the Spirit is cooperative with God in active anticipation of the eschatological transformation. If our work fails to achieve this, then it is not *good* work.

Third, work as a vocation can suffer ideological misuse. If *all* work is in Divine service then even dehumanizing work is ennobled; consequently, there is no motivation to improve. Again, we see the outcomes of such a view in our modern industrial society. Cheap labor, soulless production lines, and hazardous working conditions have all been justified at one stage or another as being worthy in themselves or necessary for an even worthier goal—the bottom line. Perhaps this idea is no more prevalent than in the relationship between industry and the environment. Here, for example, the adage of profit maximization has enabled companies and the managers within them to treat creation as a free and limitless good with little motivation to change their behavior. The consequences of such actions are only beginning to be experienced now. Starting with the Spirit and acknowledging how he transforms work so that it integrates with the new creation while anticipating the future creation would suggest two things. First, that we preserve what we have—we must act as stewards of God's creation. Second, our labor is Spirit inspired and Spirit filled and therefore should be concerned with the renewal of God's creation, not its further destruction.

Finally, our modern interpretation of vocation has become synonymous with gainful employment. This reduction, coupled with the belief that vocation is the service of ordinary Christians to God, has contributed to elevating work to the status of a religion. Indeed, Max Weber famously foresaw this. He argued that the Reformers' idea of vocation was one important element in the "Protestant work ethic." Simply put, this idea has the worker called to do good works and to perform one's duties *religiously* as if pleasing God. For Weber such a person is capable of ceaseless disciplined work and is the combination of the religious man and the economic man.[57] When work becomes a religion, it assumes religious-like goals. People believe their work will set them free or at least

---

57. This merger, contends Weber, enabled the rise of industrial capitalism. See Casey, *Work, Self & Society*, 28.

give freedom enough to consume and find an identity (as opposed to true freedom found in Christ). The result is that people work more. This has certainly been the case in the Western world. The secondary outcome of this religious metamorphism of work is the commodification of human relationships. As Jensen puts it, "home becomes work and work becomes home." This objectifies relationships, which then become "quasi-disposable commodities that I negotiate according to my self-interest."[58]

While vocation/calling theology has been the prominent Protestant view, several other alternatives have arisen. By critically adopting Volf's proposals, we may comment on various recent attempts to account for the Spirit at work. Within Catholic social teaching, *Laborem Exercens* by Pope John Paul II is seminal as it views work as a means to physical and spiritual ends. Cosden asserts that *Laborem Exercens* is overly foundationalist in its anthropology and conception of work and so underplays the doctrine of creation and eschatology.[59] In this way, it reflects early ascetic and ethical views of work. Unfortunately, there appears little role for the Spirit in this process.

Jensen's theology of work, on the other hand, does have a Trinitarian focus.[60] Using Karl Rahner's concept of the economic Trinity, Jensen contends that the persons of the Trinity act as an open economy participating fully and abundantly in the life of creation. Jensen notes several things in particular about the Trinity as it relates to work. Making the gloomy observation that scarcity, efficiency, standardization, avariciousness, lack, and overwork epitomize the economies of the West, he contends that God's self-disclosure as Trinity in the economy of salvation counters this "reality" by pointing to the inherent value of difference, abundance, interdependence, just distribution, and fun in work.[61] In other words, God's work redeems our labors and the economies of which they are part. As we faithfully believe and act in the triune God, we hope for "the transformation of alienated human work as it is enfolded in God's very life."[62]

Jensen also presents a lengthy presentation on the Eucharist as the definitive example of God's triune work and of humanity's liturgical re-

58. Jensen, *Responsive Labor*, 15
59. Cosden, *Theology of Work*, 29–35.
60. Jensen, *Responsive Labor*, 43
61. Ibid., 51
62. Ibid.

sponse to it.⁶³ The Eucharist presents us with a vision of work that disrupts the separation of the secular and the sacred. As a eucharistic people who encounter Christ in all that we do, work can no longer be seen as a place foreign to the Christian faith. However, work is not simply sacred because Christians happen to be doing it, but rather, as Jensen notes, because the Eucharist and the liturgy "tear open heaven" ensuring God's holiness envelops all that we do.⁶⁴ The workplace has worth because it is *God's place*, where one's work belongs not only to oneself but also to God.

Jensen's Trinitarian theology of work and his use of the eucharistic theme is a significant theological improvement on ascetic or vocational views of work. However, from a pneumatological perspective there are concerns. First, it underplays eschatology. While the Eucharist is a sign of God's work for us, there is little written about how this relates to the future creation and how our work contributes to that. In fact, the strong emphasis on God's sovereignty implies that creation is somehow already completed and our work is merely an act of worship and thankfulness for this gift.⁶⁵ Second, there is no discussion as to what role the Spirit actually plays in this transformation; rather the Divine persons and their intra-Trinitarian relations are used as models for human work. Here Jensen is guilty of drawing too long a bow when he appeals to the notion of *perichoresis* to describe the similarity between the intra-Trinitarian relations and between that of inter-human relations. The reality, however, is that human beings do not participate in a common substance and consequently remain separate individuals even in the most intimate of their relations. *Perichoresis*, when applied to human relations, can only be done so analogously and not literally. Finally, if work is merely a response to God's already finished work, does this render work ultimately meaningless? Moreover, what is the role of the Spirit in the distribution of *charisms*? After all, if work is eucharistic and consequently all God wanted it to be from eternity, then what is the purpose of the individual gifts that the Spirit of God bestows? The risk of alienation that exists in vocational theologies raises its ugly head here. As Volf notes,

> The point is not to simply interpret work religiously as cooperation with God and thereby glorify it ideologically, but to

63. Ibid., 67.
64. Ibid., 75.
65. Ibid., 84.

transform work into a charismatic cooperation with God on the "project" of the new creation.⁶⁶

Another well-known set of reflections on work are those of Jürgen Moltmann.⁶⁷ Essentially, Moltmann believes that human beings can improve themselves through their work. In this way work serves an instrumental function. However, he is wary of economic utility encroaching upon work's ultimate meaning.⁶⁸ Moltmann also suggests that work aids human socialization. For Moltmann, this is the "human significance of work . . . and becomes the comprehensive sense of work."⁶⁹ Although these points are interesting, Moltmann extends his notion of work further, adding a transcendent meaning related to all of life:

> In his or her work, a person corresponds to the creating God. In their work, people participate in God's self-emptying for the purpose of liberating humanity. In his or her work, even if not alone, a person realizes his or her call to freedom. In his or her work and through it, a person is on the promised road to the kingdom of freedom and human worth.⁷⁰

After which, he goes on to to paint an eschatological picture of work that sounds vaguely similar to that of Volf:

> If one seeks a concept that includes the significance of work for the person and for society, then the expression "work in the kingdom of God" is near at hand . . . it is also able to show the eschatological meaning of all work and of society itself in its historical dealings with the natural world.⁷¹

Even from these brief examples it is clear that work for Moltmann is eschatological: work is participation in God's history.⁷² Christ's act on the cross grounds Moltmann's emphasis on human work corresponding to

---

66. Volf, *Work in the Spirit*, 116.

67. Moltmann's reflections on work are found primarily in two works: *Theology of Play*, trans. Reinhard Ulrich (New York: Harper & Row, 1972) and *On Human Dignity: Political Theology and Ethics*, trans. M. D. Meeks (Philadelphia: Fortress, 1984). For details see Cosden, *Theology of Work*, 47.

68. Jürgen Moltmann, *On Human Dignity*, 54–55.

69. Ibid.

70. Ibid., 56.

71. Ibid.

72. Cosden, *Theology of Work*, 60–61.

Divine activity. Christ's sacrifice brought about the eschatological realization of creation and affirmed the joyful and grateful nature of work.

Unfortunately, there appears minimal requirement for the Spirit in this process. Instead, what Moltmann offers are new ways of understanding work based on an eschatological Christomonism.[73] In later works, Moltmann accentuates the importance of the Spirit in all areas of life including work. In his *The Spirit of Life: A Universal Affirmation*, he develops a holistic doctrine of the person and work of the Holy Spirit within a Trinitarian framework. He defines experience of the Spirit as "an awareness of God's fellowship, friendship, and love."[74] Such a doctrine, according to Moltmann, must comprehend human beings in their totality and embrace the whole of the community of creation. This holistic pneumatology has allowed him to explore the experiences of a wide range of liberation movements and suffering peoples many of whom exist in subsistent working conditions.

However, there are concerns with Moltmann's approach to the Spirit. First, Moltmann implies that God is inseparable from the world. Creation is a result of God's desire to create but this resolve is a necessary part of God's nature. As Moltmann puts it, "creation is the outcome of the rapturous abundance of his divine Being, which longs to communicate itself and is able to communicate itself".[75] In the power of the Spirit, God creates and pervades his creation. Moltmann considers this a *perichoretic* relationship, what Kärkkäinen calls an "immanent transcendence."[76] This need to necessarily perceive God in all things, and all things in God, exposes him to the charge of panentheism.[77] The doctrine of *creatio ex nihilo* has a long biblical and apostolic history. Both the Old and the New Testaments portray God as the Creator separate from his creation.[78] Moltmann's position intimates that God is not the ultimate reality because

---

73. Ibid., 62

74. Jürgen Moltmann, *The Spirit of Life: A Universal Affirmation*, trans. Margaret Kohl (Minneapolis: Fortress, 2001), 17.

75. Ibid., 295.

76. Veli-Matti Kärkkäinen, *Pneumatology* (Grand Rapids: Baker, 2002), 127.

77. On Moltmann's identification as a panentheist see Donald G. Bloesch, *The Holy Spirit* (Downers Grove, IL: InterVarsity, 2000), 236.

78. See for example Gen 1; Isa 45:7, 18; Prov 8:22–24; Matt 13:55; 25:34; Luke 11:50; John 17:24; Acts 14:15; Rom 4:17; Eph 1:4; Heb 4:3; 9:26; 1 Pet 1:20; and Rev 13:8; 4:11; 17:8.

he is mutually dependent upon creation. As Christians, we affirm that God has no fundamental need for the world, that his act of creating the world was gratuitous and contingent and not a metaphysical or rational necessity. Applying this to the idea of human work, participating in God's history suggests that humanity physically participates in God by the Spirit in creation. Taking this absurd idea further entails worshipping a God who, as part of or dependent on a fallen creation, is in need of redemption himself.[79] Further, it implies that human work somehow contributes to God's redemption.

Furthermore, Moltmann views God creating by producing a space for the world and then filling it with the energy of his Spirit.[80] This view effectively divinizes the world and as such brings Moltmann to the brink of pantheism.[81] Such a view leads to what Erickson calls the "de-emphasizing [of] the independent status of specific objects, even to view independent existence as illusionary."[82] Instead of being real entities with their own status, the individual elements of the world become adjectives attaching to the ultimate reality, God. In other words, work is not individual, nor charismatic, nor does it participate in the new creation or look forward to the future; rather, our individual labors are just facets of the one God. The irony is almost palpable. Moltmann has developed a theology of the Spirit that is in danger of achieving the antithesis of what he originally intended—the recognition and elevation of creation.

Another critique revolves around Moltmann's understanding of the Spirit and the Trinity. The Spirit's personhood is "the loving self-communicating, out-fanning and out-pouring presence of the eternal divine life of the Triune God."[83] The cosmic Spirit resides "in, with and beneath creation" through a kenotic act in which "God is alienated from

---

79. See Ron Highfield, "Divine Self-Limitation in the Theology of Jürgen Moltmann: A Critical Appraisal," *CSR* 32 (2002) 66.

80. Moltmann, *Spirit of Life*, 252.

81. In an earlier work Moltmann resists this label. He contends that creation in the Spirit of God "simultaneously takes creation into God, though without divinizing it." Jürgen Moltmann, *God in Creation* (San Francisco: Harper & Row, 1985), 258. However, in *The Spirit of Life*, 212, his language betrays him when he states that "the emanation of all things [come] from the All-One and their re-emanation into the All-One."

82. Millard J. Erickson, *Christian Theology* (Grand Rapids: Baker, 1983), 377.

83. Moltmann, *Spirit of Life*, 289.

God."[84] While referring to it as a source of supernatural transformation, he clearly views the Spirit from a naturalistic and vitalistic perspective.[85] Furthermore, this S/spirit reflects Hegel's movement of the Absolute into human history, although not as a single subject but the interaction of three subjects. While not seeing the evolutionary world process in terms of the transformation of matter in S/spirit (Hegel), Moltmann views it as the transformation of the cosmos into the S/spirit of love.[86] This view has more in common with contemporary secular spirituality in the workplace than it does with Scripture or orthodox Christianity.

A PNEUMATOLOGICAL CRITIQUE OF CONTEMPORARY SECULAR SPIRITUALITY IN THE WORKPLACE

The link between S/spirit/spirituality and work is not new. As we have seen, for centuries people have strived to interpret work through religious lenses. In recent times, however, a significant paradigm shift has seen S/spirit/spirituality play a more central and explicit function in the workplace. Several reasons may exist for this including a societal shift from a modernist to a postmodernist worldview, large-scale socio-demographic changes, and socio-cultural trends towards deinstitutionalization and individualization.

The general definition of spirituality in the psychology of religion literature is "subjective feelings, thoughts, and behaviours that arise from a search for the sacred," where the sacred is broadly understood as "a divine being, divine object, ultimate reality, or Ultimate Truth as perceived by the individual."[87] However, when spirituality enters the work context, then the question relates to the lived experiences and expressions of individuals in the organization. This is problematic since very

---

84. Douglas B. Farrow, "In the End Is the Beginning: A Review of Jürgen Moltmann's Systematic Contributions," *Modern Theology* 14 (1998) 431.

85. Similar to Henri Bergson, *Creative Evolution* (1911; reprint, New York: Dover, 1998), 66, the Spirit is "the principle of evolution" or the "principle of creation," the *élan vital* that is the creative force within duration that moves the world to completion.

86. Bloesch, *Holy Spirit*, 238. The use of "S/spirit" here indicates the ambiguity in Moltmann's work: is this the Holy Spirit, a sub-personal spirit, or the human spirit?

87. Peter C. Hill, Kenneth I. Pargament, Ralph W. Hood, Michael E. McCullough, James P. Swyers, David B. Larson, and Brian Zinnbauer, "Conceptualizing Religion and Spirituality: Points of Commonality, Points of Departure," *Journal for the Theory of Social Behavior* 30 (2000) 68.

few scholars categorically agree on what S/spirit/spirituality in the workplace is. For example, in a recent sample of definitions from the management literature, six different definitions of spirituality in the workplace were identified.[88] Mitroff and Denton's influential work *A Spiritual Audit of Corporate America* listed eleven dimensions.[89] Moreover, if this was not confusing enough, Freshman's analysis of employee emails, survey responses, and the literature resulted in over twenty constructs linked to spirituality at work. Her conclusion: "perhaps, the most useful part of what has been demonstrated here is that there is no one answer to the question 'what is spirituality in the workplace?'"[90]

Sheep argues that, despite these differences, there is a conceptual convergence in the literature as to what spirituality in the workplace is.[91] This convergence occurs in four recurring themes. The first, self-workplace integration, may be conceptualized as "a personal desire to bring one's whole being into the workplace."[92] Individuals wish to integrate work into their lives and in so doing connect to themselves and others in their workplace community. The second dimension, meaning in work, reflects this desire for integration and holism, but directed at the work itself. As Ashmos and Duchon wrote, "spiritual beings . . . express inner life needs by seeking meaningful work."[93] Consequently, the meaning of one's life must converge with the meaning one obtains from work in order for spiritual growth and development to occur. Third, self-transcendence has the spiritual individual rising above themselves to become part of an integrated whole and involves conferring their work and the workplace with the quality of connection to something greater than the self. As Mitroff and Denton put it, "Spirituality is the basic feel-

---

88. A. Amin Mohamed, Amin M. Hassan, and Joette M. Wisnieski, "Spirituality in the Workplace: A Literature Review," *Journal of Global Competitiveness* 9 (2001) 646.

89. Ian Mitroff, and Elizabeth A. Denton, *A Spiritual Audit of Corporate America: A Hard Look at Spirituality, Religion, and Values in the Workplace* (San Francisco: Jossey Bass, 1999).

90. Brenda Freshman, "An Exploratory Analysis of Definitions and Applications of Spirituality in the Workplace," *Journal of Organizational Change Management* 12 (1999) 326.

91. Matthew L. Sheep, "Nurturing the Whole Person: The Ethics of Workplace Spirituality in a Society of Organizations," *Journal of Business Ethics* 66 (2006) 360–62.

92. Ibid., 360.

93. Ashmos, and Duchon, "Spirituality at Work," 136.

ing of being connected with one's complete self, others and the entire universe."[94] Such a practice allows workers to rise above their differences and naturally look to their organization as a communal center.[95] Finally, growth and development of one's inner self connects to the other three dimensions of workplace spirituality, but it is distinct in that it imposes a quality of vitality upon the spirituality construct. A maturing process must occur in the workplace if the human life at work is to be integrated and whole. As Neck and Milliman assert, the main goal of workplace spirituality "is seen as being able to reach one's full potential and to have positive attitudes and relationships with the world."[96]

From a pneumatological perspective, contemporary spirituality in the workplace has several difficulties. First, it confuses the human spirit with the Holy Spirit. In the New Testament, Paul for example uses the adjective "spiritual" for objects that were somehow under the influence of or were manifestations of the Spirit of God, the Holy Spirit. Thus he speaks of the Law (Rom 7:14), truth (1 Cor 2:13); gifts or *charisms* (1 Cor 12:1), blessings (Eph 1:3); hymns and songs (Eph 5:19), and understanding (Col 1:9). However, most interestingly, in 1 Cor 2:14–15, Paul contrasts the "spiritual person" (*pneumatikos anthrōpos*) with the "natural person" (*psychikos anthrōpos*). In light of what has been said about the work of the Spirit in 1 Cor 2:6–13, Paul sets forth the negative side of the antithesis: what it is like for those who do not have the Holy Spirit. The people of this age, those who in their merely human wisdom miss God's wisdom, are designated "the natural man/woman" in contrast to those with the Spirit.[97] Paul describes natural persons in three ways. First, they reject the things that come from the Spirit of God. Second, the reason for this rejection is that the things of the Spirit are foolishness to them; their view of everything is corrupted. Third, without the Spirit they lack the necessary quality for them to know God and his ways.[98] The Spirit alone distinguishes the believer from the unbeliever in Pauline theology.

94. Mitroff, and Denton, *Spiritual Audit of Corporate America*, 83.

95. Philip H. Mirvis, "Soul Work," *Organization Science* 8 (1997) 198.

96. Christopher P. Neck and John F. Milliman, "Thought Self-Leadership: Finding Spiritual Fulfillment in Organizational life," *Journal of Managerial Psychology* 9 (1994) 10.

97. Robert P. Meye, "Spirituality," in *Dictionary of Paul and His Letters*, eds. Gerald P. Hawthorne and Ralph F. Martin (Downers Grove, IL: InterVarsity, 1993), 909.

98. Fee, *God's Empowering Presence* (Peabody, MA: Hendrickson, 1994), 106.

This is why the latter "are perishing" and consider the cross foolishness; this is why they do not understand the ways of God in Christ. The Spirit differentiates between what is of Christ and what is not.

For Paul, the "spirit" within the human person is what is influenced by the *Pneuma Theou*, whereas he portrays *sarx* ("flesh")[99] as everything in a person that is opposed to this influence. Thus, *sarx* could be a person's mind, will, or heart. It could also be their physical flesh.[100] Paul's usage makes it clear that he is not contrasting a living person who possesses a human spirit with one who lacks a spirit—that is, a dead person. Both the spiritual and the unspiritual person are alive, possessed of body and spirit. This opposition, for Paul, is also not between the incorporeal or non-material and the corporeal or material, but between two ways of life. The "spiritual" person (*pneumatikos*) is one whose life is under the influence of, or is a manifestation of, the Spirit of God. The "natural" person (*psychikos*) is one whose life is opposed to the working and guidance of the Spirit of God.

Contemporary spirituality in the workplace is human centered. Its focus is not on the things of God but on the things of man. For example, McKnight defines it as "an animating life force, an energy that inspires one toward certain ends or purposes that go beyond the self."[101] Giacalone, Jurkiewicz, and Fry refer to it as "a personal set of values that promote the experience of transcendence through the work process, facilitating a sense of connectedness to others in a way that provides feelings of completeness and joy."[102] Moreover, the instrumental nature of spirituality in the workplace reflects the modern organization's need for productivity and profit. Brown sarcastically elaborates on this:

> [Spirituality is] "sacred/ultimate whole system values" which enable the human spirit to grow and flourish. The benefits of these

---

99. Paul uses "flesh" (*sarx* or *caro*) in a variety of ways throughout his epistles. However, the most common use is to describe rebellious human nature, most of which are found in 1 Cor 2, Gal 5 and 6, and Rom 8. This is the understanding emphasized in this section.

100. Principe, "Toward Defining Spirituality," 45.

101. Richard McKnight, "Spirituality in the Workplace," in *Transforming Work*, ed. John D. Adams (Alexandria, VA: Miles River, 1984), 12.

102. Robert A. Giacalone, Carole L. Jurkiewicz, and L. W. Fry, "From Advocacy to Science: The Next Steps in Workplace Spirituality Research," in *Handbook of the Psychology of Religion and Spirituality*, eds. Raymond F. Paloutzian and Crystal L. Park (New York: Guilford, 2005), 518.

> time-honoured, life-affirming, and unifying values are that [sic] can enhance profit and productivity. The benefits further include truth and trust (which liberate the soul), freedom and justice (which liberate creative and co-creative genius), creativity/innovation, collective harmony and intelligence, wholeness, synergy, deeper meaning and higher purpose. In short, introduce spirituality to your organization and you have utopia on a plate.[103]

Essentially, this type of spirituality is about satisfying the existential needs of the individual and the needs of the organization for profitability and growth. Unfortunately, such a discourse simply "reinforces the idea of work providing a path to enlightenment through the notion of self-actualisation"[104] and contradicts the biblical view of spiritual work, that is, work under the influence of the Holy Spirit.

The second area of confusion in contemporary spirituality in the workplace exists between the subjective with the objective. The contemporary focus is on experience instead of the fuller reality that is God. For example, Ashar and Lane-Maher refer to spirituality in the workplace as

> A personal, inner, and deep domain within us that we can experience as a state of extraordinary calm and happiness, of awareness that is beyond the ordinary waking consciousness, or a state of harmony and oneness with the universe.[105]

Such an experiential approach results in the reverence of human esoteric moments or points of wonder. This, in turn, places the triune God, the *Creator ex nihilo* of all things and the One who sustains all things, in a subordinate position to his creation (cf. Rom 1:25).[106] The biblical witness rejects any such notion. The Holy Spirit, as opposed to the human "spirit," points us towards the incarnate Christ, who was crucified and resurrected from the grave thereby inaugurating a new beginning, a

---

103. Reva B. Brown, "Organizational Spirituality: The Sceptic's Version," *Organization* 10 (2003) 395–96.

104. Emma Bell, and Scott Taylor, "The Elevation of Work: Pastoral Power and the New Age Work Ethic," *Organization* 10 (2003) 336.

105. Hanna Ashar and Maureen Lane-Maher, "Success and Spirituality in the New Business Paradigm," *Journal of Management Inquiry* 13 (2004) 252.

106. Edith M. Humphrey, *Ecstasy & Intimacy: When the Holy Spirit Meets the Human Spirit* (Grand Rapids: Eerdmans, 2006), 5.

beginning where our experiences of work, can for the first time, be fully, really spiritual—centered on and empowered by the Holy Spirit.

Donald Bloesch might label this type of secular spirituality in the workplace a type of "secular mysticism."[107] The focus on the inner person calls for a self-adoration and exaltation of "our own rational self-awareness—the divinity operating within us [and . . .] arrives at no more interesting destination than spiritual narcissism."[108] This spirituality rests upon metaphysics of *becoming* as opposed to *being*; we are all in a process of change and evolution as we seek continual interrelation between the individual and a larger reality in which we transcend our personal existence. We transcend it not by leaving it behind for some separate realm of existence but by realization of its enlarging and transformative potentiality.[109] In this way, the infinite, states Bloesch, is known only in the finite, the absolute only in the relative.[110] Consequently, this spirituality becomes inherently pantheistic.

When we turn to Volf's pneumatological theology of work we uncover other limitations of contemporary secular spirituality in the workplace. The two central ideas in the literature, personal development and communal interconnectedness and well-being, are inadequate contexts for theological reflection on human work. According to Volf,

> To do justice to the nature of its subject (work) and its source (Christian revelation), a theology of work must investigate the relation of work to the future destiny of the whole creation, including human beings as individual and social beings, and the nonhuman environment. The appropriate theological framework for developing a theology of work is not anthropology but an all-encompassing eschatology.[111]

In Scripture humanity is made in the image of God (Gen 1:26–27) but is never confounded with divinity (Job 4:17; Rom 9:20–21). God is

---

107. A secular mysticism is characterized by the affirmation of human life, the will to power, pre- and post-Christian thought, and is this-worldly as opposed to other-worldly. See Donald G. Bloesch, *Spirituality: Old and New* (Downers Grove, IL: InterVarsity, 2007), 102.

108. James A. Herrick, *The Making of the New Spirituality: The Eclipse of the Western Religious Tradition* (Downers Grove, IL: InterVarsity, 2003), 259.

109. Robert M. Torrance, *The Spiritual Quest: Transcendence in Myth, Religion and Science* (Berkeley: University of California Press, 1994), 3.

110. Bloesch, *Spirituality*, 105.

111. Volf, *Work in the Spirit*, 85.

always wholly other and humanity exists in relationship with God by virtue of its election and incorporation in Jesus Christ by the gift of the Holy Spirit. Furthermore, in the biblical view, the tragic flaw of sin blights all humanity (Isa 64:6; Rom 3:23). This is not something incidental to human life but affects us at our core. Bloesch calls it a "forward drive toward the enthronement of the self."[112] Any view of spirituality that accentuates personal development of the self or community well-being simply falls into the trap of sin. Work is not the savior of the human race; Jesus Christ is. Moreover, work is not a replacement for the communal fellowship that exists through the Holy Spirit which joins believers to Christ and to fellow believers. This is not to say that human beings should not work. The biblical account (see e.g., Gen 1:26; 2:15; Psalm 104:23; Matt 20:1–16) is clear: work is a fundamental dimension of being human. It is part of God's intention for us to fulfill his original plan in our lives. Work is an act of worship to God for the work he has done and is doing in achieving his purposes in creation.[113] However, the contemporary religion of work "has little to do with either worship of God or with God's demands on human life; it has much to do with 'worship' of the self and human demands of the self."[114]

In a pneumatological understanding of work, all human skills stem from the operation of the Spirit of God.[115] Furthermore, according to Volf, we are to continually seek new *charisms* (1 Cor 14:12) and develop existing ones (2 Tim 1:6) whether at work or not. In the New Testament, these gifts are accompanied by the fruit of the Spirit (Gal 5:22), which represent the values of the new creation; consequently they determine how we use our gifts in our work.[116] Such a paradigm removes any notions of individualistic human-centered (and therefore corrupted) self-development from our work while ensuring that our labor is "put in the context of concern for God's new creation."[117] When this occurs personal development does not cease, rather it is fulfilled as part of the new creation. Indeed, fulfillment can only occur when the whole creation has

---

112. Bloesch, *Spirituality*, 127.
113. Jensen, *Responsive Labor*, 22.
114. Volf, *Work in the Spirit*, 129.
115. Ibid., 130.
116. Ibid., 131.
117. Ibid.

found its fulfillment too. Therefore, development "must be attuned to the well-being of the whole creation."[118] Work that fails to consider its negative environmental and social impacts not only resists God's new creation but also limits humanity's development within that creation.

Thomas Torrance uses the image "priest of creation" to describe the function humanity plays in creation. As its priest, humanity's job is to "assist the creation as a whole to realize and evidence its rational order and beauty and thus to express God."[119] Similar to Volf, Torrance views humanity as co-creators with God. Our work brings forth "forms of order and beauty of which it would not be capable otherwise."[120] Human beings must realize this priestly call to co-create and act as stewards of the creation. However, the primary means of doing this, according to Torrance, is through natural science.[121] Natural science attests to the order and beauty of the creation thereby pointing towards and praising the Creator. In fact, natural science becomes a religious duty, "for it is part of [humanity's] faithful response to the Creator and Sustainer of the cosmos."[122]

Habets notes that while this notion of humanity as priests of creation has value, it is not without its problems. By taking too narrow an approach, Torrance has limited this idea to that of natural science alone while failing to address the wider realm of what this function may entail.[123] I would suggest that Volf has something to add here. Humanity's function, as priests of creation, is broader than simply maintaining and/or developing the creation through natural science. Our daily work also participates in the new creation through the Spirit, cooperates with God in the redemption of the world, and looks forward with hope to the future renewal of the heavens and the earth. Consequently, our daily work matters whatever task it is we perform. All work has value if it anticipates God's transformation of the world.[124] From a pneumatological perspec-

---

118. Ibid.

119. Habets, *Theosis in the Theology of Thomas Torrance*, 45.

120. Thomas F. Torrance, *Divine and Contingent Order* (New York: Oxford University Press, 1981), 130, cited in ibid.

121. Torrance, *Reality and Evangelical Theology* (Philadelphia: Westminster, 1982), 25–26, cited in ibid.

122. Torrance, Space, *Time, and Resurrection* (Grand Rapids: Eerdmans, 1976), 179–80, cited in ibid.

123. Habets, *Theosis in the Theology of Thomas Torrance*, 46.

124. Jensen, *Responsive Labor*, 40.

tive, all Christians are priests of creation and our daily labors are our ministry and worship to God.

CONCLUSION

Historical views of work as a vocation or calling limit the role of the Spirit, while contemporary notions of spirit/spirituality are essentially humanistic and pantheistic. Volf's pneumatological theology of work gives the Holy Spirit a central role in human labor and is thoroughly eschatological in nature. As priests of creation, humanity is enabled to glorify God through daily labor. Humans are invited to become co-creators with God in the stewardship of his creation. This is our response to the work the triune God has done and is doing for us. However, we are more than merely responsive; our mundane labors empowered by the Holy Spirit allow us to cooperate with God in his kingdom in a way that completes creation and contributes to the renewal of heaven and earth. This is the reality of the Holy Spirit and spirituality in the workplace.

12

The Spirit and Particularity

by Judith Brown

I believe in the Holy Spirit: the Lord and Giver of Life[1]

... but the essence of the world is cheerful spirit
and the urge to creative shaping ...[2]

The story is well known: in 1919, on leave from the trenches, a young chaplain in the German army encountered a painting entitled *Madonna and Child with Singing Angels*. The painting was by Sandro Botticelli. Of this experience Paul Tillich wrote:

> In the beauty of the painting there was Beauty itself. It shone through the colours of the paint as the light of day shines through the stained-glass windows of a medieval church....
> I turned away shaken. That moment has affected my whole life ... brought vital joy and spiritual truth. I compare it with what is usually called revelation ... I know that no graphic artistic experience can match the moments in which prophets were

---

1. Nicene Creed.

2. Ernst Bloch, *The Principle of Hope*, trans. Neville Plaice, Stephen Plaice, and Paul Knight (Cambridge: MIT, 1995), 1:xx.

grasped in the power of the Divine Presence, but I believe there is an analogy between revelation and what I felt. In both cases, the experience goes beyond the way we encounter reality in our daily lives. It opens up depths experienced in no other way.[3]

In 1955 another noted theologian wrote this in response to a work of art: "Whenever I listen to you, I am transported to the threshold of a world which in sunlight and storm, by day and by night, is a good and ordered world."[4] Nor are such remarks the preserve of theologians. The literary critic and author Mark Schorer believed that any given act of human creativity is impelled by the need for realization.[5]

This chapter reflects on the work of the Spirit, though without focusing on any particular doctrine. Rather, it will reflect primarily on creativity. Creativity stands over against the pressures of our lives toward disengagement from the other and, more fundamentally, from community. In the binding and bringing together of creativity there is an implicit recognition and concern for the particular:

> St. Thomas called art "reason in making." . . . The artist uses his reason to discover an answering reason in everything he sees. For him, to be reasonable is to find, in the object, in the situation, in the sequence, the spirit which makes it itself.[6]

This function is at the least analogous to the Spirit's work of reconciliation. The basis of the discussion is with the ways in which the arts have an integrative and constituting function. Thus, "[t]he arts open up a dimension of reality which is otherwise hidden, and they open up our own being for receiving this reality."[7] Some of the ways this may in fact occur will be investigated in the rest of this chapter.

3. Paul Tillich, "One Moment of Beauty," in *On Art and Architecture*, ed. John Dillenberger with Jane Dillenberger (New York: Crossroad, 1987), 235.

4. Karl Barth, "A Letter of Thanks to Mozart," in *Wolfgang Amadeus Mozart* (Grand Rapids: Eerdmans, 1986), 22.

5. Mark Schorer, *The World We Imagine: Selected Essays* (New York: Farrar, Straus and Giroux, 1968), 388. Later he quotes Lionel Trilling: "The function of literature through all the mutations has been to make us aware of the particularity of selves . . ." Ibid., 402.

6. Flannery O'Connor, "The Nature and Aim of Fiction," in *Mystery and Manners* (New York: Farrar, Straus and Giroux, 1961), 82.

7. Tillich, "Address on the Occasion of the Opening of the New Galleries and Sculpture Garden of the Museum of Modern Art," in *On Art and Architecture*, 11.

On the one hand, it is not taken as a mark against creativity that its products sometimes become a replacement for God, a disarticulation of the divine. In effect such a displacement is a mark of respect for a mystery that remains as the substance of these phenomena. It is this situation exactly that characterizes the writings of the Marxist utopian Ernst Bloch. His philosophy of hope expresses a profound appreciation for *Geist*, and the revelatory capacity of creativity. This will be discussed briefly further below.[8]

SPIRIT AND THE ARTS

Before proceeding it must be acknowledged that the Spirit and the arts have not always been seen as necessarily related. This has been the case in both the world and the church. As the misjudgments of faith regarding the arts and the creative function are not the focus of this essay, let us review some typical uses of the word "spirit" elsewhere. "Spirit" is a common enough term in theories about the arts and creativity. For example the Romantics speak of inspiration in a manner that is resonant with religious associations. But much of their language is at best ambiguous. Inspiration is not of the everyday: in this condition one is taken outside of oneself.[9] It is a state where one is "not in one's right mind," and the source of this state is in the sub-rational, an involuntary spirit regarded as the same one active in nature.

G. W. F. Hegel was committed to the idea that spirit (*Geist*) was "the universal mark of being."[10] Hegel contended that spirit has its highest existence in the Absolute Spirit, whose greatest expression is, in ascending order, in art, religion, and philosophy. These are differing forms of Absolute Spirit. Absolute Spirit is a totality, a unity transcending the dialectic of spirit and it's alienated others. Its unity takes the form of a total incorporation that transcends otherness yet preserves it. And only

---

8. While I do not wish to make this an essay on Bloch, his magpie philosophy is a magical reconfiguration, within the Marxist this-worldly horizon, of many theological trajectories. Hence his understanding of creativity is a significant aid here.

9. The untranslatable German *Geist* has one basic meaning of "being in a state of excitement." See the chapter "Against Reason's Despair" in Dorothy Sölle, *The Truth Is Concrete* (London: Burns & Oates, 1969).

10. The phrase is Colin Gunton's. *The One, the Three and the Many: God, Creation and the Culture of Modernity* (Cambridge: Cambridge University, 1993), 184.

in philosophy is this unmediated—in all other expressions its essence is trapped in imaginative forms.

Ernst Bloch, both an admirer and critic of Hegel, in his work *The Spirit of Utopia* (one of whose original titles was to be *The Eschatological Man*)[11] presents spirit as that which summons us. We are summoned to responsibility for our own human condition, presenting the ultimate encounter with the self as the "final dream of the world." The work begins with an imperative, borrowed from Nietzsche, to "embark," *incipit vita nova*. Bloch states that "in this book, a new beginning is posited, and the unlost heritage takes possession of itself."[12] The goal is "the real, where the merely factual disappears."[13] A kind of meta-reality, a meta-history, rises beyond the concrete forms of human existence, and is characterized by Bloch as the "eternal goal," the "one conscience, the one salvation," which, rising into the blue, actually "rises from our hearts."[14] The drive to transcendence is shaped by a living relationship to tradition. This is what fruitful cultural creativity is. It is the human spirit itself embarking on its path to its authentic being.

There are many possible points of dialogue between such notions and theology. In the latter creativity is first in God. God is essentially creative. This dynamic essence is manifest in the work of the person of the Trinity revealed to us as the One named Holy Spirit. The action of God in the Spirit reveals a concern for the particular that stands over against the fragmentation of social and epistemic reality in contemporary Western culture. The Spirit, in saying no to our culture, redeems it. The Spirit's action realizes the unity-in-diversity of the Divine economic involvement in the world, drawing us up into the dialogue of Father and Son, of a relationality that is a movement of exchange within God's own life.

The point of congruence is in the work of the Spirit, which makes us more ourselves, more authentic through becoming more particular. There is no homogenization in the body of Christ, but greater distinction. This is how our freedom is understood in biblical terms—we are reintegrated by the Spirit into a nature that has become afflicted with fragmentation

---

11. Wayne Hudson, *The Marxist Philosophy of Ernst Bloch* (New York: St. Martin's, 1982), 29.

12. Ernst Bloch, *The Spirit of Utopia*, trans. Anthony Nasser (Stanford: Stanford University Press, 2000), 3.

13. Ibid.

14. Ibid.

and distinction based on isolation. In the Spirit our movement is toward engagement rather than isolation, reduction, and anomie.

The locus of this analogy of the Spirit in the arts is taken to be the process of making art itself, together with selected facets of the arts. These features have some bearing on the moral quality of art—it is presupposed in this essay that where these qualities are present the work of art, in its motivation and presentation, will at least incline toward the good, which is also truth. Henry James located the truthfulness of a work of fiction on the amount of "felt life" in it.[15] O'Connor expands this to show that we cannot demand "goodness" from the writer unless we are prepared to limit their "freedom to observe what [we] have done with the things of God."[16] Truth cannot thrive when the good is compartmentalized.

Those forces and structures that facilitate, support, and enable fragmentation and our separation from one another are the enemies of integrity. This is more than mere economic structures, such as the functional division of labor, which is not morally neutral anyway. What is at work in such philosophies is a moral postponement, a diffusion that is essentially atomization. On the other hand, good art testifies to abundance and the flourishing of life and so honors God, whether by explicit intent or not. It has the integrity that is a mark of authenticity because it proclaims "here I am" and "here you are," and we meet.

The work of the Spirit is always going forth, as well as, with apologies to John Taylor, "going-between." One finds much to agree with in Barth's procedural analysis of first the no, the dissolution, from which reconstitution arises in the experiential engagement "with us" of the God who cannot be subsumed by our conceptual orderings. Dietrich Bonhoeffer's example of musical polyphony gives us an image of this divine-human relationship.[17] The *cantus firmus* (which enables the music to go forth and flourish) is God's summons to love him eternally with all our heart, the counterpoint woven about it being "all the other melodies of life," our living completely to and in the world. We are being called to a destiny centered on the one who says, "Behold I make all things new." Because the Holy Spirit is first of all a Divine person, an Other, his otherness is the

---

15. Cited in O'Connor, "Nature and Aim of Fiction," 146.
16. Ibid., 151.
17. Dietrich Bonhoeffer, *Letters and Papers from Prison*, ed. Eberhard Bethge (New York: Macmillan, 1972), 302.

very guarantee of our own particularity—our autonomy is established by specific structuring.

An important effect of the Holy Spirit's work is that it points to an interdependence of the social and personhood that counteracts the perceived pressures to both fragmentation and homogeneity in contemporary society. Relationality in the universal activity of the Spirit toward the world takes a form, or manner, which fulfills the integrity of the world's being by opening it up to participation in the Other's particularity. Boundaries are crossed in this dynamic. The results are often startling juxtapositions and links. And for us, a new way of seeing can ensue—a new seeing that is both a cognitive shock and an ontological refiguring. As John McIntyre says, the Holy Spirit is God's imagination let loose and working with all the freedom of God in the world.[18]

THE ABUNDANT SPIRIT

A brief review of theological precedents raises for us the admirable Irenaeus of Lyons, from whom we have the concept of the particularizing (making unique, special, distinct) character of the will of God. God, by his will, creates a *particular* world. According to Irenaeus, creation is held in continuing relationship to God by the Son and the Spirit (the Son and the Spirit are, to use a term of Gerald Manley Hopkins, the world's "inscape"). In other words, the Spirit shapes the world for it to be received by the Father from the Son. The Spirit has, as one of his modes of action, the work of rendering particular, which is to say the Spirit is the *Perfector*.

This Trinitarian understanding of the divine economy allows the world to be itself, by its very relation to God. It maintains the richness and diversity of the ways of God toward the creation. One way in which the Spirit's ongoing shaping of the world, to be received by the Father from the Son in perfection, is expressed is in the creation's abundance (or diversity) and joy as witness to this work of the Spirit.[19]

Secondarily, from Basil of Caesarea comes the notion of the Spirit as the *perfecting* cause of creation. One of the most attractive aspects of Basil is his celebration, in his *Hexameron*, of the sheer variety of creation as a

---

18. John McIntyre, *Faith, Theology, and Imagination* (Edinburgh: Handsel, 1987).
19. Genesis 1:22ff.

work of wonderful or good order. This order "reigns in visible things."[20] A number of his passages are so full of enthusiasm for the abundance of the created world that he himself remarks, "But I perceive that an insatiable curiosity is drawing out my discourse beyond its limits."[21]

The cause of this abundance and diversity in the *Hexameron* is the Spirit, who maintains the distinction that constitutes the "wonderful order." The Spirit's perfecting work fulfills, but not in a singular act of perfecting. It involves task. The work of the Spirit does not result in a product. This work is a movement toward. It is characterized by joyful anticipation. It is right then to say that creativity is a process that is a little anticipation of creation's end. Further, all creation has ontological equality before God as the object of his creating will and love as manifested in the Spirit.

CULTURAL ANALOGIES

This very brief and selective summary of theological material gives us a context within which we can explore some cultural analogies. The first of these comparative reflections is in the way the Spirit's dynamic directedness turns us from our self-absorption. A multitude of associated concepts and insights gather around this. The arts are, as Solzhenitsyn said, the only way we have into the experience of a life we have not lived; art "transmits . . . the . . . accumulated load of another being's life experience . . ."[22] For each of us it is a unique encounter with "nothing like him before, nothing like him after."[23] This is how the church is, the body that is formed by the Spirit of particularity—possibly incomprehensible to an era that failed to see that becoming one is only possible through each becoming more definitively a self. The means of attaining this distinction

---

20. Basil *Hexameron* 1.1 (*NPNF2* 8; online: http://www.ccel.org/ccel/schaff/npnf208.viii.ii.html).

21. Ibid., 5.9 (*NPNF2* 8; online: http://www.ccel.org/ccel/schaff/npnf208.viii.vi.html).

22. Alexander Solzhenitsyn, "The Nobel Prize Lecture on Literature," quoted in Alain Finkielkraut, *In the Name of Humanity: Reflections on the Twentieth Century* (New York: Columbia University Press, 2000), 78.

23. Part of Michelet's epitaph for the duke of Orleans, quoted in Finkielkraut, *In the Name of Humanity*, 80.

models the integration of structure and vitality that characterizes a work of art.

There are consequences arising from encounter. A personal relationship is inescapable when a work of art engages us. This does not occur in an arbitrary manner. There is a character to a work—a character that only arises because the work is purposeful and formed.[24] In the process of creative work something is recognized and uncovered: "the artist can and perpetually does create an order that did not exist before he made it."[25] William Butler Yeats called this the love "of all life at peace with itself."[26]

Ernst Bloch speaks of creativity as "venturing forth."[27] Creativity arises from the dialectical movement that is of course the Marxist engine of history. Creativity is this-worldly, but is not constituted by material relations. Rather, it is itself constitutive of the condition of the transformation of our human condition. It brings us into relation with the new. It occurs when "participating reason" suffers the recognition of forms that are signposts of the future. Creativity is the function that gives material expression to our yearnings in ways that make those yearnings more clearly seen.

The interaction of artist and material reality occurs within constraints that mark our human condition itself. For each of us these include space, time, physicality, and cultural context. Constraints are "structures that prevent us from being indeterminate and amorphous creatures."[28] Art does not make being. But in its particular making, and in the finished work, a discernable interaction occurs that in its tendency counters the isolation of each from the other. The imagination of the art maker cannot bring about just anything—there are always limitations to what can be made, but these are only the givens, and in that sense they are the very possibility of creative realization. The Spirit makes of these constraints the basis for freedom.

---

24. Where the work arises from the use of chance operations this is less present. Even so, decision remains the originating cause.

25. Schorer, *World We Imagine*, 402.

26. Quoted in ibid.

27. In "Venturing beyond the Most Intense World of Man in Music," in *Principle of Hope*, 3:1057, Bloch titles the section on music, the most utopian of the arts.

28. Jeremy Begbie, *Theology, Music, and Time* (Cambridge: Cambridge University, 2000), 198.

REDEMPTIVE ART

We have already stated that art is task: all creative activity involves struggle with its material. This active wrestling involves us in a figurative, sometimes literal, tearing down and building up. This is a potential source of redemption—fitting or discovering a new reality for, and in, the discarded. This is something we literally see in Ralph Hotere's art.[29] What has been lost, or declared outmoded, or no longer fits is found to have new use and function. It is only a matter of orientation and purpose in the creating imagination. In such a struggle the presence of what endures is achieved, as is transformation. Paul Tillich was not entirely wrong when he spoke of a period of disintegration as a *kairos* moment in which there is the potential of creation.

Task and toil are kin of play. They are necessary for the work to be achieved in that no art work is natural. Spirit engages in a process of deeper encounter with form. Play, which in essence is an acknowledgment of gift, of givenness as freedom and as superfluity, immerses us in the participatory enlargement of ourselves and cosmos. Among the philosophers Friedrich Schiller spoke of *Spieltrieb* ("play-drive"), a term he used for a structured engagement with the world. Schiller's *Aesthetic Letters* reveal his faith that art, and the imaginative faculty that produces it, is uniquely able to unify and reconcile the divided. In a conflicted and fragmented society, in which the organic has been replaced with "ingenious clockwork," art restores the "totality of our nature."[30] *Spieltrieb* satisfies impulse and reason, which manifests in creativity as form. In this it mirrors true philosophy.[31] And true philosophy has as it subject matter all of reality. Its object is original unity. By extrapolation, then, creativity is functional reconciliation. We bear witness through our acts of creativity, which re-shape the dis-order of the world. The Spirit is the

---

29. For example in *Black Window—Towards Aramoana* (1981). This frames the painting with a salvaged window frame from a demolition site. Hotere leaves the catch on the top and by this device, as well as the frame itself, opens up a range of possible readings of the interior of the work. Gregory O'Brien, *Hotere: Out the Black Window: Ralph Hotere's work with New Zealand Poets* (Auckland: Godwit, 1997), 13.

30. See Schiller's sixth *Aesthetic Letter*, in M. H. Abrams, *Natural Supernaturalism: Tradition and Revolution in Romantic Literature* (New York: Norton, 1971), 211–12. This concept can be found in, among others, Schelling, Novalis, and Coleridge.

31. See Alan White, *Schelling: An Introduction to the System of Freedom* (New Haven: Yale University Press, 1983), 8.

one who interweaves or braids together what might otherwise be thought disconnected and distinct, in such a way that the truth is discovered as connective.[32]

Many artists have recognized this consequence of creative endeavor. Coleridge spoke of art as the "mediatress between, and reconciler of man and nature."[33] In this the imagination is the productive faculty. Similarly, Friedrich Wilhelm Schelling regarded the imagination as a uniting faculty. It is the sense of significance, or depth of meaning, beyond the articulate that the imagination as creative act can give us. The imagination has the capacity to recognize the authentic character of the thing—it does not arbitrarily impose order but brings it to light. In this we are "reading into" the world in the sense of "interpretation." The Spirit enables us by "opening our eyes."[34]

This aspect of creativity is a constant in discussion of the subject—the artist as someone who discovers. Structures that form reality are recognized: one feels a sense of coming home, of scales falling from the eyes. This is by no means a contradiction of the truth that "the artist can and perpetually does create an order that did not exist before he made it."[35]

Change and order may co-exist. This is what happens in improvisation. Specific givens are particularized for a contingent "now."[36] Freedom is experienced as a "description of the proper relationships and configurations between particularities."[37] Temporal and relational particularities are the essence of improvisation; in fact the essence of all musical activity. In music we hear the "impossible" reconciliation of pure flow and pure present moment.[38] Jeremy Begbie points to a model for the Spirit's work

---

32. See for example Daniel Hardy, "The Spirit of God in Creation and Reconciliation," in *Christ and Context*, eds. Hilary Regan and Alan J. Torrance (Edinburgh: T. & T. Clark, 1993), 237.

33. Samuel Taylor Coleridge, "On Poesy or Art," *English Essays: Sidney to Macaulay*, Harvard Classics 27 (New York: P. F. Collier), 1909–14.

34. John V. Taylor, *The Go-Between God* (London: SCM, 1974), 19.

35. Schorer, *World We Imagine*, 402.

36. Begbie, *Theology, Music, and Time*, 202, 215.

37. Ibid., 199.

38. Catherine Pickstock, *Radical Orthodoxy*, eds. John Milbank, Catherine Pickstock, and Graham Ward (London: Routledge, 1999), 269. In her discussion of Augustine, Pickstock comments that for Augustine "every creature is perpetually seeking to be 'like itself' or to occupy more precisely its proper position in time and space. Every creature is a specific rhythm." Ibid., 249.

in the technique of improvising not on the chord being played but on the one immediately to come.[39]

Creativity then draws us out from ourselves; even in looking inward first we must then proceed:

> ... every truly creative act, transcends ... the order of the world and the potential order within the subjective life, is now, goes beyond what has been. This is not to say that it is better, only that it is itself ... .[40]

And so we may, in going forth, arrive at joy. The dynamic of joy is *ek-stasis*. In the Spirit we are blessed with an understanding of the superfluity of life. Creativity has a quality of insistence that is like grace. It is an immersion in the "grain of the world." And in its directionality one can contend that creativity is an act of praise, akin, at least, to the character of worship. The capacity to give response is promoted by the Spirit. This is the ground of joy. In a true if limited way we are most truly ourselves in this time.

THE CREATIVE SPIRIT

In conclusion, the notion that artistic creativity illuminates in various ways the reconciling and particularizing work of the Spirit offers a reading of the human condition that redeems it from interpretations typical of much twentieth-century thought. Even though Bloch believes we have what it takes, his reading of our condition is that of a "hard, far from paradisiacal ... age."[41] We are weary, atomized, collapsed into ourselves in a world that has the quality of juxtaposition rather than integration; diverse things are present, but unrelated. There is dissociation and the feeling that "in our strangely weary and obscure life something important [is] not right."[42] Elsewhere: "I am aware of something within me that that gleams and flashes before my soul; were this perfected and fully established within me, that would surely be eternal life."[43]

39. Begbie, *Theology, Music, and Time*, 221–23.
40. Schorer, *World We Imagine*, 385.
41. Bloch, *Principle of Hope*, 3:1091.
42. Bloch, *Utopia*, 168.
43. Ibid., 195. This is a quotation from a sermon on the *Wisdom of Solomon* once thought to be by Augustine (but now considered spurious).

In fact, it is the artist and most critically the surplus in the creative arts that nurtures unalienated relationships. Creativity establishes a template that may be termed salvatory. In his Marxist terminology Bloch declares that the arts show us our authentic self as the "We." The arts are prophetic: they show us that in our unalienated and authentic being we are no less than the revolutionary vanguard. That who we shall be is who we are, if we but act on it, and that this being is one in which we are at "home" (*Heimat*),[44] a place that "shines into the childhood of all and in which no one has yet been."[45] For our being to know completion we must be joined to "a body of corporate knowledge and a tacit 'fiduciary framework' of basic attitudes . . . [by which] we are able to come to terms with the world we inhabit."[46]

The Spirit is the presence of Being (*Sein*) surpassing death, the final exile. (Digressing briefly, perhaps too this is part of the sting of death. And its promise: for somehow that which is departed from us is encompassed about with a negative space of concrete particularity. Nor clearly does the unique particularity of the person depend upon their embodied presence). For Bloch disengagement and subjectivism are two sides of the same coin. Fragmentation and displacement are a veiling but not an erasure.

Creativity has the fragrance of the divine. Together with beauty and truth it forms a compelling witness to the intentionality revealed, rather than first established, in the redemption. Rather, as the artist brings into being something that has not been in the world before, yet does so from the things at hand. Though we have not even spoken of truth and beauty, they are the real conclusion of this essay. The Spirit "communicates God's beauty to the world"[47] through the creation and through the inspiring of artistic beauty (a reflection of the divine and a sign of eschatological sig-

---

44. This is an absolutely crucial term in Bloch's philosophy, which we cannot fully deal with here. Though it means "home" (in the Austro-German context, which is Bloch's point of origin) the English word conveys little of the emotional charge of the term. This "home" is much more than a living space. It involves the full spectrum of the human sense of belonging and completion. Its resonances are immense in the context of Bloch's investigation into how to "complete the world."

45. Bloch, *Principle of Hope*, 3:1376.

46. Begbie, *Theology, Music, and Time*, 218.

47. Patrick Sherry, *Spirit and Beauty: An Introduction to Theological Aesthetics*, rev. ed. (London: SCM, 2002), 2.

nificance). For surely any instance of beauty captures us exactly because it manifests the height of particularity. This may be why when we encounter this it evokes not just joy but an intermingled sadness: this supports the notion of those like Bloch who claim our essence is longing—and that this longing is ontological but known in the particular, the embodied. It is only encounter with that which is present in its self that fragmentation is seen as possibility rather than endless postponement.

Beauty is an anticipation of the restored and transfigured world. "Beauty crosses boundaries,"[48] and this makes it the true epitome of the Spirit of the God who works to remove all boundaries so that each being, gathered in the One, shines forth as itself.

---

48. David Bentley Hart, *The Beauty of the Infinite: The Aesthetics of Christian Truth* (Grand Rapids: Eerdmans, 2003), 20.